THE *PAST & PRESENT* BOOK SERIES

General Editor
MATTHEW HILTON

Status Interaction during the Reign of Louis XIV

Status Interaction during the Reign of Louis XIV

GIORA STERNBERG

OXFORD
UNIVERSITY PRESS

OXFORD
UNIVERSITY PRESS

Great Clarendon Street, Oxford, OX2 6DP,
United Kingdom

Oxford University Press is a department of the University of Oxford.
It furthers the University's objective of excellence in research, scholarship,
and education by publishing worldwide. Oxford is a registered trade mark of
Oxford University Press in the UK and in certain other countries

© Giora Sternberg 2014

The moral rights of the author have been asserted

First Edition published in 2014

Impression: 1

Published in the United States of America by Oxford University Press
198 Madison Avenue, New York, NY 10016, United States of America

British Library Cataloguing in Publication Data
Data available

Library of Congress Control Number: 2013951732

ISBN 978–0–19–964034–8

As printed and bound by
CPI Group (UK) Ltd, Croydon, CR0 4YY

To My Parents

Acknowledgments

To name all persons and institutions that have aided me in several years of research and writing in three continents is an impossible task that inevitably leads to faux pas of omission. Nevertheless, it is a ritual that is hard to resist.

At Tel-Aviv, I decided to pursue historical studies due to the inspiring example of Gadi Algazi and the unfailing support of Miriam Eliav-Feldon. I also enjoyed there the guidance of Hava Bat-Zeev Shyldkrot and David Katz. At Oxford, David Parrott made me a better scholar and has offered kind and constant support, well beyond the call of duty of a supervisor. I am extremely grateful to Lyndal Roper for supporting my work so generously ever since the beginning of the D.Phil. At its end, the thesis received thought-provoking examination from Robin Briggs and William Doyle; Robin has been a source of insights and guidance from my first trip to Oxford. In the UK, Colin Jones offered generous advice and support. At Harvard, Mario Biagioli has supported my work from an early stage, and I am especially grateful to Ann Blair, who introduced me to other academic horizons.

Special thanks to Oded Rabinovitch for invaluable advice, comments, and suggestions on countless occasions. Jeroen Duindam and Guy Rowlands generously offered advice at several junctures. Avi Lifschitz has guided my path in Oxford, while Olivier Chaline and Lucien Bély kindly welcomed me in Paris. Alexandre Tessier lent a hand with some of the translations from the French and Samuel Pollack in the preparation of the index. The project also benefitted from Yehonatan Alsheh, Bernard Bailyn, Sara Barker, Élie Barnavi, Naor Ben-Yehoyada, Mark Bryant, Peter Campbell, James Collins, Nick Davidson, Jonathan Dewald, John Elliott, Peter Galison, Anthony Grafton, Sam Haselby, Daniel Hershenzon, Leonhard Horowski, Howard Hotson, Daniel Jütte, Thomas Kaiser, Vera Kaplan, Sharon Kettering, Mark Kishlansky, Joseph Koerner, Nadine Kuperty-Tsur, Judith Loades, Phil McCluskey, Roger Mettam, Yair Mintzker, Siobhan Phillips, Robert Priest, Jeff Ravel, Nicole Reinhardt, Thierry Sarmant, Daniel Smail, Jonathan Spangler, Rachel Stern, Julian Swann, William Todd, Shulamit Volkov, Evelyn Welch, colleagues at the Harvard Society of Fellows, and many others, including convenors and audiences at various venues in Europe and in the US. My thanks go to numerous librarians and archivists, and in particular to those whose willingness to help went beyond their institutional obligations. I am also grateful to Alexandra Walsham at Past & Present, to Stephanie Ireland and Cathryn Steele at Oxford University Press, and to the anonymous readers for the careful scrutiny of the manuscript and many helpful and insightful suggestions.

Indispensable support was provided at Tel-Aviv by the Adi Lautman Interdisciplinary Program, the Graduate School of Historical Studies, and the Lessing Institute; at Oxford by the Clarendon Fund, the History Faculty, the Reynolds Fund and New College, the Colin Matthew Fund (St Hugh's College), the Zaharoff Fund (Faculty of Medieval and Modern Languages), and the Harding Fund and Hertford College; elsewhere in the UK by the Overseas Research Students Award

Scheme, the Society for the Study of French History, the Royal Historical Society, and the Institute for Historical Research; and at Harvard by the Society of Fellows (special thanks to Diana Morse and Kelly Katz) and the Milton Fund.

I owe a huge debt of gratitude to friends and family in three continents. Ofra has brightened the darkness of the final stages of the project with the light of true partnership. My sister and, above all, my parents have supported me throughout in ways I cannot even begin to thank them for.

Contents

List of Illustrations

List of Abbreviations

AAE	Archives du ministère des Affaires étrangères, La Courneuve
AC	Bibliothèque et archives du château de Chantilly
AD	Archives départementales
AM	Archives municipales
AN	Archives nationales, Paris
Arsenal	Bibliothèque de l'Arsenal, Paris
BM	Bibliothèque Mazarine, Paris
BN	Bibliothèque nationale de France, Paris
CP	Correspondance Politique
Dangeau	*Journal du marquis de Dangeau*, ed. Soulié et al. (19 vols, Paris, 1854–60)
FF	Fonds français
MD	Mémoires et Documents
NAF	Nouvelles acquisitions françaises
SHD/DAT	Service historique de la Défense, Département de l'armée de terre, Vincennes
Sourches	*Mémoires du marquis de Sourches sur le règne de Louis XIV*, ed. le comte de Cosnac and Édouard Pontal (13 vols, Paris, 1882–93)
SSB	*Mémoires de Saint-Simon*, ed. A. de Boislisle et al. (43 vols, Paris, 1879–1930)

Introduction

In the autumn of 1679 the new queen of Spain set out for a royal tour de France from the chateau of Fontainebleau to her kingdoms. Like Emperor Charles V before her and other sovereigns since, she was regaled by numerous towns and communities on her passage. The king of France nominated the prince and princess of Harcourt to escort the Catholic Queen across his realm and ordered his Master of Ceremonies, Nicolas Sainctot, to ensure that she received the honours due to her rank. Municipal authorities at Orléans, Poitiers, and other towns greeted her at the gates and offered to bear a canopy over her head. In Bordeaux, they prepared a magnificently decked ship to conduct her across the Gironde estuary from Blaye to their home port. Ecclesiastical and judicial authorities paid their respects and gave solemn harangues in her honour. At the border, the French retinue ceremoniously delivered the queen to a Spanish delegation, in a building specially designed for the occasion. The Harcourts accompanied her into Spain as extraordinary ambassadors, until she was finally united with her new husband, Charles II.

This account echoes many familiar descriptions of early modern ceremonies. Like them, it smooths over an important part of the picture. In Orléans, local officers also quarrelled over precedence at the queen's entry. The *jurats* of Bordeaux demanded—in vain—the right to wear their vestments of authority at Blaye and to hold the queen's hand as she embarked their ship. In the cathedral of Saintes, the canons expressed their independence vis-à-vis the local bishop in complimenting the royal guest. Judges and treasurers disputed the right of first visit in several provincial towns; the treasurers of Poitiers liaised with colleagues from other provinces, tried to influence Sainctot in their favour, and, when unsuccessful, did not pay their respects at all. These concerns, moreover, did not stop at the border. Rank disputes among the Spanish delegation delayed the delivery ceremony, and the long-awaited union of their Catholic Majesties saw a jostle for placement in church between Spanish grandees and French ambassadors.[1]

Such instances of 'status interaction' may seem strange to modern eyes, but they abound in early modern sources. They might appear amusing or trivial now, but contemporaries took them very seriously. The symbolic expression of social position was an ever-present source of concern and conflict, across geographical and

---

[1] The context and sources of 1679 are discussed in detail in Chapter One. For the provincial disputes, see BM, MS 2741, fos. 45v–69v, *passim*; Adrien Bonvallet, 'Le bureau des finances de la généralité de Poitiers', *Mémoires de la société des antiquaires de l'ouest*, 2nd ser., vi (1883), 261 n. 1; Tillet, *Chronique bordeloise* (Bordeaux, 1703), pp. 64–6, 69–70. For the Spanish ones, AAE, CP, Espagne 64, esp. fos. 177–208; *Gazette* (1679), pp. 617, 628.

temporal boundaries and within a wide range of political and social configurations: from Ireland in the north to Naples in the south and from Russia in the east to colonial America in the west;[2] in the eighteenth as in the sixteenth centuries;[3] in city-states, in centralizing monarchies, and in the fragmented Holy Roman Empire;[4] from the level of local communities to the international 'Society of Princes'.

On the local level, status interaction was not limited to the salient moments of incursion by sovereigns and by other grand personages. Communities lived their own share of ceremonial highlights, routines, and contestations, as magistrates, municipalities, confraternities, and other parties regularly interacted and contended in civic processions, religious services, and social occasions. The symbolic contention between treasurers and judges in Poitiers, for example, raged on from well before 1679 to the town's Corpus Christi celebrations in the next century.[5] On state level, status interaction marked changes and continuities in the relations among rulers and elites. In the international arena, it was—and to a certain extent remains— part and parcel of diplomacy and power politics. Clashes over the minutest points of protocol regularly disrupted international relations and occasionally threatened war. In the most famous example, an earlier Franco-Spanish dispute from the 1660s, the order of ambassadorial carriages on the street delineated a new European order, as a Spain in decline gave way, under pressure, to a rising France.[6]

---

[2] Brendan Kane, *The Politics and Culture of Honour in Britain and Ireland, 1541–1641* (Cambridge, 2010), esp. ch. 6 on precedence disputes; Gabriel Guarino, *Representing the King's Splendour: Communication and Reception of Symbolic Forms of Power in Viceregal Naples* (Manchester, 2010), esp. ch. 2; Jan Hennings, 'The Semiotics of Diplomatic Dialogue: Pomp and Circumstance in Tsar Peter I's Visit to Vienna in 1698', *International History Review*, xxx (2008), 515–44; Tamar Herzog, *Upholding Justice: Society, State, and the Penal System in Quito (1650–1750)* (Ann Arbor, 2004), pp. 221–32; Alejandro Cañeque, 'On Cushions and Chairs: The Ritual Construction of Authority in New Spain', in Laurie Postlewate and Wim Hüsken (eds), *Acts and Texts: Performance and Ritual in the Middle Ages and the Renaissance* (Amsterdam-New York, 2007), pp. 101–48.

[3] Besides the examples cited in this and in the following paragraph, see the discussions of the longer *durée* of status interaction in the final section and in the Conclusion.

[4] Richard C. Trexler, *Public Life in Renaissance Florence* (New York, 1980), esp. chs. 8 and 9; Edward Muir, *Civic Ritual in Renaissance Venice* (Princeton, 1981), esp. pp. 201–3, 235–7; Barbara Stollberg-Rilinger, 'La communication symbolique à l'époque pré-moderne: Concepts, thèses, perspectives de recherche', *Trivium*, ii (2008) (<http://trivium.revues.org/1152>); Barbara Stollberg-Rilinger, 'On the Function of Rituals in the Holy Roman Empire', in R. J. W. Evans, Michael Schaich, and Peter H. Wilson (eds), *The Holy Roman Empire, 1495–1806* (Oxford, 2011), pp. 359–73.

[5] Bonvallet, 'Le bureau des finances', pp. 268–81. Notable studies include Stuart Carroll, *Blood and Violence in Early Modern France* (Oxford, 2006), esp. chs. 2 and 3; Robert Darnton, 'A Bourgeois Puts His World in Order: The City as a Text', in Robert Darnton, *The Great Cat Massacre and Other Episodes in French Cultural History* (New York, 1984), pp. 107–43; Robert Descimon, 'Le corps de ville et le système cérémoniel parisien au début de l'âge moderne', in Marc Boone and Maarten Prak (eds), *Statuts individuels, statuts corporatifs et statuts judiciaires dans les villes européennes* (Leuven, 1996), pp. 73–128; Roger Mettam, 'Power, Status and Precedence: Rivalries among the Provincial Elites of Louis XIV's France', *Transactions of the Royal Historical Society*, 5th ser., xxxviii (1988), 43–62; Robert A. Schneider, *The Ceremonial City: Toulouse Observed 1738–1780* (Princeton, 1995), esp. ch. 4.

[6] William Roosen, 'Early Modern Diplomatic Ceremonial: A Systems Approach', *The Journal of Modern History*, lii (1980), 452–76; Lucien Bély, *La société des princes: XVIᵉ–XVIIIᵉ siècle* (Paris, 1999), esp. pt 3; Alexandre Tessier, 'Des carrosses qui en cachent d'autres: retour sur certains incidents qui marquèrent l'ambassade de Lord Denzil Holles à Paris, de 1663 à 1666', in Lucien Bély and Géraud Poumarède (eds), *L'incident diplomatique (XVIᵉ–XVIIIᵉ siècle)* (Paris, 2010), pp. 197–240; Hennings, 'The Semiotics of Diplomatic Dialogue'.

Hierarchy was inherent in all these early modern arenas, and the open pursuit of its external manifestations both widespread and legitimate. Social reputations and political authority depended on such status symbols, and contemporaries invested in them a great deal of time, effort, and resources. While most did not question the general principle of hierarchy, few regarded their particular position as an immutable given. Status was open to contestation. Far from a unitary, consensual, or static chain of being, the early modern world was a patchwork of overlapping, competing, often poorly-defined hierarchies: lay and ecclesiastical, local and foreign, old and new. In these circumstances, status symbols did not simply reflect a predefined social and political order; they continually defined and redefined positions and identities.

Status regularly materialized at the level of concrete interactions, among persons and between persons and objects. These interactions occurred in solemn ceremonies as on everyday occasions, in public arenas and in private settings. Anything could figure in status interaction: from precedence in three-dimensional space to the temporal order of events; from canopies and pews to nightshirts and drinking cups; from the length of a textile train to the number of adjectives in a verbal formula. It involved diverse and subtle distinctions and gradations, which reflected—and shaped—the intricacy of early modern socio-political structures, identities, and relations. Such a micro-level, multifaceted, and complex object of historical inquiry calls on us to zoom in on a specific arena, where the political stakes, the social relations, and the cultural practices can be properly discerned on the basis of available sources.

This study accordingly offers an in-depth analysis of status interaction among the French aristocracy during the reign of Louis XIV. The court society of the 'Sun King' is among the most famous historical arenas of status interaction. Already at its time, it was perceived as a focal point and a model, in France and in Europe at large. As the centre of government, the court combined the social and the political, or the micro-political and the macro-political. Its hierarchy led up to the throne, and its stakes extended from localized contexts to wider 'national' and international ones. The temporal focus on a single yet remarkably long reign balances the need for an overall coherence of framework with scope for considering diachronic evolution and change. Last but not least, aristocrats have left traces more abundant and more diverse than have other strata of society, in their own writings and archives and in other contemporaneous accounts of the minutest aspects of their existence. They thus lend themselves better to the formidable challenge of deciphering and reconstructing codes of behaviour that are often subtle and implicit.

How instructive is this arena? Status interaction probably reached its highest level of intensity and complexity in aristocratic society. The French court in particular might seem exceptional in the degree of 'ritualization' of its daily life, most famously during the monarch's morning rising, the *lever*. Even the rising of the Sun King, however, has parallels elsewhere on the historical horizon.[7] More generally,

---

[7] See Chapter Five.

as the opening paragraphs have already emphasized and as subsequent discussions will further demonstrate, most aspects of status interaction were by no means peculiar to Versailles. Solemn occasions like marriages or processions and everyday routines such as courtesy calls or letter-writing engaged the status of participants in a myriad of social, geographical, and temporal contexts. The insights to be gleaned from this highly influential and richly documented historical arena can thus contribute towards a better understanding of the significance of status interaction in the early modern world in general.

PRELIMINARIES (I): HISTORIOGRAPHICAL AND CONCEPTUAL

Such a key arena has of course attracted the attention of a vast number of scholars from a variety of disciplines, including the burgeoning sub-discipline of court studies.[8] Surprisingly, though, court society at the time of Louis XIV has yet to receive its definitive treatment. In the domains of status, ceremony, and etiquette in particular, many studies continue to work with the same old paradigms, perspectives, and sources. There has been no satisfying account of status interaction 'on the ground', in all its complexity and multifacetedness, as experienced in practice by its various protagonists. Not least, even after decades of 'revisionism' by social and political historians, the ceremonial court is still primarily considered as a reflection of the monarchy's designs and interests.[9] Completeness being obviously impractical, the following paragraphs review the most influential past projects dealing with status and ceremony in early modern France, and the main studies of recent years. The subsequent discussion will consider general conceptual issues in relation to the aims and defining terms of this study.

The seminal work in this context has been Norbert Elias's analysis of court society, which played a pivotal role in the emergence of court studies and of cultural history in general.[10] Critics have subsequently exposed the historiographical and

---

[8] For an analytic overview, see Jeroen Duindam, 'Early Modern Court Studies: An Overview and a Proposal', in Markus Völkel and Arno Strohmeyer (eds), *Historiographie an europäischen Höfen (16.–18. Jahrhundert)* (Berlin, 2009), pp. 37–60. See also John Adamson (ed.), *The Princely Courts of Europe: Ritual, Politics and Culture under the Ancien Régime, 1500–1750* (London, 1999).

[9] A pioneer of the 'revisionist' paradigm of social collaboration between monarchy and elites has recently perpetuated the image of the 'total control' of Louis XIV, who 'invented a whole science of petty distinctions that kept the courtiers competing among themselves and turning to him as arbiter': William Beik, *A Social and Cultural History of Early Modern France* (Cambridge, 2009), pp. 330–1.

[10] The most relevant work is Elias's *Die höfische Gesellschaft* (*The Court Society*), written in the early 20th century, first published in 1969, and first translated into English by Edmund Jephcott in 1983. This study was part of the foundation for his most famous work, *Über den Prozess der Zivilisation*. Both have recently reappeared as volumes ii and iii (respectively) of new German and English editions: *Gesammelte Schriften* (Frankfurt, 1997–); *The Collected Works of Norbert Elias* (Dublin, 2006–). See also Roger Chartier's preface to the French edition: *La société de cour* (Paris, 1985), pp. i–xxviii; English translation by Lydia G. Cochrane in Roger Chartier, *Cultural History: Between Practices and Representations* (Cambridge, 1988), ch. 3.

methodological flaws in Elias's model.[11] However, since his ideas continue to reson-
ate in recent scholarship, and since some remain valid despite the general critique,
it is worth noting how they relate to our inquiry. Elias has been hugely instrumental in transforming ceremony and etiquette from 'a dusty exhibit in an historical
museum' to legitimate objects of scholarly inquiry.[12] Rightly accused of many
anachronistic readings, he nonetheless had the vision to insist on the significance
of status in early modern society, a significance that modern observers still tend to
underestimate.[13]

Elias pioneered in relating codes of behaviour and micro-interactions to macro-
historical questions like the structure of society and the nature of political power.
But while he was right to insist on the broad implications of minute ceremonial
gestures, his analysis of these implications suffered from his reliance on dated historiography and on a highly partial sample of sources—notably the enticing yet
problematic memoirs of the duke of Saint-Simon.[14] Elias famously posited etiquette as an instrument of power that enabled monarchs to domesticate nobilities
obsessed with status competition. The domestication thesis appears questionable,
however, in light of increasing evidence that the old 'sword' aristocracy retained
dominance after 1661.[15] Granted, this does not rule out the potential for instrumental use of ceremony and etiquette, but by privileging the monarch's perspective
as master manipulator of the system, Elias's interpretation has relegated courtiers
to an essentially passive role.[16]

Two other influential projects that have dealt with ceremony and status in early
modern France are known as the 'American Neo-Ceremonialist School' and the
'Society of Orders'. The Neo-Ceremonialists produced in-depth analyses of individual ceremonies, beginning with Ralph Giesey's monograph on the royal funeral
and continuing with works dedicated to the *lit de justice*, the coronation, and the
royal entry.[17] Drawing extensively on series of contemporary sources, this school

---

[11] See esp. Jeroen Duindam, *Myths of Power: Norbert Elias and the Early Modern European Court* (Amsterdam, 1995); Emmanuel Le Roy Ladurie with Jean-François Fitou, *Saint-Simon, ou le système de la Cour* (Paris, 1997), pp. 515–20.

[12] *The Collected Works of Norbert Elias*, ii, 91.

[13] 'One does not need to share the values of court people to understand that they formed part of the constraints of their social existence, and that for most of these people it was difficult if not impossible to step out of the competition for socially valued opportunities': *The Collected Works of Norbert Elias*, ii, 83.

[14] Much of this literature was already dated at the time of composition and was hardly updated for publication in the 1960s: Duindam, *Myths of Power*, pp. 184–7. On Saint-Simon, see later.

[15] Roger Mettam, *Power and Faction in Louis XIV's France* (Oxford, 1988); Katia Béguin, 'Louis XIV et l'aristocratie: coup de majesté ou retour à la tradition?', *Histoire Économie et Société*, xix (2000), 497–512; William Beik, 'The Absolutism of Louis XIV as Social Collaboration', *Past & Present*, clxxxviii (2005), 195–224; James B. Collins, *The State in Early Modern France*, 2nd edn (Cambridge, 2009).

[16] See also Chapter Five, which revisits one of Elias's key examples of the function of etiquette.

[17] Ralph E. Giesey, *The Royal Funeral Ceremony in Renaissance France* (Geneva, 1960); Sarah Hanley, *The* Lit de Justice *of the Kings of France: Constitutional Ideology in Legend, Ritual, and Discourse* (Princeton, 1983); Richard A. Jackson, *Vive le roi!: A History of the French Coronation from Charles V to Charles X* (Chapel Hill, 1984); Lawrence M. Bryant, *The King and the City in the Parisian Royal Entry Ceremony: Politics, Ritual, and Art in the Renaissance* (Geneva, 1986). Another work associated with this school is Michèle Fogel, *Les cérémonies de l'information dans la France du XVIᵉ au XVIIIᵉ siècle* (Paris, 1989). See also Ralph E. Giesey, *Rulership in France, 15th–17th Centuries* (Aldershot, 2004).

established the study of symbolic forms and their evolution on a firmer empirical basis. The range of forms, however, was largely limited to the special case of state ceremony in the period preceding what they saw as a shift in ceremonial idiom with the advent of absolutism. Analytically speaking, the main problem lies in their tendency to reduce ceremony to a single abstract framework of 'constitutional ideology'. The resulting analyses appear forced at times, and in any case do not convey the complexity of occasions that involved multiple meanings, protagonists, and agendas, practical as well as ideological.[18]

In the 'Society of Orders', Roland Mousnier and his followers interrogated status through a model of social stratification. Rejecting Marxist models of a 'Society of Classes', they argued that the social hierarchy of early modern Europe was ordered by an ideological principle of 'social function' rather than in relation to the means of production. In seeking non-economic measures of social position, proponents of this model experimented with methods that would remain useful for subsequent scholars, such as the sampling of honorific titles as status-markers. Ultimately, however, they too forced empirical measures to fit pre-conceived theoretical moulds. Mousnier's Society of Orders, especially in its later formulations, rested on an idealized notion of a unitary, consensual, and static hierarchy. In such a framework, status symbols become attributes of social essences rather than objects of social dynamics.[19]

Among more recent treatments, Jeroen Duindam has provided the best analysis of the early modern French court, opening up fresh avenues and archival sources for comparative research. Integrating the insights of the 'revisionist' critique of absolutism, he offers a nuanced reassessment of the use of ceremony and etiquette as an instrument of power. His main interest, however, lies in rulership and court organization rather than in the agendas and practices of courtiers or in status interaction per se.[20] Emmanuel Le Roy Ladurie, in contrast, has focused on the courtier's viewpoint, illustrating the pervasiveness and subtlety of status and its symbols. Yet his 'system' of hierarchy and ranks is rather a brilliant reading of Saint-Simon and a few other celebrated sources than a systematic account of the court of Louis XIV.[21]

---

[18] See esp. the critique of Alain Boureau e.g. in his 'Les cérémonies royales françaises entre performance juridique et compétence liturgique', *Annales ESC*, xlvi (1991), 1253–64. See also Philippe Buc, *The Dangers of Ritual: Between Early Medieval Texts and Social Scientific Theory* (Princeton, 2001), pp. 229–37.

[19] For a review of Mousnier's project and of other approaches to the social order, see 'À propos des catégories sociales de l'Ancien Régime', introduction to Fanny Cosandey (ed.), *Dire et vivre l'ordre social en France sous l'Ancien Régime* (Paris, 2005), pp. 9–43; for a pungent critique, see Armand Arriaza, 'Mousnier and Barber: The Theoretical Underpinning of the "Society of Orders" in Early Modern Europe', *Past & Present*, lxxxix (1980), 39–57. See also M. L. Bush (ed.), *Social Orders and Social Classes in Europe since 1500: Studies in Social Stratification* (London, 1992); Gail Bossenga, 'Estates, Orders, and Corps', in William Doyle (ed.), *The Oxford Handbook of the Ancien Régime* (Oxford, 2011), pp. 141–66; Gilles Chabaud (ed.), *Classement, DÉclassement, REclassement de l'Antiquité à nos jours* (Limoges, 2011).

[20] Duindam, *Myths of Power*, and Duindam, *Vienna and Versailles: The Courts of Europe's Dynastic Rivals, 1550–1780* (Cambridge, 2003), esp. chs. 5 and 6; cf. the more traditional account in Jean-François Solnon, *La Cour de France* (Paris, 1996[1987]), esp. pt 3.

[21] Le Roy Ladurie with Fitou, *Saint-Simon, ou le système de la Cour*, esp. ch. 1. An earlier Saint-Simon-based system of ranks is Henri Brocher, *À la cour de Louis XIV: le rang et l'étiquette sous l'ancien régime* (Paris, 1934).

Drawing on a mass of archival sources, Frédérique Leferme-Falguières has provided a vast panorama of court ceremonial in the seventeenth and eighteenth centuries, from state ceremonies to everyday life. Such an ambitious scope has, however, inevitably strained the reliability of her findings.[22] In a series of articles, Fanny Cosandey has interrogated the question of precedence in the French monarchy during the sixteenth and seventeenth centuries, based primarily on the manuscript compilations of later early modern erudites. She too highlighted the efficacy of ceremonial as an instrument of royal power, albeit in a more nuanced way than had Elias or the Neo-Ceremonialists. Cosandey has forcefully argued for the importance of the quarrels of precedence and delineated some of their complex mechanisms. Her analysis, though, has focused more on the level of social ranks than on that of symbolic codes, and on the question of order and sequence more than on other aspects of status relations.[23]

This study explores status interaction during the reign of Louis XIV: how and why individuals and groups expressed, shaped, and contested social positions in moments of interpersonal contact, from high ceremonies to everyday occasions. Since there never was a consensual or coherent Society of Orders, the symbolic dimension of social occasions became determinant. Certain aspects of these occasions—spatial, material, gestural, linguistic—signified the respective positions of interacting parties. To gain the upper hand in these *de facto*, micro-level orderings was thus to advance one's particular version of the social hierarchy at large. The 'Culture of Orders' created as much as reflected the Society (or societies) of Orders.

This book traces some of the major codes of status interaction and how contemporaries used them to achieve social and political objectives. By 'codes' I mean models or patterns of contemporary practices and of their associated meanings, not of normative or necessarily explicit sets of rules. For each status code, I have attempted to detect the relevant vocabulary and grammar, so to speak: which aspects of a ceremony, a dress item, a gesture, or a letter were meaningful with regard to status, and how they combined to signify social positions on concrete occasions. Given the arbitrariness of the symbol, any aspect could in theory be relevant; in fact, only a subset of potential aspects were consistently so in any given context.[24] Once deciphered, these codes reveal underlying regularities—and irregularities—in what had previously seemed like an undifferentiated sea of detail. Since the sources themselves do not usually explicate the codes, one could not tell the significant from the incidental in a given text, image, or object without systematic inquiry; the results of this study should thus prove helpful to readers of early

---

[22] Frédérique Leferme-Falguières, 'Le monde des courtisans: la haute noblesse et le cérémonial royal aux XVIIᵉ et XVIIIᵉ siècles' (Univ. of Paris I Ph.D. thesis, 2004); the first half was published in Frédérique Leferme-Falguières, *Les courtisans: une société de spectacle sous l'Ancien Régime* (Paris, 2007). For a more detailed critique, see Giora Sternberg, 'The Culture of Orders: Status Interactions during the Reign of Louis XIV' (Univ. of Oxford D.Phil. thesis, 2009).

[23] For a useful summary and references to her main articles, see Fanny Cosandey, 'Classement ou ordonnancement? Les querelles de préséances en France sous l'Ancien Régime', in Chabaud (ed.), *Classement, DÉclassement, REclassement*, pp. 95–103.

[24] To give a simple example, in our historical context the upper margin of pages in letters was meaningful with regard to status, but the right-hand margin was not: see Chapter Six.

modern sources even when status is not their primary concern. I have also looked for cross-code regularities, or recurring principles that characterize status interaction in general.[25]

Although some of the resulting categories and generalizations transcend the consciousness or perspective of any individual actor, I have tried to draw as near as possible to contemporaries in order to recapture early modern perceptions of the stakes and the strategies of status interaction. In the study of symbolic forms and behaviour, there is an inherent danger of forced or anachronistic interpretations. Historians of pre-modern periods in particular are at a disadvantage compared with natural scientists or anthropologists: they cannot generate experimental data or question informants.[26] By the seventeenth century, though, the number and the nature of available sources—at least in better-documented contexts, like that of elite society—make the task arguably possible, if still formidable. Here as in other cases, the early modern period has left behind just the right balance of sources: ample and varied enough to enable us to go beyond wild conjecture, but limited enough to make the task particularly interesting.

The basic stakes of status interaction become clear already from a cursory glance. Early moderns did not conceal or sublimate the pursuit of status symbols: they quarrelled openly over a form of address and unabashedly disputed the length of a train. For us, this generates not only fascination, but also the confidence that we are dealing with intentional symbolic behaviour and not simply with a retrospective symbolic interpretation. The challenge remains, however, to go beyond such general claims as 'status was important', 'early modern ceremonies were intricate', or even 'train-length signified hierarchical position', and to make sense of specific moves and their significance. Did the trains worn on a particular occasion confirm or disrupt the status quo? Why did a journal-writer note down dress codes on some occasions but not on others? And what can all this tell us about social dynamics or power struggles? The reconstruction of 'insider' actions and perspectives requires patient and resourceful detective-work that, by piecing together extant material of diverse types and origins, can recover practices and assumptions which were often taken for granted, and hence were seldom formulated explicitly, let alone systematically.[27]

Status interaction took place in a wide variety of contexts and occasions. The Neo-Ceremonialists and others have traced a shift from state ceremonies to the ritualization of daily life in the course of the seventeenth century, in particular during the reign of Louis XIV.[28] This transformation has been overstated, and in any case the precise distinctions among 'ceremony', 'ritual', and 'etiquette' are not germane to this inquiry. Status interaction cut across these chronological and typological

---

[25] See the Conclusion, esp. pp. 159–64.

[26] Peter Burke, *The Historical Anthropology of Early Modern Italy: Essays on Perception and Communication* (Cambridge, 1987), p. 15; Buc, *The Dangers of Ritual*, p. 4.

[27] On sources, see next section. See also the more specific discussions of methodological challenges and solutions in the introductory sections of chapters.

[28] See e.g. Ralph E. Giesey, 'The King Imagined', in Keith Michael Baker (ed.), *The French Revolution and the Creation of Modern Political Culture* (4 vols, Oxford, 1987–94), i, 41–59.

divides. The handing of the chemise at the daily *lever*, already prevalent in the sixteenth century, corresponds to the handing of the regalia in the course of the coronation and of other high ceremonies that continued until the end of the ancien régime. The codes and contestations of hat-wearing (covered or uncovered?) operated similarly at court and in *lits de justice*.[29] For heuristic purposes, though, it is useful to speak of a 'ceremonial spectrum', roughly ordered by frequency: from the rarer high ceremonies, such as the state events discussed by the Neo-Ceremonialists or other dynastic occasions like marriages; through recurring events on the religious or social calendar, notably including courtesy visits; to the routines of court life and other quotidian practices like letter-writing. The book journeys across this spectrum, illustrating differences as well as similarities along the way.

There is a tendency to view such ceremonial occasions in a prescriptive or normative sense, as the observance or performance of predefined formalities. From this perspective, status contestations become an aberration: they 'mar' ceremony, 'breach' etiquette, are 'bad' ritual.[30] Behind this normative view stand influential documentary and theoretical lenses. On the documentary side, one could point to the excessive scholarly reliance on prescriptive sources, not least on early modern courtesy literature. Although readily accessible and comprehensible to outsiders, such sources do not offer a reliable key to the actual practice of contemporaries.[31] On the theoretical side, 'performative' approaches to ceremony tend to assume a predetermined script and to regard any departure from it as a 'deviation' or 'failure' that 'represents a more general failure of the ritual ordering of society itself'.[32] In a similar way, Erving Goffman's framework describes an 'interaction order' that is geared to 'face-saving' and to the reduction of friction, according to the injunctions of 'our Anglo-American society'.[33]

Though sometimes useful as a point of departure, these lenses ultimately obscure the fact that, in early modern times, it was interaction disorder that was often the norm. In an account of the proceedings of the estates of Brittany in 1636, the writer noted in passing 'some contestations *quite ordinary in all assemblies*, over the seating and precedence of some nobles'.[34] Men and women literally threatened the face of their interactants as they grappled, shoved, and scratched one another during the

---

[29] On handing, see Chapter Five; on hats, compare e.g. BN, FF 14119, fo. 278v, and Hanley, *The Lit de Justice*, p. 287.

[30] Giesey, 'The King Imagined', p. 48; Schneider, *The Ceremonial City*, p. 145; cf. Buc, *The Dangers of Ritual*, pp. 8ff., 255. 'Etiquette' especially has this prescriptive connotation and I accordingly minimize use of the term.

[31] For a detailed illustration, see the discussion of letter-writing manuals in Chapter Six. See also John Walter, 'Gesturing at Authority: Deciphering the Gestural Code of Early Modern England', in Michael J. Braddick (ed.), *The Politics of Gesture: Historical Perspectives* (*Past & Present* Supplement 4, 2009), p. 103 (there, though, 'code' is used in a prescriptive sense). Court ordinances and official paperwork are similarly popular and problematic as mirrors of actual practice.

[32] Schneider, *The Ceremonial City*, p. 12 (a discussion of classic anthropological frameworks).

[33] The most relevant work in this context is his *Interaction Ritual: Essays on Face-to-Face Behavior* (New York, 1967). For recent historical uses and reassessments of Goffman, see Braddick, *The Politics of Gesture*.

[34] Theodore and Denys Godefroy, *Le Ceremonial François* (2 vols, Paris, 1649), ii, 377 (my emphasis).

most solemn occasions, a far cry from the dictums of courtesy.[35] The ordering of society was a matter for negotiation and contestation, not just observance or performance. One party's deviation was another party's return to immemorial tradition. Those who stood to lose often boycotted the occasion, showing little regard for its general success or failure. The notion of a consensual or stable script would have been foreign to their experience.

Indeed, was there a script at all? Even at the court of the Sun King no fixed body of rules regulated all the high ceremonies and everyday routines that expressed and shaped the hierarchy in practice. In lieu of positive codification, the system operated largely by customary law: precedents served to determine subsequent occasions. This introduced enough structure and regularity to allow complexity and conscious planning, yet without the rigidity that might have ruled out contention and change. In the case of formal dispute, the monarch as arbiter would normally rule with reference to past usage rather than simply by his discretionary authority as 'master of the ranks'. This logic of the precedent meant that any interaction could potentially set, confirm, or disrupt status codes, and hence redefine social positions and relations.[36]

Closely connected to the prescriptive viewpoint is the tendency to adopt the perspective of the monarch or of the state, and to measure status and ceremony by the yardstick of their designs and interests. Noticeable already in studies of non-monarchical political units such as the Italian city-states, this tendency is particularly strong in the case of the court 'of' Louis XIV. Ceremony and etiquette are thus considered primarily as instruments of central power, either as part of a coordinated machinery of propaganda or as a means of domestication. This central perspective has both guided the selection of evidence and coloured its interpretation.[37] To be sure, the Sun King was the single most important and influential person at court: the pinnacle of the hierarchy, the master and arbiter of ranks, and the focal point of ceremonial activity. But status interaction concerned multiple actors who cultivated their own stakes even in the midst of the most monarchical state ceremony or the most heliocentric of Versailles's rituals. Much status interaction, moreover, took place outside the monarch's presence, knowledge, or indeed interest.[38] Even if we held the extreme view that the monarchy enjoyed absolute control over the system and sowed endemic contestation among the aristocracy,

---

[35] See e.g. Godefroy, *Le Ceremonial François*, ii, 127; Sourches, iii, 423; Bonvallet, 'Le bureau des finances', pp. 269, 276–7; AM Nîmes, OO 27, no. 6; Carroll, *Blood and Violence*.

[36] 'If a certain "honor" had been usurped and no one objected, the honor could be defended as an acquired right thereafter. This is why the court is also referred to as Theatrum Praecedentiae': Duindam, *Myths of Power*, p. 125. In some cases, the monarch did issue positive regulations or ordinances (e.g. on the service of the household: AN, O¹ 756), but they never amounted to anything resembling a body of ceremonial law. For a comparable constitutional situation in the Holy Roman Empire, see Stollberg-Rilinger, 'La communication symbolique'.

[37] On the machinery of propaganda, see Peter Burke, *The Fabrication of Louis XIV* (New Haven-London, 1992), and Gérard Sabatier, *Versailles ou la figure du roi* (Paris, 1999); cf. Oded Rabinovitch, 'Versailles as a Family Enterprise: The Perraults, 1660–1700', *French Historical Studies*, xxxvi (2013), 385–416. On the instrumental approach and domestication thesis, see earlier, p. 5.

[38] The proposed perspectival decentring is thus somewhat akin to Tom Stoppard's famous strategy in *Rosencrantz and Guildenstern Are Dead* (I am grateful to Paul Friedland for this analogy).

the story of the 'victims' would still be worth telling, and in their own terms. This study thus interrogates the phenomenon from the multiple perspectives of contesting actors, stakes, and strategies.

Though different in perspective and unequal in rank, these actors shared a comparable competence in status codes. In other contexts and interactions, social distinction turned on differences in knowledge as well as in behaviour, between contemporary insiders and outsiders. Aristocrats, for example, notoriously used dress, language, and comportment in a manner different from other social strata, notably from the 'rustic' provincial nobility or from the 'vile' bourgeoisie.[39] My main concern here, however, is with mechanisms of distinction that operated through codes familiar and available to all protagonists and that involved direct, explicit, and informed contestation, not just passive resistance. Such an inquiry calls for a focus on a specific milieu or community (loosely defined). Here I have chosen French aristocratic society, but analogous cases can be made for other strata, down to the smallest provincial towns. Indeed, the limits of the phenomenon may well be documentary rather than social.[40]

After all, the notion of elite too is a question of scale and perspective. Distinctions marked shifting gradations along multiple hierarchies, not a simple or stable dichotomy between superiors and subordinates. One party's superior was another's inferior. Accordingly, my use of these two terms, even as nouns, retains the comparative rather than the absolute sense. This 'relativity principle', as we shall see, is particularly pertinent on the level of codes: whether or not a train was considered long or a term of address respectful did not derive from any inherent formal characteristic, but from its use relative to other forms or to other parties. The signification of forms, moreover, was not limited to the simple issue of sequential order. The use of the term *Monseigneur*, for example, signified great deference, not just the inferiority of addresser to addressee.[41] In other words, the question of precedence is only one facet of the wider and more complex phenomenon of status interaction.

What sort of agency did status interaction involve? It is useful to distinguish here between motivations and strategies. My working assumption is that the general preoccupation with status and its symbols was, as Elias put it, 'part of the constraints of social existence' under the ancien régime. It engaged not only fanatics like Saint-Simon, but also many others not famous for status-mindedness, throughout the social hierarchy. To renounce it, as to renounce society, was always

---

[39] François de Callières, *Du bon, et du mauvais Usage dans les manieres de s'exprimer. Des façons de parler bourgeoises. Et en quoy elles sont differentes de celles de la Cour* (Paris, 1693).

[40] See e.g. Denise Turrel, 'L'identité par la distinction: les robes syndicales des petites villes de Bresse (XVᵉ–XVIIIᵉ siècle)', in *Cahiers d'histoire*, xliii (1998), 475–87. For a recent general overview, see Jean-Pascal Daloz, *The Sociology of Elite Distinction: From Theoretical to Comparative Perspectives* (Basingstoke, 2010). See also Alain Faudemay, *La distinction à l'âge classique: émules et enjeux* (Paris, 1992).

[41] And, correspondingly, on the level of social ranks: while it is true that, since 1576, no *dignité* could dispute the precedence of the princes of royal blood (Cosandey, 'Classement ou ordonnancement', p. 99), this by no means put an end to the latter's contestations with inferiors (see esp. Chapter Four; on the *Monseigneur*, see Chapter Six).

a possible course of action, but one that came at a price. Status was woven into the fabric of early modern life: it enjoyed ideological justifications, buttressed power and political authority, provided social distinction and prestige, even had economic implications.[42] Most of the time, most contemporaries must have pursued this compulsion without pausing to reflect on it, much as their modern counterparts would pursue money, a career, or family life.

This does not mean, however, that they pursued it blindly. The quest for distinction was but one of many motivations, which might call for contradictory courses of action.[43] Sometimes contemporaries would make deliberate status concessions to promote other agendas, not least in attempts to recruit support from influential persons or from potential allies. Most importantly, the pursuit itself gave much scope for creativity and ingenuity. Actors did not simply follow a rigid set of rules. The mastery and successful manipulation of the codes of status interaction involved a great deal of sophistication and cunning, as the following chapters will show. Disentangling motivations and strategies also helps to underscore that the calculated nature of manoeuvres by no means entails a lack of passion or emotion on the part of protagonists.

PRELIMINARIES (II): ANTECEDENTS, HIERARCHIES, SOURCES

Status interaction in its early modern form did not begin with the reign of Louis XIV.[44] The sixteenth century already abounds with comparable codes, contestations, and strategies. To give just a handful of examples directly related to the themes of the following chapters: in 1509, municipal and royal officials in Paris disputed two-dimensional spatial choreographies of precedence in processions. In 1553, a contestation over the hoods worn by members of the *Cour des Aides* delayed a special service at the abbey of Saint-Denis, while parties went to and fro to argue their case before the sovereign.[45] In 1570, the duke of Nevers boycotted the royal marriage ceremony after the king had ruled against his rank. A few years later, members of an ecclesiastical assembly admonished a correspondent who had

---

[42] In 1739, the treasurers of Montpellier argued that a contrary decision on the protocol of a complimentary visit would risk their investment in their venal offices: AD Hérault, C 58, no. 33. Conversely, of course, the huge amounts that contemporaries spent on ennobling and honorary positions reflect the capital importance of status. See e.g. Bossenga, 'Estates, Orders, and Corps', pp. 151–2.

[43] Studies exploring alternative aristocratic motivations in this period include Jonathan Dewald, *Aristocratic Experience and the Origins of Modern Culture: France, 1570–1715* (Berkeley, 1993), and Jay M. Smith, *The Culture of Merit: Nobility, Royal Service, and the Making of Absolute Monarchy in France, 1600–1789* (Ann Arbor, 1996). The pursuit of offices was a related yet distinct motivation: Leonhard Horowski, '"Such a Great Advantage for My Son": Office-Holding and Career Mechanisms at the Court of France, 1661–1789', *The Court Historian*, viii (2003), 125–75.

[44] Nor did it end with the reign: see the Conclusion.

[45] François Bonnardot et al. (eds), *Registres des délibérations du bureau de la ville de Paris* (15 vols, Paris, 1883–1921), i, 151–3; iv, 89–90; Godefroy, *Le Ceremonial François*, ii, 949–50; cf. Descimon, 'Le corps de ville'.

addressed them as *Messieurs* rather than as *Messeigneurs*.[46] Intricate status codes like train-bearing and ritualized daily routines like chemise-handing during the *lever* were already in place under the Valois monarchs and continued under the first two Bourbons.[47]

A sense of continuity is thus evident enough to dispel the notion of a radical transformation of the system under the Sun King.[48] The same holds for the reign of Henri III in the second half of the sixteenth century, another conventional landmark in the evolution of ceremony and etiquette.[49] Although change in the personal inclination or involvement of monarchs is easier to trace, it cannot, as argued earlier, stand for the development of status interaction as a whole. Nor can other seemingly-related and better-studied aspects of ceremony and behaviour, such as splendour, familiarity, or refinement: that the sixteenth-century court was more 'familiar' than its successors does not entail that status was less important or less contested there.[50] Quantitative and qualitative differences in documentation pose a further obstacle to detailed diachronic comparison. Not least, there is no surviving prior equivalent to the serial inside accounts of Louis XIV's Masters of Ceremonies.

In the absence of comparably systematic studies of status interaction in these earlier contexts, it remains difficult to identify precisely what did change and what did not. It would be reasonable, though, to acknowledge growing standardization and complexity, in status codes as in social hierarchies. Easier to trace, the reforms of Henri III and the authority, inclination, and longevity of Louis XIV played an important role in these processes. So did the sedentarization of the court and the growing bureaucratic apparatus for ceremony. In 1585, the creation of the posts of Grand Master of Ceremonies and of Introductor of Ambassadors formalized and elevated earlier practices for regulating high ceremony and diplomatic protocol. In the following century, these officials were joined by a small supporting staff, notably by a Master of Ceremonies.[51]

---

[46] Fanny Cosandey, 'L'insoutenable légèreté du rang', in Fanny Cosandey (ed.), *Dire et vivre l'ordre social*, pp. 171–3; Godefroy, *Le Ceremonial François*, ii, 312. Godefroy's compilation includes numerous other examples. See also Monique Chatenet, 'Quelques aspects des funérailles nobiliaires au XVIᵉ siècle', in Jean Balsamo (ed.), *Les funérailles à la Renaissance* (Geneva, 2002), pp. 52ff.

[47] See Chapters Three and Five.

[48] 'Continuity' here refers to the general principles and characteristics of the system; the specifics of ranks and codes changed all the time. Indeed, this state of continual change was a principle of the system (see later).

[49] Monique Chatenet, *La cour de France au XVIᵉ siècle: vie sociale et architecture* (Paris, 2002), esp. ch. 4; Nicolas Le Roux, *La faveur du roi: mignons et courtisans au temps des derniers Valois* (Seyssel, 2001), esp. 176–86; and the recent English synthesis in Robert J. Knecht, *The French Renaissance court, 1483–1589* (New Haven-London, 2008). The first two Bourbons have received less treatment, but see Robin Briggs, 'The Theatre State: Ceremony and Politics 1600–60', *Seventeenth-Century French Studies*, xvi (1994), 15–33; Orest Ranum, 'Courtesy, Absolutism, and the Rise of the French State, 1630–1660', *The Journal of Modern History*, lii (1980), 426–51.

[50] See Chatenet, *La cour de France*, pp. 109, 111–12; Carroll, *Blood and Violence*, p. 310.

[51] See Marie-Lan Nguyen, 'Les grands maîtres des cérémonies et le service des Cérémonies à l'époque moderne, 1585–1792' (Univ. of Paris IV *mémoire de maîtrise*, 1999); Duindam, *Vienna and Versailles*, pp. 188–93; [Auguste Boppe], *Les introducteurs des ambassadeurs, 1585–1900* (Paris, 1901).

The Grand Masters of Ceremonies hailed from a middling or rising sort of nobility, not on a par with other grand officers: the Pot de Rhodes family from 1585, then the marquis of Blainville (a younger son of Colbert) from 1685, and finally the Dreux-Brézés, from 1701 until the end of the ancien régime. The Sainctot family held the post of Master of Ceremonies since the first half of the seventeenth century. In 1691 its best-known member, Nicolas II, sold the post to the newly ennobled Michel Ancel Desgranges, whose family continued to hold it into the second half of the following century. Since the Grand Masters were often away from court, especially during the incessant wars of Louis XIV, the Masters managed the service for extended periods. While this involved direct interaction with the monarch, royal authority was channelled in many cases through the Secretary of State in charge of the king's household.

The duties of these officials concerned the higher end of the ceremonial spectrum, including, *inter alia*, state ceremonies and 'life-cycle' events of members of the royal house. They had little involvement in the daily routines of court life (these were mostly managed by other, more senior officers, such as the Grand Master of the Household or the First Gentlemen of the Bedchamber). For high ceremonies, the Masters drew up the plans, supervised the preparations, and orchestrated the events.[52] Throughout, they had to deal with streams of status claims and contestations from all sides. In many cases, especially those involving the high aristocracy, they would pass on the matter to the king who would personally decide.

Another means of standardization was the increasing reliance on writing as an aid to ceremonial memory. In a system of customary law, past precedents played a crucial role in determining future occasions, especially in deciding status contestations. But how would precedents be noted? In the mid-sixteenth century, Henri II commissioned Du Tillet, the clerk of the *parlement* of Paris, to comb parliamentary and other registers for the 'rank and order' of dignitaries in 'grand and solemn assemblies'.[53] In subsequent reigns, erudites and officials continued to collect information and to research the topic; in 1649, the Godefroys published the most cited reference-work in the field, the voluminous *Ceremonial François*. Besides such compilation of old data, Henri III instructed his officials to keep an 'accurate register' of ongoing ceremonies under their charge. Under Sainctot and Desgranges, this became a detailed and serial coverage, which enabled monarchs to make more informed decisions.[54]

While such standardization structured status interaction, it by no means put an end to contestations. Nor did it leave parties helplessly dependent on a centralizing bureaucratic state. In the absence of positive law, they could still point to contradictory precedents, argue the irrelevance of past cases due to a difference in circumstances, or introduce novel distinctions for which there was no precedent.

[52] Where there is no contrast, I use 'Masters of Ceremonies' as shorthand for Grand Masters as well as Masters.

[53] Godefroy, *Le Ceremonial François* (unpaginated).

[54] More details in the discussion of sources later. The daily routines of court life received less serial coverage and occasional positive codification: see Chapter Five.

Parties, moreover, were quick to appropriate the new informational practices. Magistrates and municipalities had already been recording ceremonies before the household did, and aristocrats soon joined in the creation and assembly of status-related writings and archives. In the most remarkable cases, they even successfully manipulated the official record of the monarchy in their favour, in real time or after the fact.[55]

Status interaction thus remained unstable and contested, as did the social structures and relations that it signified. The French aristocracy never followed a clear-cut, comprehensive, or consistent table of ranks. Throughout the early modern period, new positions appeared, old positions evolved, hierarchies changed. And they all varied with context and perspective. To delineate a single, 'true' hierarchy at any given moment, let alone for a reign that spanned almost a century, thus goes against the grain. It is essential, though, to have a grasp of the main rungs and of those of their members who will appear frequently in what follows. Thus, those who 'held rank' at court during the reign of Louis XIV can be divided into several types. They include all members of the royal house, other princes and dukes subject to the king, and holders of high office. These ranks, like many others, had a strong patrilineal and patriarchal aspect. Most were at least to some extent hereditary, and all transferred to female spouses.[56]

At the top stood Louis XIV. One of France's most celebrated monarchs, in ceremonial as in other respects, he was born in 1638, became king five years later at the death of his father Louis XIII, and was crowned in 1654 after the rebellious Fronde. His 'personal reign' followed the death of Cardinal Mazarin in 1661, and lasted more than half a century until his own death and the accession of his great-grandson, Louis XV, in 1715. There were two queens at court in the course of his reign. The Queen Mother, Anne of Austria, served as regent at its turbulent beginnings and died in 1666. In 1660, the king married Maria Theresa, daughter of Philip IV of Spain. Following her death in 1683 he secretly married Madame de Maintenon, the governess of his bastards by another mistress, Madame de Montespan; this morganatic union did not make Maintenon queen, but allowed some ambiguities of rank in her favour until the end of the reign.

Next came the dauphin, the heir to the throne by strict male primogeniture. The main incumbent of this rank was Louis's eldest son, the *Grand Dauphin*.[57] But the demographic catastrophe of the final years of the reign saw a quick succession of heirs, as the *Grand Dauphin* died in 1711, his eldest son the duke of Burgundy in 1712, and his eldest grandson shortly thereafter. Another grandson, the only legitimate offspring to survive Louis XIV, then became dauphin and finally succeeded

---

[55] See Giora Sternberg, 'Manipulating Information in the Ancien Régime: Ceremonial Records, Aristocratic Strategies, and the Limits of the State Perspective', *The Journal of Modern History*, lxxxv (2013), 239–79, and also in Chapters One, Three, and Four.

[56] In the minority of cases where princesses married beneath their birth rank, they normally retained it by special privilege. On the problematic of birth v. marital rank, see the first two chapters. For the exposition that follows, cf. Appendix I; unavoidably technical, it is nonetheless essential to make sense of subsequent discussions.

[57] Until the *Grand Dauphin*'s birth in 1661, the heir was the king's younger brother Philippe.

as Louis XV. The two dauphines of the reign were the *Grand Dauphin*'s wife, Maria-Anna-Christina-Victoria of Bavaria, from her marriage in 1680 to her death in 1690; and the duchess of Burgundy, daughter of Victor Amadeus II of Savoy. Officially dauphine only from 1711 to her premature death a year later, Burgundy enjoyed the rank of first lady of the court (and the favour of the royal couple) from her arrival in France in 1696.

The 'Children of France' (*enfants de France*) formed the following level. This most obviously applied to daughters or younger sons of French kings; in this case, to two dukes of Orléans: the king's uncle Gaston (son of Henri IV) and his brother Philippe (son of Louis XIII).[58] Both were known at court simply as *Monsieur*, and their wives as *Madame*. Gaston lived in exile from court since 1652, following his conduct at the Fronde, and died early in the reign, in 1660. Macro-politically submissive, Philippe nevertheless sought to aggrandize the house of Orléans, in rank as in other respects. He first married Henrietta-Anne, daughter of Charles I of England, who died in 1670, and then the Palatine Elisabeth-Charlotte, known for her prolific correspondence. Though impatient of ceremony, the second *Madame* was no less jealous of her rank.

Those 'of the direct eldest line, presumed heir to the throne' were also considered Children of France, even when removed from the king by more than one generation.[59] This notably applied to the three legitimate grandchildren of Louis XIV, sons of the *Grand Dauphin*, who were treated as status equals at birth and preceded *Monsieur* by virtue of their greater proximity to the throne. The eldest, the duke of Burgundy, attracted a group of aristocratic reformers critical of Louis XIV's policies (on status as in other matters), whose hopes were shattered by the news of his premature death in 1712. The duke of Anjou left France in 1700 to found the Bourbon line in Spain as Philip V. The youngest, duke of Berry, married the daughter of Philippe II of Orléans in 1710 and died of a riding accident four years later.

Whereas the rank of Children of France had existed for centuries, the following one was a creation of seventeenth-century status interaction. 'Grandchildren of France' (*petits-enfants de France*) came to denote the children of Sons of France.[60] It began with the struggle of Gaston's only child of his first marriage, the *Grande Mademoiselle*, to distinguish herself from more distant cousins of royal blood. The new rank was still far from established at the beginning of the reign, as the *Grande Mademoiselle* was joined by three half-sisters, daughters of Gaston's second wife, Marguerite of Lorraine. These married in the 1660s, to become grand-duchess of Tuscany, duchess of Guise, and duchess of Savoy. When Tuscany returned to France

---

[58] None of the other legitimate children of Louis XIII or of Louis XIV reached adulthood. Three of Henri IV's daughters were still alive when Louis XIV acceded to the throne. They had all married foreign sovereigns by then, thus espousing other countries and rank-systems, though the youngest, Henriette-Marie, the wife of Charles I of England, spent extensive periods in France and was buried in Saint-Denis in 1669.

[59] SSB, xix, 514.

[60] Excluding those of the direct eldest line, considered Children of France. Children of Daughters of France no longer belonged to the dynasty, because born outside the male line.

in 1675 following the failure of her marriage, she retained her birth rank, as had her sister Guise.[61]

Philippe of Orléans also played a key role in establishing this new rank, which concerned his own children. His first marriage produced two Granddaughters of France: the queen of Spain of the opening example and a duchess of Savoy, wife of Victor Amadeus II from 1684. Of Philippe's marriage with Elisabeth-Charlotte, two children reached adulthood. Philippe II of Orléans, duke of Chartres until his father's death in 1701 and duke of Orléans since, married a legitimated daughter of the king in 1692. Although he did not get along well with his royal uncle and father-in-law, he became regent of France in 1715. His sister, Elisabeth-Charlotte, married the duke of Lorraine in 1698. The senior unmarried Granddaughter of France was referred to simply as *Mademoiselle*, a title first held by the *Grande Mademoiselle*, and then successively by Philippe's descendants.[62] Following Sainctot, I use 'Royal Family' (*famille royale*) to denote all ranks down to and including the Grandchildren of France.[63]

All other Bourbons of the legitimate male line were known simply as 'Princes of the Blood' (*princes du Sang*). The men thus stood in line to the throne. Orléans apart, these princes and princesses all belonged to the branch of Condé, founded in the sixteenth century.[64] When Louis XIV acceded to the throne, the head of the branch, 'First Prince of the Blood', was Henri II of Bourbon. His son Louis II, known as the *Grand Condé*, succeeded him in 1646. Military hero and patron of the arts, the *Grand Condé* rebelled during the Fronde, but returned to obedience following the peace with Spain in 1659. His only surviving child, Henri-Jules, was particularly passionate about status. Henri-Jules married two of his children to legitimated bastards of Louis XIV: his successor Louis III to Mademoiselle de Nantes and his daughter Anne-Louise-Bénédicte to the duke of Maine. He and Louis III died in the space of a year, succeeded in 1710 by Louis-Henri, First Minister of Louis XV in the 1720s.[65]

The *Grand Condé*'s brother, Armand of Bourbon, refounded the cadet line of Conti. His and his wife's early death brought their two sons under the tutelage of the head of the branch. The elder, Louis-Armand, was the first legitimate Bourbon to marry a legitimated child of Louis XIV, in 1680. When he too died, in 1685, the younger and more promising François-Louis became prince of Conti, but he suffered from an early disgrace. Another Condé cadet line, Soissons, left one member only by 1643: the princess of Carignan, who retained her birth rank as Princess of the Blood notwithstanding her marriage with a prince of the house of Savoy. Towards the end of the reign, the third Orléans generation reluctantly took its

---

[61] Tuscany lived in retirement from court life, but participated in ceremonies.

[62] The Orléans usurped the title for Philippe II's daughter, even though she was not a Granddaughter of France, as part of their efforts to carve yet another new rank for the fourth generation.

[63] AN, K 1712, no. 6/3.

[64] See esp. Katia Béguin, *Les princes de Condé: rebelles, courtisans et mécènes dans la France du Grand Siècle* (Seyssel, 1999).

[65] Until 1709, the head of the branch was known as *Monsieur le Prince*, and his eldest son as *Monsieur le Duc*, but from Louis III onwards, the head was known as *Monsieur le Duc* only (because of the seniority of the Orléans).

place at the head of the Princes of the Blood, after Philippe II and his wife failed in the attempt to create yet another genealogical level, of 'Great-Grandchildren of France'.

The Royal Family and the Princes of the Blood together composed the 'Royal House' (*maison royale*) of France. What about the bastards of the royal dynasty? Legitimated princes occupied an uneasy intermediate space between the Princes of the Blood and the rest of the aristocracy. The four legitimated bastard lines that Louis XIV inherited from his predecessors (Longueville, Angoulême, Verneuil, Vendôme) had each followed its own path, periodically reconfirmed—and hence implicitly undermined—by successive rulers. The duke of Verneuil, son of Henri IV, benefitted from the early concessions that favoured Louis XIV's children. The Vendômes became a test-case for a third-generation line, receiving confirmation of their intermediate rank in 1694, in parallel with Louis's progeny.

In the course of the reign, the legitimated descendants of the Sun King gradually entered the Bourbon orbit. The daughters married into the legitimate Royal House, each union surpassing the previous in rank. The elevation of their brothers required more direct royal intervention. This process began with the count of Vermandois, son of the king's first *maîtresse en titre*, Madame de La Vallière. It reached its zenith with the duke of Maine and the count of Toulouse, the two surviving sons of Madame de Montespan, supported by their morganatic stepmother and sometime governess Maintenon. From obscurity at birth in the 1670s, these 'Legitimated Princes' (*princes légitimés*) became full-fledged Princes of the Blood at the close of the reign, triggering a constitutional crisis over the question of succession to the throne.

Such an extraordinary rise did not occur overnight. Rather, it depended on a continuous interplay between *de facto* gains in status and *de jure* promotions in rank, which powerfully demonstrates the macro-political ramifications of status interaction. Accordingly, it will occupy us throughout and will be analysed in detail at the end. By way of introduction, it would be useful to trace the main *de jure* landmarks here.[66] The first was legitimation itself, which occurred at an early age. Then, in May 1694, the *parlement* registered royal letters patent that awarded Maine, Toulouse, and their future (legitimate) children an intermediate rank between the Princes of the Blood and the rest of the aristocracy. The process was precipitated by the demographic catastrophe of the last years of the reign. In 1710, the king granted Maine's children the honours enjoyed by their father. A year later, an edict on the peerage gave the Legitimated Princes and their posterity an inter-mediate rank in state events, while private patents (*brevets*) awarded them, for life, the honours of the Princes of the Blood on all other occasions.

The rise of the Legitimated Princes culminated in the edict and declaration that made them full Princes of the Blood, complete with the right to inherit the throne. This happened in 1714–15, after the death of the duke of Berry left the future Louis XV as the Sun King's only legitimate descendant. Louis XIV's own demise reversed the fortunes of his bastard descendants, as their rivals from above and

---

[66] For details and references, see the Conclusion, pp. 164–9.

from below took power during the Orléans regency. In 1717, the Legitimated were removed from the line to the throne, retaining honours on a personal basis only. A year later, Maine and his children lost even the intermediate rank in a celebrated *lit de justice*. The end of the regency, however, signalled a partial recovery for them. In 1723, Maine and Toulouse returned to the status that they had held before 1710. Subsequent decisions improved their position and extended it to their children.

The French rank system also uneasily encompassed princes from other dynasties. The 'Foreign Princes' (*princes étrangers*) came from families established in the kingdom but recognized as having 'the potential to exercise sovereign power, by right of inheritance, but not within France'.[67] At the top of this scale stood scions of the houses of Lorraine (most famously, the branch of Guise) and of Savoy, established already in the sixteenth century. The need to recruit support in the troubled first half of the next century made the crown recognize families with more questionable claims to sovereignty, including the houses of La Tour d'Auvergne-Bouillon, Rohan, La Trémoille, and Monaco. Indeed, it was status interaction that marked differences along this scale of recognition. Like the Princes of the Blood, better-recognized Foreign Princes passed on their rank to all children in the legitimate male line.

For non-princely families, a ducal title offered the prospects of attaining a permanent rank at court.[68] The most significant and prestigious sub-group among them were peers as well as dukes (*ducs et pairs*), nominated by the king and registered by the *parlement*, where they could sit by right. Other sub-groups included hereditary dukes who were not peers, and 'patented dukes' (*ducs à brevet*) who received ducal rank as a personal favour. Peers and hereditary dukes passed on their rank by the principle of (usually male) primogeniture, and numbered a few dozen families during the reign of Louis XIV.[69] Other noble titles did not confer official rank at court. The Foreign Princes and the dukes were thus collectively known as 'titled people' (*gens titrés*), while other marquises and counts were considered 'untitled'.

By the mid-seventeenth century, members of these hereditary groups held most of the high offices that conferred a functional rank at court, including the 'Grand Offices of the Crown'. Thus, the Condés were Grand Masters of the King's Household; the Bouillons—Grand Chamberlains; the Lorraines—Grand Equerries. Titled aristocrats also came to monopolize the four posts of First Gentleman of the Bedchamber that monitored access to the king. Though not formally hereditary, high court office tended to stay in the family.[70] On the other hand, the posts

---

[67] Jonathan Spangler, *The Society of Princes: The Lorraine-Guise and the Conservation of Power and Wealth in Seventeenth-Century France* (Aldershot, 2009), p. 34.

[68] Note, however, that many princes were known by a ducal appellation (e.g. the dukes of Burgundy, Orléans, Bourbon, and Guise). See Jean-Pierre Labatut, *Les ducs et pairs de France au XVIIe siècle* (Paris, 1972); Christophe Levantal, *Ducs et pairs et duchés-pairies laïques à l'époque moderne (1519–1790)* (Paris, 1996).

[69] There were also half a dozen ecclesiastical peerages, attached to specific sees.

[70] See esp. Horowski, "'Such a Great Advantage for My Son'".

of marshal—Grand Offices of the Crown as well as military commands—were non-hereditary, and often conferred court rank on people who had not already possessed it, sometimes even on parvenus like Nicolas Catinat.[71] The ceremonially exalted and equally non-hereditary post of chancellor was the only Grand Office traditionally held by 'robe' nobles. As for female households, they were non-hereditary by definition; the two principal posts of the queen's—the Superintendent and the Lady of Honour—were also dominated by titled women.

This ordered outline idealizes a confused and dynamic reality. Although aristocrats liked to trace their claims to immemorial traditions, many ranks in the Old Regime were in fact new or renewed. The Princes of the Blood were formally set above the rest of the aristocracy in 1576 only. The rank of Foreign Prince was not much older, and most of its holders were recognized no earlier than the mid-seventeenth century. Far from resembling their medieval namesakes, the Dukes and Peers took their familiar shape—of a sizable and largely non-princely corps—only in the late sixteenth and early seventeenth centuries, and continued to absorb new blood until the end of the ancien régime. One could hardly imagine a separate rank for Grandchildren of France before Gaston of Orléans became the first younger son of a French king to produce adult legitimate offspring since the early fifteenth century. The Legitimated Princes, finally, provide the most spectacular example of the plasticity of rank.

Such instability in the rank system created both threats and opportunities; no wonder that protagonists clashed perpetually about status. Untitled nobles resented the pretensions of the nouveau-dukes. For its part, the titled nobility could look back to a time, not long ago, when Bourbon princes had not automatically outranked its members. Within it, dukes and princes argued about the ultimate source of prestige: the highest dignity a French subject could attain or dynastic claims outside the realm? In the Royal House, the Orléans established their new branch, while the Condés would not be marginalized without a fight. And the meteoric rise of the royal bastards appeared to disrupt the entire social order. Within ranks too, the question of internal precedence generated numerous intractable problems.

What is more, the principles underlying this idealized order—French-, lay-, and sword-oriented—clashed with competing status regimes. Besides the naturalized Foreign Princes, aristocrats not subject to the crown frequently interacted with their French counterparts, in France and elsewhere. Sovereigns and non-sovereigns travelled, sometimes spending extended periods outside their native court.[72] Ambassadors had become a permanent presence, in particular during ceremonial occasions. Such international encounters generated much dispute and incongruity, in ranks and in codes, with no conventional mechanism for arbitration.[73] The

---

[71] There were roughly a dozen marshals at any given time. The post of *connétable* was extinct. That of *amiral* was revived in 1669 in favour of the Legitimated Princes (first Vermandois and then Toulouse). That of *grand maître de l'artillerie* was largely held by dukes, and then by Maine's legitimated line.

[72] Including periods of exile, as in the case of the Stuarts in France, first during the civil war, then after the 1688 revolution. See Edward Corp, *A Court in Exile: The Stuarts in France, 1689–1718* (Cambridge, 2004), esp. ch. 6.

[73] See the first two chapters.

Catholic Church, a supra-national jurisdiction as well as a secular principality, formed a special case. As princes of the Church, cardinals received a rank roughly equal to the Princes of the Blood. But status also depended on context: whereas in lay settings cardinals had to remain standing in the presence of the king, in Church even clerics who had no rank at court officiated in an armchair before kneeling royalty. Given that most ceremonial occasions had some religious component, the hierarchical ambivalence between the two orders was structural.

Within the French lay framework, the sword aristocracy faced competing claims for prestige. The leaders of the *parlement* of Paris, at the apex of the nobility of the robe, famously refused to doff their hats before the Dukes and Peers.[74] Ministers proved another interesting case. Under Louis XIV, nearly all of them came from a robe background, but they enjoyed special personal status as long as they were in power.[75] Multiple regimes, moreover, could ambiguously converge in a single person. How should one treat Emmanuel-Théodose de La Tour d'Auvergne at the end of 1671: as a Foreign Prince, as a cardinal, or as Grand Almoner? Indeed, Foreign Princes repeatedly played on this ambiguity, using the cardinal's hat to demand status symbols which they believed were due to them by birth. The cardinal-ministers similarly gained pre-eminence in council through ecclesiastical rank.[76] Finally, married women frequently lived an ambiguity between their birth rank and their marital rank.

Where rank was contested, ambiguous, unstable, and—most importantly—perceived as such, its external manifestations became a powerful tool for shaping status. What is the source basis for studying such an elusive phenomenon?[77] Most works in this field have drawn mainly on a canon of published texts. For the second half of the reign in particular, there are three continuous accounts by well-placed personages.[78] Philippe de Courcillon, marquis of Dangeau, was an assiduous courtier who enjoyed intimate access to the king and to the royal family, *inter alia* as the senior male officer of both dauphines. From 1684 he made a personal record of court news on a daily basis, almost uninterrupted until his death in 1720. Dangeau's style is brief, factual, and circumspect; written for insiders, it usually lacks background and detail. Louis-François du Bouchet, marquis of Sourches and

---

[74] That is, before the non-Bourbon ones. On this *affaire du bonnet*, see Harold A. Ellis, *Boulainvilliers and the French Monarchy: Aristocratic Politics in Early Eighteenth-Century France* (Ithaca, 1988), ch. 5. As an arena, the *parlement* followed different hierarchical rules to those of the court (for example, dukes who were not peers had no parliamentary standing). On the robe, see Robert Descimon and Élie Haddad (eds), *Épreuves de noblesse: les expériences nobiliaires de la haute robe parisienne (XVIe–XVIIIe siècle)* (Paris, 2010).

[75] See esp. Chapter Six. I use 'minister' as shorthand for the four Secretaries of State and for the Controller-General of Finances rather than as a literal rendering of the partially overlapping but not identical 'ministre'.

[76] Roger Mettam, 'The French Nobility, 1610–1715', in H. M. Scott (ed.), *The European Nobilities in the Seventeenth and Eighteenth Centuries*, 2nd edn (2 vols, Longman, 2007), i, 141–2. This affected the order of opining, and hence carried macro-political significance too: Peter R. Campbell, *Power and Politics in Old Regime France, 1720–1745* (London-New York, 1996), pp. 112–13.

[77] See also later in the book for chapter-specific source evaluations.

[78] The editions used are abbreviated as 'Dangeau', 'Sourches', and 'SSB' (see List of Abbreviations for details).

Grand Provost of France, conducted a similar recording project between 1681 and 1712. Sourches was less interested in status interaction, but his account offers occasional corroboration or supplementary detail.

The third writer has had the most profound influence on the image of the court, especially as regards status, ceremony, and etiquette. Born in 1675, Louis de Rouvroy became duke of Saint-Simon following his father's death in 1693, and a full-time courtier since his resignation from military service in 1702. Saint-Simon was affiliated with the critical circles surrounding the duke of Burgundy and Philippe II of Orléans, and remained well-placed thanks to the appointment of his wife as Lady of Honour to the duchess of Berry in 1710. Following the death of Louis XIV, he became actively involved in high politics during the first years of the regency. In 1729, Saint-Simon gained access to Dangeau's journal, and in the following decade he annotated its text with 'additions' that refuted, expanded, or reflected on many of the marquis's curt entries. From 1739 to 1750 he used the journal and the additions as a scaffold for a more ambitious project: his own memoirs, covering the period from the early 1690s to 1723.[79]

Saint-Simon's testimony is far from impartial, and his writings reflect his strong opinions. He was highly critical of Louis XIV, and obsessed with status and ceremonial from an early age. Above all, he exalted his own rank as Duke and Peer and vilified its rivals, notably the Foreign Princes and the royal bastards. Written in long retrospect, the memoirs have been subjected to critical scrutiny since the second half of the nineteenth century, but have nevertheless continued to inform modern accounts. While Saint-Simon's assertions and analyses are questionable even in his areas of expertise, he crucially complements Dangeau by illuminating and explicating status interaction from an insider's perspective. His writings thus offer a valuable context of discovery; for verification, however, one must turn elsewhere.[80]

The nature and availability of other sources, in print and in manuscript, varies across the ceremonial spectrum. Predictably, high ceremonies have received more consistent coverage. First, there are the many accounts in contemporary publications and journals, such as the *Gazette* and the *Mercure*. These, however, tend to convey a harmonious image of ceremonial proceedings (along the lines of the opening paragraph), and seldom reveal the stakes and disputes of status interaction. The opposite is true of the manuscript registers of the ceremonial staff. The Masters of Ceremonies, as noted earlier, kept a detailed record of the events under

---

[79] The standard biography is Georges Poisson, *Monsieur de Saint-Simon*, now in its fifth edition (Paris, 2007). See also Hélène Himelfarb, *Saint-Simon, Versailles, les arts de cour* (Paris, 2006); Le Roy Ladurie with Fitou, *Saint-Simon*. For a recent bibliography of the 'Saint-Simonian forest', see Philippe Hourcade, *Bibliographie critique du duc de Saint-Simon* (Paris, 2010).

[80] The scholarly apparatus of the monumental Boislisle edition points the way in many cases. The problem of retrospect is somewhat mitigated by the fact that Saint-Simon relied on an extensive private archive in compiling his magnum opus. Among pieces written during his active life, the most noteworthy for our purposes is his 'Estat des changements arrivéz a la dignité de duc et pair', prepared in 1711 for the benefit of the duke of Burgundy and published in *Écrits inédits de Saint-Simon*, ed. P. Faugère (8 vols, Paris, 1880–93), iii, 3–221 (re-edited in part in le duc de Saint-Simon, *Hiérarchie et mutations: écrits sur le kaléidoscope social*, ed. Yves Coirault (Paris, 2002), pp. 37–121).

their charge. When Desgranges took over in 1691, he copied the volumes of his predecessor Sainctot, and successively produced his own accounts until 1729. This continuous record of high ceremonies during the reign of Louis XIV has fortunately survived in its original form.[81]

Although it makes dull reading at times, such serial coverage offers a precious insight into the manifold aspects of early modern ceremony, including minutely detailed descriptions of costume, spatial position, and gesture. Since this record was intended to inform future decision-making rather than for public consumption, its authors frequently noted what occurred behind the scenes as well as on stage—notably problems, dilemmas, and contestations. One should nevertheless beware of treating this source as a definitive, transparent, or neutral account. There is first the inherent difficulty of capturing the multifaceted nature of early modern ceremony, especially when composers were participants as well as observers. More intriguingly, the description itself became an object of contestation. Aware of its role in determining precedents, interested parties surreptitiously sought to influence or to modify the record. While such efforts complicate the task of verification, they also illustrate the importance of the stakes involved.

There is no equivalent testimony for the routine activities of the court, where recurrence may have made serial coverage seem redundant. Normative sources, like household ordinances, remain useful, but they can never be taken as evidence of actual practice. One must therefore look for the occasional illuminating needle in the haystacks of narrative sources and court paperwork. This problem highlights the considerable advantage of analysing codes that were embodied in the written medium in the first place. In the case of epistolary ceremonial, twenty-first-century readers can still observe with their own eyes the status interaction that took place in correspondence centuries ago.[82] Such opportunity for unmediated observation is impossible even in the best-documented instances of high ceremony, where one can only rely on textual representations of events that did not originally occur on the page.

In contrast with the retrospective and embellished nature of most standard sources, the manuscript working papers of protagonists offer glimpses of real-time actions and insider perceptions. Besides yielding fresh insights into specific themes and codes, the very existence and organization of these papers point to another dimension of the phenomenon. Documentation was not just a by-product of status interaction; it became an essential tool and target. As the system of customary law increasingly relied on the written medium, aristocrats created their own ceremonial

---

[81] BM, MSS 2737–2751. The first of these fifteen volumes is a collection of documents from the early years of the reign, emanating from Sainctot's family predecessors. Continuous coverage begins in the second volume, from 1660. I have also drawn on other copies of this record and on other working papers of the ceremonial staff, for example in AN, K 1042–1044. There is no equivalent continuous record by the Grand Masters of Ceremonies for this period. In addition, I have occasionally drawn on the registers of the Introductors of Ambassadors, especially those of Louis-Nicolas Le Tonnelier de Breteuil, who served between 1698 and 1715: Baron de Breteuil, *Mémoires*, ed. Evelyne Lever (Paris, 1992); Arsenal, MSS 3859–3865.

[82] See Chapter Six and Giora Sternberg, 'Epistolary Ceremonial: Corresponding Status at the Time of Louis XIV', *Past & Present*, cciv (2009), 33–88.

archives. They secretly copied the official record, wrote down their own accounts, and gathered other status-related evidence. These private knowledge-bases demonstrate the benefits to be gained by looking beyond the monarch's perspective.[83]

In the case of manuscript knowledge-bases as in the case of epistolary ceremonial, written objects provide material and not just textual evidence. Other types of objects, such as dress items, have proved less resilient to the ravages of time. I have nevertheless tried, as far as possible, to consider the implications of their past materiality. For this purpose, visual media (drawings, tapestries) offer a useful complement to texts, illustrating the form of lost objects, spaces, configurations, and postures. The Masters of Ceremonies and others used diagrams to illustrate spatial choreographies of precedence. For the purpose of reconstructing specific events, however, the verisimilitude of visual media can be misleading. They are often inaccurate, at times wholly fictitious.[84] Their coverage of status and ceremony is uneven, particularly sparse on the everyday end of the spectrum. An image is thus not always worth a thousand words.

*   *   *

This book investigates status interaction from four distinct but complementary angles, on successive points along the ceremonial spectrum: a key high ceremony; a quintessential ceremonial dress-item; a celebrated court routine; and an elaborate written code-system.

It begins with one of the ceremonial highlights of the reign of Louis XIV: the marriage of his niece to Charles II of Spain in 1679. Chapter One demonstrates the complex interplay, on a single occasion, among multiple status codes, regimes, and rivalries: spatial, gestural, linguistic, and sartorial; French and international. High ceremonies articulated status relations in public, in a series of special events and interactions. This included processions and parades, where spatial position indicated precedence according to elaborate three-dimensional choreographies. Any aspect of procedure or appearance, from pen-handing to dress emblems, could have a lasting effect on the rank of participants. This effect, in turn, was mediated via printed and manuscript accounts. For status interaction did not end with the event: what ultimately mattered was how it was reported and remembered. In the information warfare over ceremonial memory, even the mouthpieces of the Bourbon monarchy were not immune to partisan influence.

Chapter Two traces the anatomy of a ceremonial crisis based on a remarkable archival dossier. After the ceremonies, the transformation of the bride from French princess to Spanish queen would show in the protocol of courtesy visits, and in particular in the type of seats that she would offer her visitors: armchairs, chairs, or perhaps only stools? This seemingly minute detail brought about an intense sequence of deliberations behind the scenes, involving the king personally, the rival clans of Orléans and Condé, the Spanish ambassador, and other international parties. Scarcely mentioned in the standard sources of the period, the affair received

---

[83] See Sternberg, 'Manipulating Information'.
[84] Of course, images do not necessarily purport to represent reality. When misrepresentation is deliberate, it becomes interesting (see Sternberg, 'Manipulating Information', pp. 260–72), but this is not always the case.

real-time coverage in a neglected dossier of correspondence between the *Grand Condé* and his trusted agent Gourville. Such extraordinary coverage enables us to reconstruct status negotiation and dynastic politics to a degree of precision normally denied by the nature of surviving sources.

Whereas the first two chapters illustrate and integrate the multiple facets of a single occasion, the following ones analyse select status codes and explore their evolution in time. Chapters Three and Four examine the quintessential item of ceremonial dress in pre-modern Europe: mantles. I first consider the signification and significance of the mantles worn for high ceremonies such as obsequies and nuptials. Thus, the length of trains signalled status differences throughout the court hierarchy, from the royal couple to minor officers. Train-bearing involved the interaction among and between wearers, bearers, and others present, turning on the number, rank, and even gender of train-bearers and on choreographic subtleties of location, position, and occasion. An unravelling of the grammar of these distinctions is followed by a diachronic analysis of their dynamics in Bourbon rivalries from 1643 to 1715. Based on a serial examination of the official ceremonial registers, complemented or challenged by other inside data, this analysis reveals the cross-generational vitality, adversarial tactics, and dynastic strategies of status interaction.

Like Chapter Two, Chapter Four shifts focus from high ceremony to social protocol, by examining mantles in the context of courtesy calls. The right to wear this garment during complimentary visits on mourning occasions was a sumptuary privilege, limited in theory to select sword nobles. Yet the exercise of the privilege also signified deference, or even subordination, towards the hosts of such 'mantled visits'. The act of wearing was thus not simply a static or absolute attribute of wearer identity, but rather a dynamic interaction between wearers and others. This relational aspect could turn an otherwise prestigious garment into a liability. Pitting hosts and visitors close to one another on the social ladder, mantled visits generated bitter disputes and subtle manoeuvres. With the rapid succession of Bourbon deaths in the early eighteenth century, they became a familiar sight at court. Their tempestuous evolution in this period reflected and shaped social and political changes: the dynastic upheavals within the ruling house; the development of its relations with the rest of the aristocracy; and the social climbing of those in the margins.

Completing the journey across the ceremonial spectrum, the last two chapters turn to everyday routines of status interaction, at court and beyond. Chapter Five revisits a celebrated act of court ritual that served as a key example in Norbert Elias's classic account: the gesture of handing the king his chemise as he rose each morning. Re-contextualizing this gesture thematically, socially, chronologically, and functionally, I underscore the inherent duality of such 'honourable service' and the degree to which it was shaped by extra-royal agendas even in the heyday of the Sun King. In place well before Louis XIV, these acts occurred in sub-royal as well as in royal settings; in the former, a more complicated perception of service emerges, of a humiliating task as well as a 'prestige fetish'. Givers, moreover, were also receivers: each time an aristocrat was to hand the king his chemise, he would receive it from other persons, often high-ranking themselves; in many cases, this was the more important interaction. The final section of the chapter uncovers the macro-political stakes of these acts in the struggle of the Legitimated Princes to equate themselves with the legitimate princes of royal blood, from surreptitious beginnings early in the personal rule to the succession crisis that surrounded its end.

Chapter Six investigates epistolary ceremonial. Letters were not only vehicles of narrated information, but also social acts, a statement of addressers about their position relative to the addressee. Documented at regular exchanges as well as in moments of conflict, in prescriptive as well as in descriptive sources, epistolary status interaction enables us to compare norm and practice, equilibrium and crisis. A highly elaborate code, it manifested itself in forms of address, in ending formulae, in subtler aspects of word-choice and grammar, and—probably least self-evident to most modern readers—in non-verbal features, such as letter material, spatial layout, and graphic elements. These were no mere niceties: disputes over epistolary formulae could disrupt military chains of command and even lead to incarceration. Opening a window into everyday encounters in a variety of social and geographical arenas, epistolary ceremonial illuminates the pervasiveness of status interaction in the early modern period.

The Conclusion draws together key themes and points out inter-connections and wider implications. An analysis of the general mechanics of status interaction is followed by a discussion of the dynamics of codification: what were the relations between status symbols and status, between status *de facto* and status *de jure*, and between customary and positive law? These questions then inform a cross-code, longitudinal analysis of the Legitimated Princes, which provides a strong case for the link among status symbols, rank, and power. I end by highlighting the significance and broader ramifications of the phenomenon in this and in other social, geographical, and temporal contexts and hence the importance of developing a comparative framework of status interaction in the early modern world.

1

The Marriage of 1679: High Ceremonies as Multifaceted Status Interactions

The marriage of Marie-Louise of Orléans, daughter of Philippe I of Orléans and niece of Louis XIV, to King Charles II of Spain, at the chateau of Fontainebleau in late August 1679, was one of the ceremonial highlights of the Sun King's reign.[1] Like the two other great nuptial celebrations of this era—the king's own in 1660 and the duke of Burgundy's in 1697—it symbolically cemented a peace between parties that had just emerged from a long drawn out war. The king ordered his ceremonial staff to record the events in detail, 'as he wanted this ceremony to set a model for the future'.[2] Following months of negotiations and preparations, the proceedings began on the evening of 30 August, with the engagement ceremony and the solemn signing of the marriage contract in the king's cabinet at Fontainebleau. The next day, 31 August, the wedding was celebrated at the richly decorated chapel of the chateau, in the presence of the house of Bourbon and of a multitude of notable French and international guests. The queen of Spain then remained in the vicinity of the court for another three weeks, receiving the compliments of various personages and corporations. Finally, on 20 September she began the long journey across France to her new kingdoms.

High ceremonies were the occasion of manifold status interactions, where precedence and rank difference showed more clearly and carried more weight than usual. Nuptials are particularly interesting in this context because of the liminal status of the bride.[3] In the patriarchal order of early modern Europe, married

---

[1] In such high-level international unions, the nuptials would take place at the bride's country before she set out to join her husband. At the ceremonies, the bridegroom would be represented by a senior proxy—in this case, the prince of Conti. A second series of events would then confirm the union on the other side. See Lucien Bély, *La société des princes*, esp. pp. 195–213, 260–73; Fanny Cosandey, *La reine de France: Symbole et pouvoir XVe–XVIIIe siècle* (Paris, 2000), pp. 55–82; Leferme-Falguières, *Les courtisans*, pp. 105–41; Isabelle Poutrin and Marie-Karine Schaub (eds), *Femmes & pouvoir politique: les princesses d'Europe XVe–XVIIIe siècle* (Rosny-sous-Bois, 2007), esp. pp. 65–132; Abby E. Zanger, *Scenes from the Marriage of Louis XIV: Nuptial Fictions and the Making of Absolutist Power* (Stanford, 1997). On the macro-political context, see Henry Kamen, *Spain in the Later Seventeenth Century, 1665–1700* (London, 1980), pp. 343, 372–4; Marie-Françoise Maquart, *L'Espagne de Charles II et la France, 1665–1700* (Toulouse, 2000), esp. pp. 61–7. For a brief discussion of the ceremonies, see Yves Bottineau, 'Aspects de la cour d'Espagne au XVIIe siècle: l'étiquette de la chambre du Roi', *Bulletin Hispanique*, lxxiv (1972), 153–7.

[2] AN, KK 1430, fo. 292r.

[3] On marriage and liminality (not always in the sense meant here), cf. Zanger, *Scenes from the Marriage of Louis XIV*, esp. ch. 1.

women normally received the rank of their husband. Nuptials thus functioned as a status rite of passage. When, though, was the new rank conferred on the bride? After the engagement? After the wedding? At some stage in between? Ceremonial choreographers had to consider such questions, for status symbols suffered no vacuum. International princely unions brought further challenges: not only the endemic rank disputes among the Society of Princes, but also the incompatibilities and incongruities between different status regimes. In 1679, relations between the two monarchies were already fraught with status tensions that stirred the court and the diplomatic corps in Madrid: the newly established French ambassador could not meet the Spanish head of government, Don Juan José of Austria, due to a disagreement over who would cede the better position (*donner la main*).[4]

The marriage of 1679 is also promising in its documentation. Among the surviving contemporary narrative accounts, four prove particularly useful for our purposes. First and foremost, we have the detailed account of the Master of Ceremonies, Nicolas Sainctot, who personally attended to the ceremonial aspects, from the preparations to the journey across France.[5] We also have a partial account probably authored by the Grand Master of Ceremonies, Charles Pot de Rhodes.[6] The quasi-official *Gazette* followed events in its regular issues and in an *extraordinaire*, a special issue that appeared on 12 September. Variants of this account appear in an anonymous publication on the marriage from 1681 and in a register attributed to Michel Chabenat de Bonneuil, Introductor of Ambassadors.[7] The *Mercure Galant* too covered the marriage extensively, dedicating the second part of its October issue to the ceremonies.[8]

The source that makes the marriage of 1679 particularly valuable for our purposes is, however, of an entirely different nature. Buried among the miscellaneous boxes on

[4] Don Juan was a bastard half-brother of Charles II. The French ambassador also faced other status problems, vis-à-vis cardinals and other ambassadors. See AAE, CP, Espagne 64 (summarized in AAE, MD, Espagne 69, fos. 300r–305r); *Recueil des instructions données aux ambassadeurs et ministres de France* (Paris, 1884–), pp. xi, 275–302. On Franco-Spanish comparisons, with particular reference to ceremonial usage, see Gérard Sabatier and Margarita Torrione (eds), ¿*Louis XIV espagnol? Madrid et Versailles, images et modèles* (Versailles, 2009).

[5] I draw mainly on Desgranges's copy, certified by Sainctot: BM, MS 2741, fos. 17–69 (hereafter cited as 'Sainctot' plus folio number); other near-contemporary versions include the Condé copy: AC, MS 1176, pp. 39–158. (On their making, see Sternberg, 'Manipulating Information', pp. 243–4, 247–8.) The ornamented manuscript of this account in BM, MS 2285, is stylistically, and occasionally substantially, different from the others; is it a primitive version?

[6] AN, KK 1430: a preparatory memorandum (fos. 288r–291r) and a fragmentary description (fos. 291r–300v).

[7] The *extraordinaire* is in *Gazette* (1679), pp. 433–48 (published in English shortly thereafter as *An Exact Relation of the Grand Ceremony of the Marriage of Charles the II. The Most Catholick King, with the Most Illustrious Princess Mademoiselle Marie Louise D'Orleans* (London, 1679)). The anonymous *Mémoires touchans le mariage de Charles II., Roy d'Espagne, avec la Princesse Marie Louise d'Orléans* (Paris, 1681) draw largely on the *Gazette*. Bonneuil's version in AAE, MD, France 2192, pp. 75–87, is either a source or an adaptation of this account.

[8] Among its possible sources are the *Gazette* and a newsletter account, dated 31 August (see *Correspondance de Roger de Rabutin, comte de Bussy*, ed. Ludovic Lalanne (6 vols, Paris, 1858–59), iv, 444–8). See also AAE, MD, Espagne 73, an eighteenth-century synthesis of these and of other sources prepared at the Foreign Ministry; Sophie de Hanovre, *Mémoires et lettres de voyage*, ed. Dirk Van der Cruysse (Paris, 1990), esp. pp. 145–9, 255–7.

ceremonial in the 'K' series at the *Archives nationales* is a folder described as 'Correspondance entre le Grand Condé et Gourville, 1679' and consisting of more than twenty letters. About half of them are autograph originals from Condé to Gourville, and the rest are mostly copies and drafts of Gourville's letters to his master. All were written around the time of the marriage: probably four on 30 August, seven on 31 August, and another six or so in the next couple of days.[9] This detailed, sometimes frantic exchange is devoted almost exclusively to the ceremonies of the marriage and to their implications for the status of the Princes of the Blood.

In fact, status considerations explain the very existence of this corpus. The Condés had decided to stay away from the ceremonies—attended by almost all other members of the Royal House—after they had lost out in the question of who would hand the pen to those signing the marriage contract during the engagement.[10] The two young Conti brothers, nephews and protégés of the *Grand Condé*, did, however, attend the ceremonies, the eldest of them in the important role of proxy for the bridegroom. The Condés, therefore, sent their trusted *intendant*, Jean Hérauld de Gourville, to Fontainebleau, in order to oversee the proceedings, keep them informed, and intervene should problems arise.[11] This concern proved more than warranted, as a crisis soon unfolded over the seating protocol of the complimentary visits to the new queen.

The Condé-Gourville correspondence deals with this crisis as well as with other bones of status contention. It is an extraordinary case of an extended exchange on status interaction at the court of Louis XIV. In contrast to the quasi-official and post-facto nature of most available sources, here is a private and real-time exchange between master and trusted agent.[12] Gourville not only reported his own activities, but also served as the eyes and ears of his masters, recounting what went on at court in their absence. The Condés for their part sent him guidelines and instructions. With the breaking of the crisis, the exchange reads like diplomatic correspondence, as Gourville found himself negotiating directly with the king on behalf of his masters. This corpus thus opens a window into aspects of status interaction that normally elude us, notably including contemporary perceptions and face-to-face negotiations.

---

[9] See Appendix II. Subsequent citations refer to 'Condé-Gourville' plus reference number in AN, K 1712. Like other documents in this box, the folder was probably among the Condé papers confiscated during the Revolution. There is good reason to believe that these already impressive numbers underestimate the actual extent of the exchange, as some letters were probably lost, especially from the last couple of days.

[10] Details later.

[11] On the resourceful Gourville and his relations with the Condés, see Béguin, *Les princes de Condé*, and Béguin, 'De la finance à l'intendance: la reconversion réussie de Jean Hérauld de Gourville (1625–1703)', *Revue d'histoire moderne et contemporaine*, xlvi (1999), 435–56. On his previous experience as intermediary on behalf of Louis XIV as well as of the Condés, see Léon Lecestre, 'La mission de Gourville en Espagne (1670)', *Revue des questions historiques*, lii (1892), 107–48. Gourville's *Mémoires*, ed. Léon Lecestre (2 vols, Paris, 1894–5), do not discuss the marriage of 1679.

[12] The letters, which contain potentially compromising information (e.g. Condé-Gourville, no. 36), were probably all sent by special courier. Gourville could expect a letter written at 11 p.m. in Fontainebleau to reach his masters in their Parisian *hôtel* by 5 a.m.: Condé-Gourville, no. 39. As we shall see, this correspondence also exposes how the quasi-official sources were susceptible to partisan manipulation.

A royal marriage was many things: a diplomatic treaty, an economic transaction, and a personal crossroads as well as a ceremonial highlight.[13] From the angle of status interaction, it carried multiple meanings for multiple actors, well beyond family circles or the French court: from the First Almoner, who spun round another bishop in order to seize the better side of the Book of the Gospel during the wedding; through the anxiety of the Spanish ambassador about his interactions with the Princes of the Blood and their implications in Madrid; to the recurring local disputes between treasurers and judges over who would visit the new queen first as she passed through the provinces.[14] A single yet multifaceted occasion, the marriage of 1679 introduces some of the themes of subsequent chapters, and illustrates the diversity, complexity, inter-relatedness, and significance of the codes that made up early modern status interaction.

I begin with an exposition of the main participants and hierarchies and explore the question of their spatial and material choreographies. I then discuss the gestural and linguistic stakes of the signing of the marriage contract, and how they explain the Condé absence from the ceremonies. A third section deals with sartorial distinctions, including a first taste of the mantle problems which will occupy us in a later chapter. The last section introduces the elusive role and implications of early modern information management. The next chapter will analyse the unfolding of the crisis over seating protocol, drawing together the micro-politics of status negotiation and its dynastic and international dimensions.

PLACE AND PLACEMENT: THE CHOREOGRAPHY OF HIERARCHY

The marriage came about in what was, in more than one respect, an important moment in the life-cycle of the Bourbon dynasty. With the birth, and survival, of the duke of Chartres, the house of Orléans finally succeeded in establishing a new junior branch in the main line for the first time in two centuries.[15] Chartres made a formal appearance at court shortly before the ceremonies, receiving 'the honours due to his birth' and handing the king the chemise.[16] This gave a fresh impetus to the efforts to create a new rank of Grandchildren of France for Chartres and for the female members of the house, at the expense of the Princes of the Blood of the

---

[13] The marriage contract is in AAE, Traités, Espagne 16790010; cf. Monique Valtat, *Les contrats de mariage dans la famille royale en France au XVIIᵉ siècle* (Paris, 1953). Contemporary sources underscore the bride's grief at the prospect of leaving the French court: see e.g. Madame de Sévigné, *Correspondance*, ed. Roger Duchêne (3 vols, Paris, 1972–78), ii, 681. This, combined with her subsequent difficulties in adapting to life in Spain and with the suspicious circumstances of her death in 1689, made her an ideal heroine for historical romances, such as Sophie Gay, *Histoire de Marie-Louise d'Orléans* (Brussels, 1842). For a more historical treatment, see Marthe Bassenne, *La vie tragique d'une reine d'Espagne: Marie-Louise de Bourbon-Orléans, nièce de Louis XIV* (Paris, 1939).

[14] See later and in the Introduction, p. 1.

[15] This branch of Orléans was to oust the main line a century and a half later, and survives to this day in the counts of Paris.

[16] *Gazette* (1679), p. 407. On the chemise, see Chapter Five.

existing junior branch of Condé. Another group of Bourbons was also coming of age in this period: the bastard children of Louis XIV. Increasingly visible at court and enjoying honours previously awarded to legitimate members only, these Legitimated Princes and Princesses were now to make their first appearance at a major ceremony.

The many status interactions occasioned by a royal marriage would bring these and other contested hierarchies into sharper relief, catalysing processes of contention, negotiation, and resolution. The ordinary evasion tactic in cases of uncertainty or dispute—of conducting events informally [*sans cérémonie*]—made less sense on high ceremonies. On the other hand, the king could prove surprisingly lenient on these extraordinary occasions in tolerating individual avoidance, namely the absence of courtiers who stood to lose from the order of the day.[17] Before proceeding to the interactions themselves, let us begin with a brief survey of dramatis personae on the eve of the ceremonies—of members both present and absent.[18]

In 1679, Louis XIV stood at the apex of his glory, having just emerged triumphant from the Dutch War. His wife, Queen Maria Theresa, was by his side during the ceremonies. They were followed by their only surviving child and heir, the *Grand Dauphin*, who was to get married himself a few months later. Philippe I, head of the Orléans clan and brother to the king, known at court as *Monsieur*, was actively involved in the preparations and in the ceremonies as the proud father of the bride. His second wife, the bride's step-mother Elisabeth-Charlotte of the Palatinate, known as *Madame*, also attended. There were no other living Children of France at the time.

Next came the Grandchildren of France, all members of the Orléans clan. The seventeen-year-old bride, known as *Mademoiselle*, and her younger sister, Mademoiselle de Valois, were daughters of *Monsieur* from his marriage with Henrietta-Anne of England. The daughters of Gaston, who did not all frequent the court in this period, nevertheless showed up in full attendance: the *Grande Mademoiselle* (also known as Mademoiselle d'Orléans), the grand-duchess of Tuscany, and the duchess of Guise. The two young children of Philippe and Elisabeth-Charlotte, on the other hand, do not appear in the accounts of the marriage. Whereas the daughter (future duchess of Lorraine) was only three years old, Chartres's absence is more intriguing, especially given his publicized formal appearance at court just before the marriage.

Of course, whether these Orléans princes and princesses indeed formed a novel, separate rank of 'Grandchildren of France', or were rather merely the most senior Princes and Princesses of the Blood, goes to the heart of their differences with their Condé cousins. The terminological variation in our sources reflects the yet uncertain status of Grandchildren of France in 1679: Sainctot and Rhodes refer to the princesses as 'Granddaughters of Royalty' (*petites-filles de Roy*); in the *Mercure*, they

---

[17] See e.g. BM, MS 2742, fo. 104v. But cf. Fanny Cosandey, 'Entrer dans le rang', in Marie-France Wagner, Louise Frappier, and Claire Latraverse (eds), *Les jeux de l'échange: entrées solennelles et divertissements du XVe au XVIIe siècle* (Paris, 2007), pp. 40–5.

[18] See also the Introduction (pp. 15–20) and Appendix I.

remain 'Princesses of the Blood'; Condé and Gourville call them *Mesdemoiselles*. The Princes and Princesses of the Blood 'proper', of the branch of Condé, featured only two representatives at the ceremonies: the prince of Conti, proxy to the bridegroom, and his brother, the prince of La Roche-sur-Yon. The leaders of the branch—the *Grand Condé* and his son Henri-Jules, duke of Enghien—were conspicuously absent. Their wives, Henri-Jules's children, and the princess of Carignan do not appear in any of the narrative accounts.[19]

What about the legitimated members of the Royal House, the 'natural' children of the king? As Sainctot explains, the marriage of 1679 proved to be a landmark for their status:

> So far the legitimated children of France [*Enfans legitimez de france*] had not appeared at royal ceremonies. Since the king had accorded them the same honours enjoyed by the Princes of the Blood, such as that of handing him his chemise and presenting the serviette in preference to the Grand Officers, it was right that they should have the same honours as the Princes of the Blood on this occasion.[20]

The honours of everyday life had thus prepared the ground for the extraordinary honours of high ceremony.[21] Six legitimated members participated in the events: the count of Vermandois and Mademoiselle de Blois (the first of two princesses of that name, soon to marry the prince of Conti), children of Madame de La Vallière; the duke of Maine and Mademoiselle de Nantes, children of Madame de Montespan;[22] the duke of Verneuil, legitimated son of Henri IV, and his wife. The last two may have been invited in order to attenuate the shock of the novelty by showing that Louis XIV was not simply favouring his own progeny. The two Vendôme brothers did not enjoy the same rank, but were nonetheless singled out from the aristocratic crowd 'as grandsons of a legitimated son of France'.[23]

The narrative sources hardly account for the politics of Bourbon attendance. The two newspapers simply discuss present parties with no reference to the absent. Rhodes offers general explanations for nonattendance, without naming names: some Princes and Princesses of the Blood could not make it 'because they were too young, or because they were ill, or because they were busy elsewhere with the king's service or with their own affairs; these, I think, were the reasons that prevented them from being there'.[24] The notable exception to this general reticence is Sainctot, who, as we shall see, explains the most conspicuous absence.

Among those present, the order of ranks was inscribed in three-dimensional space, in manifold choreographies of mobile processions and stationary positions,

---

[19] A preparatory memorandum planned for the presence of Princesses of the Blood at the ceremony: AN, KK 1430, fo. 289v.

[20] Sainctot, fos. 28v–29r.

[21] On the chemise, the serviette, and their role in the ascent of the Legitimated Princes, see Chapter Five.

[22] Was Montespan particularly anxious to establish her children at this stage, when her favour was finally waning and Mademoiselle de Fontanges was establishing herself as the monarch's mistress?

[23] Of César, another son of Henri IV. Sainctot, fos. 26r, 29. This Vendôme precedence may have led to avoidance by Foreign Princes who did not have a formal role: AAE, MD, Espagne 73, fo. 55r.

[24] AN, KK 1430, fos. 296v–297r.

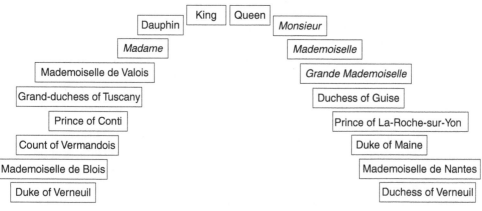

Fig. 1.1 The spatial choreography of the Royal House during the engagement of Charles II and Marie-Louise of Orléans. Members formed a standing semi-circle with the seated royal couple in the middle, according to a centre-first, right-before-left choreography of precedence (right and left are considered from the perspective of the Bourbons, not of the viewers). Thus, the dauphin stood to the right of the king, *Monsieur* to the left of the queen, *Madame* to the right of the dauphin, and so on.

of bodies and objects.[25] During both ceremonies, spatial position demarcated the Royal House from other participants: the Bourbons occupied a separate, elevated platform in a central section of the room. Only select officers and the Spanish ambassador joined them there during the engagement.[26] On the platform, spatial configuration displayed the hierarchy within the Royal House. A few days before the ceremony, the king had reset the principles of the internal ordering of the bastards along lines similar to those of the legitimate.[27] Together, all formed a standing semi-circle around the seated royal couple, according to a centre-first, right-before-left choreography of precedence.[28]

---

[25] On space, see Yves Deloye, Claudine Haroche and Olivier Ihl (eds), *Le protocole ou la mise en forme de l'ordre politique* (Paris, [1997]), esp. the contributions by Fogel and Haroche; Marcello Fantoni, George Gorse, and Malcolm Smuts (eds), *The Politics of Space: European Courts ca. 1500–1750* (Rome, 2009); Ronald G. Asch, 'The Princely Court and Political Space in Early Modern Europe', in Beat Kümin (ed.), *Political Space in Pre-industrial Europe* (Farnham, 2009), pp. 43–60. On the significance of space in another sense, see William Ritchey Newton, *L'espace du roi: la cour de France au Château de Versailles, 1682–1789* ([Paris], 2000).

[26] The significance of this boundary is underscored by Rhodes's comment that some officers mounted the platform against custom: AN, KK 1430, fos. 297v–298r. During the wedding, select officers were placed at the steps to the platform.

[27] Sainctot, fo. 20r. The ordering now followed branch first, then gender, and finally age: Louis's children preceded the children of previous monarchs; sons preceded daughters; and the elder preceded the younger.

[28] See Figure 1.1. There is some discrepancy among the reports regarding the ordering from the Princes of the Blood downwards. I follow the ordering of the ceremonial staff (e.g. Sainctot, fo. 20r); the alternative (e.g. *Gazette* (1679), pp. 436–7) does not make sense, and is probably simply mistaken.

The wedding featured a particularly elaborate configuration, on a carpeted platform elevated in the middle of the chapel.[29] A combination of objects and positions marked the division of ranks. The objects included floor-covering and seating and kneeling accessories, while the positions composed a front-first vertical axis. Thus, royalty came first, closest to the altar and enjoying a canopy, armchairs, and a prie-Dieu, covered by a fleur-de-lised violet-velvet mat (*drap de pied*) that extended backwards to the middle of the platform. Next, still on the mat, came the dauphin and the Children of France, each provided with a cushion (*carreau*) and a stool. The following ranks formed the last three rows: first, the Granddaughters of France, at the edge of the mat; then, outside it and behind them, the Princes of the Blood; and finally, the Legitimated Princes and Princesses. Each member of these three ranks received a cushion only, similar to the titled nobility outside the platform.[30] Within ranks, the horizontal axis marked internal hierarchy according to the centre-first, right-before-left choreography.[31]

The relative position of the bride changed twice in the course of the ceremonies, signifying her gradual transition in status from Granddaughter of France to queen of Spain. In the engagement ceremony, she still processed and stood according to her birth, as the highest-ranking Granddaughter of France.[32] She entered the second ceremony in an intermediate position: already preceding *Madame*, but still behind Maria Theresa. This reflected the king's decision to marry Marie-Louise, in certain respects, as though she were his own daughter. As soon as the nuptial rites were over, the queen of Spain assumed her full royal position, receiving an armchair by the prie-Dieu, on the same line as the French royal couple.[33]

Other hierarchical ambiguities created tension within and across status regimes in the course of the ceremonies. Take, for example, the interactions between the prince of Conti and the Spanish ambassador. Ambassadors were, by definition, ambiguous status entities: invested with the prestige of their ruler but also personages in their own right (in this case, a Spanish grandee). Following the dispute

---

[29] See Figures 1.2 and 1.3; cf. the diagram and explanation in *Mercure Galant*, October 1679, pt 2, pp. 175–81. On spatial choreography, contestations, and marriage ceremonies in the royal chapel, see Alexandre Maral, *La chapelle royale de Versailles sous Louis XIV: cérémonial, liturgie et musique*, 2nd edn (Wavre, 2010), esp. pp. 75, 114–17, 134–6, 219–28, and figures 13, 26, 27.

[30] Gourville emphasized the equality of objects between the Granddaughters of France and the Princes of the Blood (as opposed to the inequality of position), noting that the former were 'sans sieges': Condé-Gourville, no. 56. On seats, see the next chapter. The relative position of the last three ranks generated contestation throughout the reign. Sainctot notes (fo. 32r) that the Granddaughters of France found their cushions placed 'tellement sur le bord [of the mat] que s'estant agenouillées Elles auoient leurs pieds hors du drap de pied, c'est le lieu où Elles deuoient estre, et c'est ce qu'Elles n'auoient point obserué Jusques alors'; cf. AC, MS 1131, fos. 7, 16v–17r; *Grimoires de Saint-Simon*, ed. Yves Coirault (Paris, 1975), p. 311. In the eighteenth century, the placement of the cushions of the Legitimated Princes and Princesses—behind or beside the legitimate ones?—defined the changes in their status (see later, pp. 166, 168–9); cf. Le Roy Ladurie with Fitou, *Saint-Simon*, pp. 112–13.

[31] Thus the overall hierarchization of axes here was height first, then vertical, and finally horizontal.

[32] See Figure 1.1.

[33] See Figure 1.3. She occupied the middle position (numbered 4): as hosts, the French royal couple ceded the best place to a royal guest. The processions on both occasions observed other choreographies, including division by gender.

Fig. 1.2 The wedding of Charles II and Marie-Louise of Orléans, at the chapel of Fontainebleau, 31 August 1679. Engraving by Pierre Brissart (dedicated to one of the participants). BN, Estampes, RES ED-8B(1)-FOL. Photo: Bibliothèque nationale de France.

between Don Juan and the French ambassador in Madrid, Louis XIV authorized the Princes of the Blood not to cede spatially to Spanish ambassadors. On this occasion, however, Conti also acted as proxy for the king of Spain. Who would precede whom in the marriage processions, and—most importantly—in which capacity? The Spanish ambassador would cede only after receiving written assurance from the French foreign minister.[34]

The involvement of the Church hierarchy introduced ambivalence and tension too. In the chapel at Fontainebleau, as in other religious ceremonies at court, two spatial foci competed for centre-stage as the reference point of the hierarchical axis system: the altar, embodying spiritual authority, on the one hand, and the monarch, embodying secular authority, on the other. The king's First Almoner fruitfully exploited this duality in order to gain the upper hand against a rival bishop. The latter initially held the better position as the two approached the prie-Dieu to offer the Book of the Gospel to Their Majesties. The almoner, however, cunningly made his colleague turn round to salute the altar first, grabbed the better side of the sacred object, and refused to relinquish it afterwards: a volte-face indeed.[35]

---

[34] AAE, CP, Espagne 63, fo. 35; Sainctot, fos. 17v, 20v–21r, 37v; AAE, MD, France 2192, pp. 76–8; Condé-Gourville, nos. 45, 56; AN, KK 1430, fos. 292–295. Here too, interactions involved elaborate choreographies of meeting, greeting, and processing and multiple participants and terrains.

[35] Sainctot, fos. 33v–34r; AAE, MD, Espagne 73, fo. 64. For other dilemmas of ecclesiastical presence and precedence on this occasion, see e.g. Sainctot, fo. 29r; F. de Bojani, *Innocent XI: sa correspondance avec ses nonces* (3 vols, Rome, 1910–13), i, 148 n. 1.

Fig. 1.3 Detail from Figure 1.2, showing the spatial and material choreography of the Royal House in the course of the wedding. The Bourbons spent most of the ceremony on a platform, elevated in the middle of the chapel and covered with a Persian rug. The most high-ranking among them were positioned on a fleur-de-lised mat that extended on and behind a prie-Dieu (numbered 3). After the nuptial rites, the king and the two queens knelt on the prie-Dieu or sat on armchairs at the front (4–6), closest to the altar. Behind them, the dauphin (7) and the Grandchildren of France (8–9) received stools (and cushions, not shown). The Granddaughters of France, supplied with cushions only, were placed at the edge of the mat (10–13). The Princes of the Blood (14–15) and the Legitimated Princes and Princesses (16–21), also on cushions, formed the last two lines, behind the mat. As the numbers in each line indicate, ranks were internally ordered centre-first, right-before-left.

THE MARRIAGE CONTRACT, *LA PLUME*, AND THE FOUNTAIN OF POWER

The formal acts of the ceremonies began with the public signature of the marriage contract during the engagement. After all parties had assumed their position in the king's cabinet, the French Secretary of State for Foreign Affairs, Arnaud de Pomponne, started reading out the contract. The ceremonial of signing followed immediately, as detailed by Sainctot:

> Monsieur de Pomponne had hardly read the titles [*qualités*] of the contract when the king said that that was enough and had the contract brought to him for signing. The king and the queen signed seated, Monsieur de Pomponne having presented the pen [*la plume*] to them and taken it back from their hands. *Monseigneur* the dauphin, *Monsieur, Madame, Mademoiselle* [the bride], Mademoiselle de Valois, Mademoiselle d'Orléans, *Madame* the grand-duchess [of Tuscany] and Madame de Guise all signed in the same column where the king and the queen had just signed, the pen having also been presented to them by Monsieur de Pomponne, who took it from the hands of Madame de Guise and returned it to the ink well. Then the prince of Conti took it and

signed immediately below Madame de Guise as Prince of the Blood. This status was more advantageous to him than that of proxy, which would have made him sign in the second column, a little below Madame de Guise. The prince of La Roche-sur-Yon, Monsieur de Vermandois, the duke of Maine, Mademoiselle de Blois, Mademoiselle de Nantes, Monsieur and Madame de Verneuil all signed in the first column too, taking the pen themselves from the well and returning it there after signing. The ambassador alone signed in the second column, opposite the space between the signature of Madame de Guise and that of the prince of Conti.

During the signature of the contract, the king and the queen remained seated, the princes and the princesses approached the table to sign according to their rank and saluted the king and the queen as they drew back.[36]

In this choreography, rank was inscribed in time and in space, in gesture and on paper. King and queen remained seated; others approached in the order of their rank and saluted the royal couple on their way back to their standing positions. The spatial order of signatures on paper represented the temporal order of signing in space, expanding it, moreover, into two dimensions, horizontal as well as vertical.

The most controversial aspect of these proceedings was *la plume*—the handling of the pen. It divided the Royal House into two distinct groups. The king, queen, dauphin, Children of France, and Granddaughters of France received the pen from the hands of the Secretary of State, whereas the Princes of the Blood and the Legitimated Princes and Princesses had to take it themselves from the ink well. It was for this reason, Sainctot explains, that the senior Condés did not attend the ceremony:

> *Monsieur le Prince* [Condé] and *Monsieur le Duc* [Enghien] were not present in Fontainebleau at the time of the ceremony, because they claimed that the pen ought to be presented to them by the Secretary of State, as to the Granddaughters of Royalty. However, since *Monsieur le Duc* had signed some marriage contracts without receiving the pen from the hands of a Secretary of State, he has rendered recent usage contrary to his claims.[37]

This explanation introduces some central stakes, principles, and tactics of status interaction, which we will encounter time and again in the following chapters: the Orléans-Condé rivalry, the logic of the precedent, and the avoidance tactic. The pen drew a line between the Grandchildren of France and the Princes of the Blood. The Condés, first Princes of the Blood, refused to accept this line, but since recent usage did not support their claim, they stayed away from the ceremony in order to avoid yet another self-incriminating precedent.

---

[36] Sainctot, fo. 22 (in rendering names and titles, I have modernized orthography and abbreviation unless there was reason to believe that the original variant had been meaningful). In the actual contract (AAE, Traités, Espagne 16790010), the ambassador's signature in fact appears opposite Guise's, and Nantes's is missing (she could not write yet: AAE, MD, Espagne 73, fos. 29v–30r). On textual space, see also BM, MS 2285, p. 14; on signatures, cf. BN, FF 14120, fos. 333ff.; on both, see Chapter Six.
[37] Sainctot, fo. 22v; cf. the more tentative version in BM, MS 2285, p. 14.

Though the avoidance tactic technically put off an unwanted outcome, fleeing the ceremonial battlefield in this way could nonetheless be perceived as an acknowledgement of defeat. Avoiders would therefore try to cover up their act from the public and from posterity. A convenient 'pretext' (as Gourville called it) for absence came up when the duchess of Enghien caught smallpox shortly before the marriage. Her father-in-law and her husband joined her in Paris, attending her there and rousing the fear that they carried the 'smallpox air'.[38] At the same time, they strove to keep the *plume* out of the narrative accounts of the ceremonies (see later).

This case also introduces the duality of service. Viewed from the perspective of its potential Bourbon recipients, the *plume* seems a prestigious honour and an object of rivalry. But this act of service also involved another party, a not insignificant status-group of pen-handers: the Secretaries of State.[39] A later entry in the ceremonial register of the Condés suggests that it was in fact the ministers who made the difference:

> The Secretaries of State have presented [the pen] to the Princes of the Blood in the past, but in some recent ceremonies they dispensed themselves; and *Messieurs* the Princes pretended not to have noticed it [*nauoient pas fait semblant de le remarquer*] in order not to quarrel with them, because of their great authority.[40]

From the perspective of the Secretaries of State, the privilege consisted in *not* handing the pen to the Princes of the Blood. In the acts of service that made up many ceremonies and routines, at court and elsewhere, one party's honour could be another party's humiliation.[41] This also reminds us that an intra-Bourbon rank rivalry cannot be isolated from other status interests, or indeed from other types of interests, like the concern over the 'great authority' of ministers.

The marriage contract created status problems in text as well as in context. Thus, the Spanish wanted to use the honorary form *Madame* in reference to the yet unmarried princess, wishing that she be treated as a Daughter of France.[42] While agreeing to such treatment in certain respects (dowry included), Louis refused the pre-nuptial *Madame*, and 'Princesse Serenissime' was adopted as a compromise.[43] More notorious and complicated was the issue of appellations of the *haut et puissant* type, where lexical variants finely differentiated the status of contracting or present parties. These appellations appeared in the opening paragraphs, before the 'body' of the contract, and carried great significance, at court and in wider

---

[38] AC, P lxxv, fos. 166, 223; Condé-Gourville, nos. 33, 52, 53. Earlier, Henri-Jules's trip to the meeting of the Estates of Burgundy (as governor) also served as a reason for absence (cf. *Correspondance de Bussy*, ed. Lalanne, iv, 428). I thank Julian Swann for helping me clarify this point.

[39] See Breteuil, *Mémoires*, ed. Lever, p. 291 n. 2, p. 293 n. 2. Another pen-handing issue was the signing of the parish register after the wedding: Maral, *La chapelle royale de Versailles*, pp. 227–8.

[40] AC, MS 1217, pp. 239–40. For a precedent from 1678, see AC, MS 1174, pp. 266–8.

[41] On the duality of service, see esp. Chapter Five.

[42] *Mémoires touchans le mariage de Charles II*, p. 26. Daughters of France received the *Madame* irrespective of their marital status (see Chapter Six, p. 137).

[43] Sainctot, fos. 21v–22r. On a lower level, the unmarried Mademoiselle de Grancey received the privilege of the *Madame* address via her appointment as *dame d'atour* of the new queen during the journey to Spain: Sainctot, fo. 42v; Sévigné, *Correspondance*, ed. Duchêne, ii, 658.

society.[44] As we have seen, instead of 'skipping the preliminaries', the king had these titles read out loud, and then interrupted Pomponne and proceeded to sign the contract—leaving unread what modern readers might consider the truly important part.[45] An illustration, this, of early modern priorities and of the short-comings of an anachronistic dichotomy between form and substance.

The Royal House had indeed vigorously debated this question of appellations. A fortnight earlier, Condé emphasized to Gourville that 'the matter is very important and I pray you to do your best about it; if it is necessary that I go to Paris for this, I will do so as soon as you tell me'.[46] He instructed his agent to argue for the best appellation that they could find in past cases, which was *très haut, très excellent et puissant prince*. However, since the king himself appeared in the contract this time, with his standard appellation of *très haut, très excellent et très puissant prince*, reference to other members of the Royal House had to be adjusted accordingly. The dauphin thus received *très haut et très excellent prince*, and the Children of France—*très haut et très puissant prince*. Other members of the Royal House, down to and including the Legitimated Princes, received one adverb less than the Children of France—*très haut et puissant prince*.[47]

The king was heard to remark that it was only for lack of an intermediate form that the Granddaughters did not enjoy an advantage in this domain too.[48] The bottom line, in any case, favoured the Princes of the Blood, somewhat mitigating the inequality of the *plume*. As for the Orléans, the equality of appellations may explain the absence from the ceremonies of the highest-ranking Grandchild of France, the duke of Chartres.[49] It may also have increased their anxiety to establish an edge over their rivals in other status codes—not least in the domain of dress.

THE ROYAL HOUSE'S NEW CLOTHES

At a court famous for sumptuousness even on everyday occasions, high ceremonies called for particularly spectacular sartorial efforts. French aristocrats vied with each other in personal and patrimonial magnificence, and foreign ambassadors—in vicarious consumption for their sovereigns.[50] Heads of princely clans supervised

[44] See Robert Descimon, 'Un langage de la dignité: la qualification des personnes dans la société parisienne à l'époque moderne', and Laurence Croq, 'Des titulatures à l'évaluation sociale des qualités: hiérarchie et mobilité collective dans la société parisienne du XVIIe siècle', both in Cosandey (ed.), *Dire et vivre l'ordre social*. These matters have left an endless paper trail: e.g. AN, K 577, no. 61.

[45] The details of the contract had, of course, been agreed in advance, but choice of parts to be read out loud is nonetheless revealing; cf. BM, MS 2746, fo. 258v.

[46] Condé-Gourville, no. 36.

[47] Or female equivalent. AAE, Traités, Espagne 16790010. This did not leave the dauphin a clear edge over the others, and on subsequent occasions he was upgraded to *très haut, très puissant et excellent*: BM, MS 2741, fos. 78–79.

[48] Condé-Gourville, no. 45.

[49] Conversely, when Chartres did appear at a subsequent marriage (in 1684) in spite of a failure to secure more than *très haut et puissant*, the Condés were happy to attend and thus to underscore the equality of appellations: BM, MS 2742, fos. 104v–105r.

[50] See the remarks of the English ambassador in *Savile Correspondence*, ed. William Durrant Cooper ([London], 1858), p. 121.

the preparation of garments in person, in an attempt to outshine their rivals. *Monsieur* adjusted the gems on the Orléans outfits with his own hands, while the Condés had the prince of Conti dazzlingly decked with royal jewels inherited from the queen of Poland.[51] In the pages of the fashion-oriented *Mercure*, male attire receives by far the most detailed attention.[52] It is female dress, however, that figures most prominently in the less publicized manoeuvres of status interaction.

Marie-Louise's wedding clothes underscore her liminal status as bride: Grand-daughter of France by birth, Daughter of France in certain respects for the ceremony, queen of Spain at its end.[53] On her head, she bore a closed crown, signalling the sovereign dignity and ornamented with Spanish fleurons. She should only have been crowned 'at the moment of her marriage', the Master of Ceremonies noted, but it would have been too bothersome to attach the crown in the chapel. Her attire 'was not a proper royal mantle or outfit [*habit*]', but rather 'the outfit that princesses of this rank wear for coronations'.[54] But what was 'this rank'? The ambiguous attire played with the ceremonial idiom of the French Royal House:

> Her mantle was of violet velvet lined with ermine, three fingers in width, joined to three rows of golden fleurs-de-lis. The train trailed six ells in length; its edge was spangled with four dozen golden fleurs-de-lis, full or empty, besides the three rows just mentioned.
>
> …
>
> *Mademoiselle*'s dress was of the same fabric and colour as her mantle. The skirt was covered in front with a band of ermine, six fingers in width, joined to three rows of golden fleurs-de-lis on each side; on the bottom, it was lined with a band of ermine, three fingers in width, and above it three rows of golden fleurs-de-lis.
>
> The body and the sleeves were spangled with golden fleurs-de-lis, full and empty in roughly equal number; the sleeves were lined with three fingers of ermine, and all the seams, of sleeves as well as body, were covered by a one-finger band of ermine.
>
> Her shoes and stockings were violet, spangled with golden fleurs-de-lis.
>
> …
>
> Mademoiselle d'Orléans carried the right side of the mantle, Madame the grand-duchess the left side, and Madame de Guise the edge.[55]

---

[51] Sophie de Hanovre, *Mémoires et lettres de voyage*, pp. 147–8. Gourville reported to his masters the preparations and subsequent acclaim of Conti's outfits: AC, P lxxv, nos. 141, 195; Condé-Gourville, nos. 44, 56. See also Condé-Gourville, no. 38. Both clans used the same designer: see n. 53.

[52] The only woman whose attire receives more than a few sentences is the bride, compared with several pages devoted to the king (24–6, 101–5), the prince of Conti (15–17, 85–8), and the duke of Crussol (94–8).

[53] See Figure 1.4, reportedly based on the original design by Jean Berain (*Mercure Galant*, October 1679, pt 2, pp. 82, 216–17). The latter also designed the Conti and Crussol outfits. See Roger-Armand Weigert, *Jean I Berain, dessinateur de la chambre et du cabinet du roi (1640–1711)* (2 vols, Paris, 1937), i, 47; ii, 247–8.

[54] Sainctot, fos. 27v, 28r. On marriage mantles, see Chapter Three. On the traditions of nuptial dress at court, see Monique Chatenet, 'Habits de cérémonie: les mariages à la cour des Valois', in Poutrin and Schaub (eds), *Femmes & pouvoir politique*, pp. 221–4. More generally, see Pierre Arizzoli-Clémentel and Pascale Gorguet-Ballesteros (eds), *Fastes de cour et cérémonies royales: le costume de cour en Europe* (Paris-Versailles, 2009); Isabelle Paresys and Natacha Coquery (eds), *Se vêtir à la cour en Europe, 1400–1815* (Villeneuve d'Ascq, 2011).

[55] Sainctot, fos. 27v–28r; cf. *Gazette* (1679), pp. 441–2; *Mercure Galant*, October 1679, pt 2, pp. 78–82.

Fig. 1.4 The wedding outfit of Marie-Louise of Orléans. Engraving by Antoine Trouvain, reportedly based on the original design by Jean Berain. *Mercure Galant*, October 1679, pt 2. Photo: Film S 803, Lamont Library, Harvard University.

First note the golden lilies, emblem of the dynasty. Spangling the mantles of kings and queens from head to foot, *fleurs-de-lis* appeared in single rows at the edges of sub-royal Bourbon mantles. Correlating with rank, the number of rows became an object of intra-dynastic contention. The three rows on *Mademoiselle*'s outfit and mantle equalled her with the Daughters of France, and surpassed the two rows allotted to the Princesses of the Blood. A decade later, Sainctot cited this precedent as the reason for the addition of a fourth row to the dauphine's mantle—according to the same inflationary logic.[56] As usual with signs, the absolute number of rows was meaningless in itself; it was their relative distribution among ranks that counted.

In 1679, though, Sainctot mentioned the three rows matter-of-factly. The spangled edge of the bride's mantle, on the other hand, elicited the following note: 'the king found fault with these four dozen *fleurs-de-lis*, and ordered me to remark in my registers that this had not been his intention'.[57] Here is our first example of an

[56] BM, MS 2742, fo. 226v. On the evolution of row number as status symbol see *Mercure François*, xi (1625–26), 363–5; *Lettres, mémoires et instructions de Colbert*, ed. P. Clément (7 vols, Paris, 1861–73), vi, 275–7; BN, FF 16633, fos. 172v, 411; Sourches, ii, 28–9; BM, MS 2745, fos. 153–154, 163–164. The abbey of Saint-Denis holds early nineteenth-century exemplars of Bourbon mantles with rows of fleurs-de-lis on their edges. Louis XIV's famous portrait by Rigaud shows the royal lily-spangled mantle.

[57] Sainctot, fo. 27v.

interesting method for dealing with unwelcome ceremonial novelty: rather than simply censor the record as one might have expected, the king instead had the precedent acknowledged in the official register—but immediately countered by his express disapproval. Thus, if usurpers tried to invoke the precedent on subsequent occasions, the crown would be prepared.[58]

Mantle edges did not end with the golden lilies. Even more contentious was the issue of trains—especially their length and their bearing. Following decades of contestations, the king had tried to regulate the matter in 1666. Lengthwise, he had allotted seven ells to the Daughters of France, and five only (and equally) to the Granddaughters of France and to the Princesses of the Blood.[59] *Madame*, the only genuine Daughter of France in 1679, indeed wore a seven-ell mantle. The queen wore her traditional nine ells for the wedding. What about other female members? Several Granddaughters of France were present—the bride, her sister, and Gaston's daughters—but no Princess of the Blood. Also present, for the first time at a major ceremony, were the Legitimated Princesses. Their train distinctions on this occasion would thus set a precedent for this rank-on-the-rise.

The accounts of the engagement ceremony specify the train-length of the bride only: her gold-lined gauze mantle extended to six ells that day. On the wedding, her ermined violet mantle reached six ells again according to the official accounts (see earlier), or seven according to others.[60] The other Granddaughters of France wore six-ell trains, as explained by Sainctot:

> In the engagement ceremonies [*les Ceremonies des fiançailles*] the Granddaughters of Royalty had had mantles with a five-ell train only; the Princesses of the Blood had had this in common with them; but since in this event there were no Princesses of the Blood, the king said nothing in their regard.[61]

The ceremonies of 1679 thus introduced a novel, intermediate train-length for the Granddaughters of France—six ells, midway between the previously prescribed five and the seven granted to the next rung, the Daughters of France. The Legitimated Princesses, on the other hand, had to content themselves with five ells only.

What was the rationale of these decisions? Instructed to look into the matter, Gourville managed to get hold of the Master of Ceremonies shortly before the engagement:

> I spoke to Monsieur de Sainctot, who told me that there had been much deliberation on the length of the trains. Since Monsieur the cardinal of Bouillon had a four-ell [train] at the service of Monsieur de Turenne, the legitimated daughters were given

---

[58] Interestingly, the *Gazette* (1679, p. 442) briefly mentions the spangled edge without noting royal disapproval, while the later published *Mercure Galant* does not mention it.

[59] On trains, ells, and bearers, see Chapter Three.

[60] *Correspondance de Bussy*, ed. Lalanne, iv, 445; Condé-Gourville, no. 56. Or six and a half: AAE, MD, France 948, fo. 178r.

[61] Sainctot, fo. 28v. Does 'les Ceremonies des fiançailles' refer to the specific proceedings that took place a day earlier or to engagement ceremonies in general? The next phrase, on past equality between the two ranks, must refer more generally, given that the Princesses of the Blood did not attend either ceremony.

five and *Mesdemoiselles* six. His opinion is that *Mesdames* the Princesses of the Blood will have six [on future occasions], and that he thought that it was good that the natural daughters have five, because there remained no [other] difference between *Mesdemoiselles* and the legitimated daughters: they will all have just one squire and one gentleman train-bearer each.[62]

Again, we have a multi-rank, cross-ceremony inflationary process. The four ells worn by the Foreign Princes of the house of Bouillon at the memorial service for Turenne back in 1675 had a bearing on the question of train-length within the Royal House in 1679. The bastards of the house of France were thus awarded an advantage over members of other sovereign houses. But five ells for the Legitimated Princesses threatened to leave no difference between these newcomers to high ceremony and the Granddaughters of France, given the equality between these two ranks in yet other aspects of the mantle code, such as train-bearing. Hence the introduction of the sixth ell.

This summary report did not, however, reveal all of the 'much deliberation' that went on behind the scenes. It is not inconceivable that the Orléans envisioned an advantage over the absent Condés as well as over the present bastards. With this implication in mind, Gourville further inquired whether the king had explicitly stated an intention to grant a sixth ell to the Princesses of the Blood too, on future occasions. Sainctot replied in the negative, but added that he did not doubt that this would be the case. Gourville, accordingly, advised his master not to intervene at this juncture: first, since it would be impossible to effect any changes; and second, because one could always demonstrate both the equality 'throughout the entire past' with *Mesdemoiselles* and the difference vis-à-vis the natural daughters. Condé concurred: 'since the king has decided the matter, one must say nothing more for the present'.[63]

After length, the most contested aspect of trains was their bearing, another act of service. Here again choreography created both external and internal distinctions. The right to have mantles carried demarcated the Royal House from other participants.[64] A single gentleman bore the train of each Granddaughter of France or Legitimated Princess during the wedding. For the three highest-ranking princesses, the gender of the bearer functioned as an additional status marker. The queen's train was born by the duchess of Richelieu, her Lady of Honour. *Mademoiselle* had her engagement train born by her sister, Mademoiselle de Valois. And during the wedding, no less than three princesses carried the train of the future queen of Spain—the same treatment awarded to Maria Theresa when she married Louis XIV.[65]

Such service by women was normally restricted to queens, but *Madame* enjoyed it too on this occasion by virtue of a special exception. When *Monsieur* asked his

---

[62] Condé-Gourville, no. 33; see also nos. 45, 34.
[63] Condé-Gourville, nos. 33, 48.   [64] Sainctot, fo. 29r.
[65] According to an eighteenth-century commentator, this was why the bride wore Bourbon dress: French princesses would have refused to bear the royal mantle of Spain. AAE, MD, Espagne 73, fo. 50r; cf. AC, MS 1176, pp. 65–6.

royal sibling to approve a female train-bearer for his wife, based on a sixteenth-century precedent, Louis had Sainctot verify the matter. The precedent, it turned out, did appear in the *Ceremonial François*, but was contradicted by the account of a Secretary of State. Nevertheless, wishing to please *Monsieur* on the day his daughter was to be married, the king consented to female bearing—provided that some precedent involving the dauphine's mantle was also found. Sainctot 'immediately' came up with another sixteenth-century example, and *Madame*, accordingly, had her train carried by the *maréchale-duchesse* Du Plessis, her Lady of Honour.[66] An interesting example, this, of ceremonial decision-making—both standard procedure (admissible data sources, weighing of contradictory evidence), and what happened when the king wanted to stretch it.

Status distinctions did not operate in a void, however. In awarding royal treatment to *Madame*, the king eroded his own wife's position. Consequently, he decided to upgrade the rank of the queen's train-bearer from Lady of Honour to Superintendent. And this decision, in turn, threatened to disrupt the delicate balance between the two office-holders. In the end, the switch was for the record only: the duchess of Richelieu carried the queen's train at the actual ceremonies. Did she insist on maintaining her ancient duty as Lady of Honour, or did the Superintendent waive the service task? Whatever the answer, the question illustrates how a single ceremonial action could affect multiple rivalries in different segments of the social spectrum.[67]

In summing up the sartorial balance-sheet, Gourville tried to look on the bright side:

> *Mesdemoiselles* have one ell only more than the natural daughters. There is every reason to hope that on the first occasion *Mesdames* the Princesses of the Blood should have six ells. The three rows of *fleurs-de-lis* of the queen of Spain may not be consequential, because she was married as Daughter of France, and I was told that her train was one ell longer than that of *Mesdemoiselles*.[68]

This dense and convoluted statement demonstrates how the liminal position of the bride and the multifaceted nature of high ceremonies made the hermeneutics of status even more complicated than usual on this occasion.[69] Paradoxically, a Condé agent wanted to believe here that an Orléans train extended to seven ells rather than to six. For this would imply exceptional treatment of the bride as Daughter

---

[66] Sainctot, fos. 18v–19r. Godefroy, *Le Ceremonial François*, contains both versions: two accounts confirming *Monsieur*'s claim (ii, 37–8, 41), and a contradictory and more official account by Secretary of State Pinart (ii, 25). In fact, Sainctot's second example was no good either, since the dauphine in question was also queen of Scots (ii, 15). And in any case, of course, a simple Daughter of France was no dauphine.

[67] That the Superintendent was Madame de Montespan (mistress, and hence rival to the queen; and marquise, and hence inferior in title to Richelieu) further complicates the picture. The record is in Sainctot, fo. 27r. See also Condé-Gourville, no. 45. More on the multi-dimensional relations between and among wearers and bearers in Chapter Three; and on the rivalry between Superintendent and Lady of Honour in Chapter Five, pp. 114–15.

[68] Condé-Gourville, no. 56.

[69] cf. the bewilderment in AAE, MD, France 2192, pp. 82–3; *Mémoires touchans le mariage de Charles II*, pp. 75–6.

of France rather than the standard fare of a Granddaughter, and hence invalidate the potential consequence of another aspect of her garment—namely, the number of fleur-de-lised rows. Both aspects fell short of royal treatment; only the handling of the garment—the number of train-bearers—signified the ultimate rank of the bride. On the other hand, the intermediate train-length of six ells, shared by the non-liminal Granddaughters of France, might prove more consequential for the future. The legacy of this precedent would depend, however, on whether, and how, it would register in present and future perceptions.

THE MANIPULATION OF CEREMONIAL MEMORY

So far, we have considered ceremonial registers and newspaper reports straightforwardly, as sources of information for our inquiry. But these accounts, of course, were not simply produced for the sake of modern history-writing. In the customary-law system of early modern status interaction, written records served to store and to retrieve ceremonial precedents. In documenting the details of the marriage, Rhodes and Sainctot created a blueprint that the monarchy could draw on in future events, uncertainties, or controversies. This was internal state paperwork, intended for royal decision-making rather than for external consumption.[70] The *Gazette* and the *Mercure*, on the other hand, reached a wider contemporary readership and had an immediate impact on public images as well as future evidential value. Aristocrats and officials alike obtained their issues, annotated ceremonial reports, and stored cuttings and copies in their archives.[71] But like their more confidential counterparts, newspapers too served the early modern state, and the *Gazette* in particular is known as an organ of royal propaganda.[72]

One of the most striking revelations in the Condé-Gourville correspondence is the degree to which official records and centrally-controlled media were susceptible to unofficial manipulation. Aware of the importance of these repositories of royal and public knowledge, parties clandestinely moulded them to serve partisan interests. Rather than a simple reflection of status interaction, the recording process became one of its objects, sometimes to the point of overshadowing the actual occurrences 'on the ground'.

The Condé agent was already thinking about the record a fortnight before the event. In meeting Sainctot on 16 August, he learned that the latter was planning to write his account of the ceremonies only after the departure of the queen of Spain.[73] In their subsequent discussion of the delicate issues of *plume* and train-length,

[70] See the Introduction, pp. 14, 22–3, and Sternberg, 'Manipulating Information', pp. 241–7.
[71] See e.g. AN, K 577, nos. 79, 138 (duke of Penthièvre); BM, MS 2750, fos. 113–125 (Desgranges); AN, O¹ 3262 (*Argenterie* papers).
[72] Joseph Klaits, *Printed Propaganda under Louis XIV: Absolute Monarchy and Public Opinion* (Princeton, 1976), esp. pp. 58–67; Peter Burke, *The Fabrication of Louis XIV* (New Haven-London, 1992); Gilles Feyel, *L'Annonce et la nouvelle: la presse d'information en France sous l'Ancien Régime (1630–1788)* (Oxford, 2000), pp. 460–75.
[73] AC, P lxxv, no. 97.

Gourville secured from the Master of Ceremonies the promise 'to show the account before writing it down in his book', thus providing the Princes of the Blood with a potential opportunity to influence the final wording of the official register.

Gourville also approached the abbé Dangeau (brother of the journal author), who was in charge of the *Gazette* reports. The latter

> had decided to write down all the details...he promised me not to speak of the *plume*. As for the trains, he would like to note them. I don't know if one should write that there was no Princess of the Blood [present], or try to persuade him not to mention the matter, but he would find it a bit difficult. He will only speak in general terms in Saturday's *Gazette* and put off [the rest] to an *extraordinaire*, so there is time.[74]

By tampering with the virtual event on the ceremonial record, the Princes of the Blood could temper their actual drawbacks on the ceremonial battlefield. In the matter of the *plume*, any but the most general mention would reveal that the Grand-daughters of France received the pen from the hands of the Secretary of State, while the Conti brothers had to take it from the well. To eliminate the *plume* from the public record thus seemed the best solution. To rob the Granddaughters of France of their virtual sixth ell would similarly serve the Condé purpose. In the case of trains, though, the absence of Princesses of the Blood from the ceremonies meant that there was no positive evidence of inequality. Therefore, Gourville thought, a note of this absence might do, as it would imply that the Condé princesses would have equally enjoyed the novel intermediate train-length had they appeared.

The *Grand Condé* replied the same day:

> I will be delighted that Monsieur the abbé Dangeau not go into detail that could cause us pain concerning the *plume*, the mantles, and the trains. I think of him as someone who is enough of a friend of ours to take a bit of trouble and to please us in this way. I pray him to pass this all over in as general terms as he will be able. I will be obliged to him for it.[75]

The First Prince of the Blood, then, preferred to minimize discussion of trains (and absence?) as well as *plume*. Partisan censorship of the official mouthpiece seemed the best course in the circumstances. Accordingly, he harnessed his powers of patronage to the cause of documentary manipulation, framing the message to Dangeau in the idiom of 'friendship' and 'obligation'.[76] Gourville contacted the abbé again, and reported the results to his master:

> Monsieur the abbé Dangeau promises not to speak of the trains of *Mesdemoiselles* nor of the natural daughters. He will not speak of the *plume*, but he will restrict himself to the liberty of speaking of the train of the two queens and of *Madame*'s.[77]

Condé, in turn, approved this solution.[78]

---

[74] Condé-Gourville, no. 33. On Dangeau as *de facto* editor of the *Gazette*, see Feyel, *L'Annonce et la nouvelle*, pp. 445–50.

[75] Condé-Gourville, no. 48.

[76] On the Condés' effective use of patronage in general, see Béguin, *Les princes de Condé*.

[77] Condé-Gourville, no. 56.   [78] Condé-Gourville, no. 38.

The relevant issues of the *Gazette* show that Dangeau indeed proved himself a worthy 'friend' of the Princes of the Blood. As promised, 'Saturday's *Gazette*' (the first regular issue to appear after the nuptials, on Saturday, 2 September) summarized the ceremonies in a few sentences only, noting that 'the public will be given the details of the queen of Spain's engagement and wedding'. The detailed *extraordinaire* that followed ten days later contains no mention of the *plume*, nor of any engagement train but the bride's. The wedding account points out the train-lengths of the bride, of the queen, and of *Madame*; for all other female Bourbons, only the less controversial parameter of train-bearing is mentioned.[79] The *Mercure* shows the same omissions. Rhodes, as we have seen, accounted for Bourbon absences without alluding to ceremonial problems. On the *plume*, he merely noted that the Secretary of State handed the pen to king and queen, without specifying what happened with the other, more controversial signatories. Nor did he mention any train-length but the bride's.[80]

The Condé cover-up operation thus met with considerable success. It seems to have stopped short, though, with Sainctot. As we have seen, the Master of Ceremonies' account shattered the *plume* pretensions of the Princes of the Blood. He recorded the procedure in detail, complete with the handing of the pen to the Granddaughters of France and its denial to the Princes of the Blood; he tied the matter to the absence of the Condés, exposing and thus weakening their avoidance; and he noted that recent precedent went against them. Again, his is the only report that disclosed all Bourbon train-lengths. Although he did refer to past equality between the Granddaughters of France and the Princesses of the Blood, at the same time he noted the king's silence regarding the latter rather than his own confidence (according to Gourville) about future cases. And he implicitly contradicted this assumption of equality by placing his explanation of how the bastards received the same honours as the Princes of the Blood immediately after a passage that noted the Legitimated Princesses' *five*-ell trains.[81]

Had Sainctot indeed shown his account to the Condés before writing it down in his register? The final wording of these entries seems harsh enough from their perspective. The Master of Ceremonies, then, enjoyed relative independence vis-à-vis his administrative (and social) superior, the Grand Master of the Household. Sainctot, it appears, was not 'enough of a friend' of the Condés. Whether this stemmed from personal alignments or from a 'higher' loyalty to king or to professional integrity is a moot point. Be that as it may, in other instances ceremonial officials would prove more accommodating.

Status interaction, then, did not end with the event. What ultimately mattered was not the actual occurrence, but how it was remembered. As the written word

[79] There is also no mention of the Condé absence. *Gazette* (1679), pp. 420, 435–8, 441–2; cf. *Mémoires touchans le mariage de Charles II*, p. 57.

[80] AN, KK 1430, fos. 298v, 288v, 289r. The wedding account in this copy is, however, confused and fragmentary. The newsletter account in *Correspondance de Bussy*, ed. Lalanne, also limits itself to the train-length of the three highest-ranking ladies (iv, 445–7).

[81] Sainctot, fos. 22, 28v–29r.

was becoming a primary instrument of communication and memory, public news-papers and private registers became primary targets for interested parties. Gour-ville's machinations reveal that even the mouthpieces of the Bourbon monarchy were hardly immune to partisan influence. Even at the heart of the fabrication of absolutism it is worthwhile to extend our gaze beyond the sovereign or the state. State organs were, at least in part, the product of covert processes of negotiation, independent of—if not opposed to—their official purpose. In such clandestine dealings, humble redactors could gain the friendship and obligation of exalted princes.[82]

An understanding of these processes is crucial for assessing what our sources can tell us, and, no less important—what they would not tell us. For the most contro-versial issues, and hence often the most interesting ones, are also most liable to manipulation, and to suppression in particular.[83] We cannot always expect to recover positive evidence of such controversial issues, let alone precious 'meta' evi-dence like the Condé-Gourville correspondence. And if we are to spot meaningful omissions without positive evidence, it is essential to know more about the rela-tionships between actors and redactors, and, above all, to develop an intimate familiarity with the ins and outs of the codes themselves.

---

[82] For other cases of partisan interest involving the *Gazette* and other official media, see BM, MS 2744, fos. 87–88; BM, MS 2748, fos. 164–165; BM, MS 2750, fos. 2v–3r; AC, MS 1131, fos. 7v, 18r; AC, MS 1217, pp. 286–7; Saint-Simon, 'Estat des changements', pp. 119–21. For the perspective of the fabricators of absolutism, see the overview and case-studies in Rabinovitch, 'Versailles as a Fam-ily Enterprise'.

[83] As another gazetteer noted: 'Le principal moyen est de dire la verité, quoy que toutes ne doivent pas estre dites' (Eusèbe II Renaudot, cited in Feyel, *L'Annonce et la nouvelle*, p. 468).

2

The *affaire des sièges*: The Anatomy of Ceremonial Crisis

Status interaction did not end with high ceremonies. In the aftermath of the wedding of 1679, the parties faced the more mundane, but no less controversial implications of the status transformation of the bride. The dilemma that features most prominently in the Condé-Gourville correspondence concerns one such aspect of post-nuptial reorientation: what type of seats would the new queen of Spain offer her Bourbon relatives in the complimentary visits that customarily followed weddings? This seemingly minute detail brought about an intense sequence of secret deliberations, involving the king personally, the Condés, and the Orléans. It also acquired an international dimension that concerned the Spanish ambassador, cardinals, and—indirectly—other states and princes whose past and potential interactions informed and influenced the controversy. Absent from the usual narrative sources, the secret deliberations receive an intimate, almost live coverage in the Condé-Gourville letters. Thanks to the unusual circumstances of the Condés' absence from court, matters that were normally negotiated face-to-face surface in the confidential correspondence between the princes and their 'ambassador' in Fontainebleau. Such extraordinary coverage allows us to reconstruct the anatomy of ceremonial crisis to a degree of precision normally denied by the nature of available documentation.[1]

The second section of this chapter traces the outbreak and initial stages of the crisis. The third deals with its critical phase, drawing especially on two remarkable documents: a lengthy dispatch by Gourville that reports, almost verbatim, two negotiation sessions with the monarch; and a detailed autograph instruction by the *Grand Condé* that vehemently argues the position of the Princes of the Blood. The subsequent two sections analyse what the *affaire des sièges* reveals about dynastic politics and status negotiation, while the final one discusses the outcome and consequences of the affair. But first, an introduction of the early modern code: how did seat type map social standing?

ARM-RESTS AS ARMS RACE: THE TYPOLOGY OF SEATS

In the occasions discussed thus far, status rivalry usually played out indirectly, in comparisons between co-present but not necessarily confronted protagonists, at

---

[1] On the Condé-Gourville correspondence, see the previous chapter, esp. pp. 28–9, and Appendix II.

multilateral and multifaceted events. In contrast with such indirect, sometimes ambiguous, symbolic battles, visits distilled status interaction into a duel, pitting hosts and guests in what tended to be a zero-sum game. Issues at stake in these rank-dependent, often asymmetrical interactions included who visited whom, whether a return visit was required, and the choreography of reception, meeting, and farewell. Here again, examples abound throughout the early modern period and the early modern world. In 1737, the chapter of the cathedral of Montpellier refused to pay an unprecedented complimentary visit to the son of the First President of the Chamber of Accounts on his reception of the *survivance* of his father's office.[2] In 1679, the diplomatic dispute between the Spanish head of government and the French ambassador in Madrid turned on the thorniest aspect of visit choreography: the *main*, or who would maintain the better spatial position.[3]

A basic accessory of early modern meetings, seats signified and shaped status differences, whether in the Holy Roman Empire, in England, or in the New World: from the very right to sit down, through the distinction between communal and individual seating, to variation in the shape, size, or material of the objects themselves.[4] In 1700, an Introductor of Ambassadors alerted Louis XIV to the fact that his royal armchair was lower than that of his guest the king of Spain. The Introductor noted that 'at all the courts of Italy and at all the courts of Europe the different height of the back-rest of armchairs makes a difference between the persons'.[5] The *faux pas* of the royal household on this occasion is understandable, since at the French court at this time it was the shape of seats rather than their size that made the crucial difference. More specifically, distinction turned on a hierarchy of rests: first came the armchair, equipped with both arm-rests and a back-rest; then the back-chair (*chaise à dos*), equipped with a back-rest only; and finally, the rest-less stool.[6] Such a structural typology created discrete and hence more easily apparent distinctions than did continuous parameters like size.[7]

---

[2] AD Hérault, G 1757, fo. 393. More generally, accounts of visits appear very frequently in provincial ceremonial registers; cf. Mettam, 'Power, Status and Precedence', p. 46; SSB, xii, 5–11.

[3] See previous chapter, pp. 28, 34–5; cf. Patricia Waddy, 'Many Courts, Many Spaces', in Fantoni, Gorse, and Smuts (eds), *The Politics of Space*, pp. 209–30.

[4] Tim Neu, 'The Importance of Being Seated: Ceremonial Conflict in Territorial Diets', in Jason Philip Coy, Benjamin Marschke, and David Warren Sabean (eds), *The Holy Roman Empire, Reconsidered* (New York-Oxford, 2010), pp. 125–42; Robert Tittler, 'Seats of Honor, Seats of Power: The Symbolism of Public Seating in the English Urban Community, *c.*1560–1620, *Albion*, xxiv (1992), 205–23; Cañeque, 'On Cushions and Chairs'. See also in Naples: Guarino, *Representing the King's Splendour*, p. 32.

[5] Breteuil, *Mémoires*, ed. Lever, p. 260.

[6] The fourth possible combination, a seat with arm-rests but no back-rest, was less common, typically occupied by state officials (e.g. the chancellor during the wedding: Sainctot, fo. 25r).

[7] See Figure 2.1. Differences in make or in style were likewise secondary as far as status was concerned. Non-folding *tabourets* and folding *sièges pliants* (or *ployants*) were equivalent from this perspective: Dangeau, vi, 44; AC, MS 1201, p. 38. I thus translate both as 'stool'. Similarly, whether or not there was a stylistic distinction between *fauteuil* and *chaise à bras* is beside our point, and I translate both as 'armchair'. Like the modern 'chair', 'chaise' without qualification or addition usually denoted *chaise à dos*, but could also refer to *chaise à bras*. I use 'seat' for the generic *siège*. See the definitions of these terms in the *Dictionnaire de l'Académie Françoise* (1694), and in the rich, though not always accurate, Henry Havard, *Dictionnaire de l'ameublement et de la décoration* (4 vols, Paris, 1894). See also Guillaume Janneau, *Les Sièges* (Paris, 1967), esp. pp. 30–53.

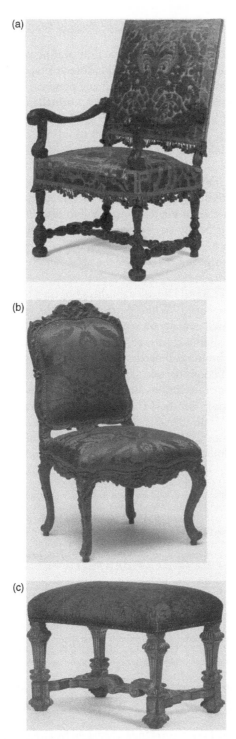

Fig. 2.1 The hierarchy of seat type. All items are from Les Arts Décoratifs, Paris: **a)** arm-chair (*c.* 1650, inv. 12056); **b)** back-chair (*c.* 1730/1740, inv. 36422); **c)** stool (*c.* 1690/1700, inv. PE 715). Photos: Les Arts Décoratifs, Paris/Jean Tholance.

Following the golden rule of status interaction, seating privileges were relative, not absolute: the same person would occupy different types of seats in different circumstances, depending on occasion and on present parties.[8] Typically, the highest-ranking person present would sit in an armchair, while others would occupy seats commensurate with rank and gender differences. In the exalted presence of the French king, most attendants could not even sit down; among those who could, all but royalty had to make do with a stool. Among Frenchmen, the right to sit before the king did not extend beyond the Royal Family, thus distinguishing Grandsons of France from Princes of the Blood. Among Frenchwomen, the privilege further applied to Princesses of the Blood and to titled noblewomen: a case of gender courtesy, but also of women representing their families. For this highly-coveted right of *tabouret* was arguably the most distinctive sign of the highest echelon of the nobility at court. In 1649, several houses fought for this right in the 'war of the *tabourets*', testing the limits of the regency government.[9]

Other members of the Royal House established—or tried to establish—analogous gradations in their presence.[10] When parties could not reach agreement, these seating distinctions could actually obstruct face-to-face contact, notably in international cases.[11] But alternative expedients to wholesale avoidance were often found, such as that of limiting all parties to stools, or simply standing. Here again there were subtle distinctions between keeping up appearances and hinting at the artifice: whereas in some interactions all controversial pieces of furniture would be removed from the room, in others the superior would receive guests 'with her armchair behind her'.[12] In the eighteenth century, the Princes of the Blood adopted an extra-protocolar expedient through variation in seat material, by introducing straw-upholstered chairs that overcame the inconvenience of mutual

---

[8] For a discussion and tabulation of 'who sits (or not) before whom and on what' (Le Roy Ladurie with Fitou, *Saint-Simon*, p. 48), see Brocher, *À la cour de Louis XIV*, pp. 24–34. For a more international perspective, see AAE, MD, France 1851, fos. 16–29. Here I focus on formal social occasions at court. Other settings, such as the royal council or chapel, were similar in logic but different in detail. Private or informal occasions could relax rank injunctions, but did not necessarily eliminate them (witness the reluctance of a nonagenarian to sit in the presence of the princess that he had raised and instructed for half a century: *Madame Palatine: Lettres françaises*, ed. Dirk Van der Cruysse ([Paris], 1989), pp. 424–5).

[9] See Labatut, *Les ducs et pairs*, pp. 203, 366, 373; Fanny Cosandey, 'Les préséances à la cour des reines de France', in Poutrin and Schaub, *Femmes & pouvoir politique*, pp. 267–78. For the early seventeenth century, see Simon Hodson, 'The Power of Female Dynastic Networks: A Brief Study of Louise de Coligny, Princess of Orange, and Her Stepdaughters', *Women's History Review*, xvi (2007), 347. A special initiation rite marked the first time this status symbol was awarded to a noblewoman: Brocher, *À la cour de Louis XIV*, p. 26; Leferme-Falguières, 'Le monde des courtisans', p. 552. In court jargon, the term 'seated women' (*femmes assises*), or even simply *tabourets*, was a metonym for titled noblewomen.

[10] And these extended to others with princely pretensions: François de Callières, *Des mots à la mode, et des nouvelles façons de parler*, 3rd edn (Paris, 1693), pp. 155–6.

[11] e.g. *Madame Palatine: Lettres françaises*, ed. Van der Cruysse, pp. 155–6; AAE, MD, France 1851, fos. 18v–19r.

[12] Sainctot, fos. 40v–41r (the new queen of Spain receiving the French *compagnies supérieures*); cf. BM, MS 2745, fo. 45v. To remove all controversial items from reach could be a defensive mechanism too, since unsatisfied visitors might literally grab a seat: Havard, *Dictionnaire de l'ameublement*, ii, 729, 731.

stools.[13] This underscores the structural advantage of hosts, who were familiar with the terrain and controlled the accessories. Indeed, in most visits, and in particular during the first encounter that set the tone for the status relationship, the host was the higher-ranking party.

Harnessing the seating code to their dynastic agenda, the Grandchildren of France would not give armchairs to anyone below their new rank. Princes and Princesses of the Blood received back-chairs only from them, as did cardinals and titled noblewomen; titled noblemen and untitled noblewomen received stools; and untitled men had to remain standing.[14] The Condés naturally did not approve of this further manifestation of inequality with the Grandchildren of France and sought to eradicate it. The customary duty to pay complimentary visits to the newly-weds would thus inevitably lead to contention in the days that followed the nuptials of 1679. Would the bride treat her relatives according to her French birth rank or according to her Spanish marital rank? Would she offer the Princes of the Blood different seats than she would the Granddaughters of France? These questions most immediately concerned the Orléans princesses and the Conti brothers, lodged with the bride in Fontainebleau, but they also affected the senior Condés, who could not avoid the world in their Parisian *hôtel* forever.

INITIAL DELIBERATIONS (30–31 AUGUST)

The first mention of the matter in our corpus appears in a letter by the *Grand Condé*, of 30 August at noon. There, he instructs Gourville to find out how the bride would treat the Granddaughters of France when she became queen.[15] That evening, Gourville replied that he has not yet inquired into the matter, for fear of 'donner quelques veües' (presumably, alerting the Orléans), but that he would strive to find out what type of seats would be given to the Granddaughters. He assured his master that the Conti brothers would not visit the bride before the king declared his intention in the matter. If the monarch introduced difference in treatment, Gourville, as instructed, would opt for avoidance and ask to dispense the brothers from seeing the bride.[16] The next morning, Condé approved this course of action and reiterated the need to follow his (previous) instructions.[17]

That same morning of 31 August, the matter gained momentum. The king spotted Gourville in the royal apartment as the cortège was preparing to make its way

---

[13] See the complaints of Saint-Simon, apropos a mid-eighteenth-century seating quarrel between the Princes of the Blood and the titled nobility: 'Matériaux pour servir a un mémoire sur l'occurrence présente—aoust 1753', transcribed in Jean-Pierre Brancourt, *Le duc de Saint-Simon et la monarchie* (Paris, 1971), p. 246; cf. AC, MS 1217, p. 28; AN, K 577, no. 72, fos. 2v–3r.

[14] *Mémoires de Mme de Motteville*, ed. F. Riaux (4 vols, Paris, 1855), i, 221; Brocher, *À la cour de Louis XIV*, p. 28. The duchess of Guise allegedly did not allow her husband (a Foreign Prince) more than a stool, even in the intimacy of their home.

[15] Condé-Gourville, no. 34.

[16] Condé-Gourville, no. 44.

[17] Condé-Gourville, no. 35. The instructions mentioned had either been given orally or in letters that have not survived.

to the chapel. An initial negotiation session thus took place in the somewhat unusual setting of the solemn wedding procession. As this session set the stage for what followed, Gourville's account of it—which also gives a flavour of the nature of our corpus—is worth citing in full:

> [The king] asked me which treatment *Messieurs* the Princes of the Blood claim from the queen of Spain. I told him that YMSH[18] had had a chair at the late Queen Mother of England's and that Madame de Carignan had had an armchair in Madrid. His Majesty had understood that I was telling him that YMSH had had an armchair in the presence of the queen of England, and said smiling: 'would you give me your word that *Monsieur le Prince* had an armchair in the presence of the queen of England?' I replied that YMSH had told me a chair, but that Madame de Carignan had assured YMSH of having had an armchair in Madrid. His Majesty replied: 'If the ambassador denies it, it will be quite difficult for us to prove this'. I replied that if she had had a chair it had been an armchair, because there were no other [chairs] in Spain. I then begged His Majesty to agree that *Messeigneurs* the princes of Conti not see the queen of Spain before he has ordered their treatment, since he had been kind enough to say that it was his affair. And [I told the king] that the [affair] of YMSHH was to beg His Majesty very humbly that there be no difference between the treatment of *Mesdemoiselles* and that of *Messieurs* the Princes of the Blood, since [the king] had always been kind enough to rule for complete equality in all public ceremonies. His Majesty finished by telling me: 'be well assured of what you will have to tell me about the manner in which *Monsieur le Prince* was treated by the queen of England and in other cases, if there are any'. I replied that I was heading off to write to YMSH, and that I was certain that [YMSH] would tell the truth. [His Majesty] replied that he did not doubt it, and that *Messieurs* the princes of Conti should not see the queen of Spain before he has talked to me [again].[19]

The king subsequently continued processing to the chapel, while Gourville went to his room to report. He asked his masters to supply him with the required information regarding previous precedents, 'so that it would be possible to show the letter of YMSH if necessary'.[20]

Louis XIV, then, entered the stage of status negotiations, making the question of seating protocol 'his affair' (and not uninformed about past precedent, as his rejoinder on the queen of England demonstrates). Furthermore, the affair of seats has clearly acquired an international dimension, and its negotiation would have to take into account the complex ceremonial of the Society of Princes and the position of foreign ambassadors.[21] Complexity stemmed not only from the difficulty of reconciling diverse precedents involving different protagonists in the international

---

[18] 'YMSH' = 'Your Most Serene Highness' ('VAS' = *Votre Altesse Sérénissime*): this is how Gourville addressed each of his masters in writing (in bound address—see Chapter Six, pp. 131–40). Since the *Grand Condé* is the primary addressee, this singular form refers to him, while the plural 'VAASS' (*Vos Altesses Sérénissimes*), which I denote by 'YMSHH', includes Henri-Jules too.

[19] Condé-Gourville, no. 54.

[20] Condé-Gourville, no. 55.

[21] In fact, the international picture gets even more complicated if we question the assumption that Carignan was treated according to her birth rank as a Princess of the Blood rather than according to her marital rank as a princess of the house of Savoy.

'pecking order' (France versus England as opposed to France versus Spain), but also from the cultural incongruities among 'national' status regimes. The Spanish regime, it appears, did not recognize the distinction between a chair and an arm-chair as hierarchically meaningful.[22]

The *Grand Condé* responded in two letters, undated but most probably written the same day. In the first, he clarified the English precedent, as requested. He and his son, it turns out, had received stools only from the late Queen Mother of England—but so had the Granddaughters of France.[23] Accordingly, the Princes of the Blood would not mind receiving the same equal treatment from the new Spanish queen. However, if *Monsieur* wished to upgrade the treatment of *Mesdemoiselles*, 'we would have reason to claim the same things, and I would hope that the king in his kindness would agree not to abandon us on this occasion; you would beg him to this effect very humbly on our behalf, with all the respect that we owe him and all the confidence that we should also have in his acts of kindness towards us'.[24] The 'obsequious mode' of the last phrases may well have been strategic, bearing in mind that Gourville had requested a letter that could be shown if necessary.

The second letter, on the other hand, was intended for Gourville's eyes only.[25] In effect the brief of a status barrister, it identified three possible scenarios, and deline-ated the lines of argument to be pursued in each case. If Granddaughters of France and Princes of the Blood were to receive seats equally, whatever the type, Gourville should not bring up the precedent of Carignan's armchair in Madrid. Internal Bourbon equality with the Granddaughters of France thus outweighed inter-national considerations here. In the second scenario, where the Granddaughters demanded preferential treatment, bringing up Carignan's precedent would become essential. If the other side then tried to dismiss this precedent by arguing that there was no distinction between seat types in Spain, Gourville was instructed to rejoin that the bride should be considered Spanish after her marriage, and therefore would have no authority to make distinctions in France that did not apply in her own country. Only in the last resort was he to plead for permission that the Princes of the Blood refrain from seeing the new queen. The avoidance tactic, the absent Condé realized, amounted to admission of failure: 'I am telling you again,' he wrote in the postscript, 'not to propose the expedient of not seeing her unless there was no way of succeeding with the rest'.[26]

---

[22] On Spanish usage, see Sabatier and Torrione (eds), *¿Louis XIV espagnol?*, pt 2; Hugo Coniez (ed.), *Le Cérémonial de la Cour d'Espagne au XVIIᵉ siècle* (Paris, 2009).
[23] Condé-Gourville, no. 43; this is confirmed in *Mémoires de Mˡˡᵉ de Montpensier*, ed. A. Chéruel (4 vols, Paris, 1858–59), iv, 406 (both texts use 'sièges' for *sièges pliants*). See Corp, *A Court in Exile*, pp. 171–5, on subsequent Stuart refusal to grant chairs to anyone below the Children of France; Corp even implies that Philippe II of Orléans's resentment of the Stuart stool contributed to his anti-Jacobite policy as regent.
[24] Condé-Gourville, no. 43.
[25] Condé-Gourville, no. 46. The material evidence hints that the two letters were sent together. All of Condé's autographs in the dossier contain traces of seals on the address page, except these two letters and nos. 47 and 50, where joint sending is almost certain (see later, pp. 67–8). Presumably, when sending more than one item, Condé had the seal applied on a separate cover (which has not survived in the dossier). On seals and covers, see Chapter Six.
[26] Condé-Gourville, no. 46.

Gourville sent another update in the afternoon of 31 August, with intelligence from the rival camp. A member of *Monsieur*'s household who had 'some obligation' to the Condé agent told him that when the bride rehearsed her new treatment with her three-year-old sister, the latter was placed on a stool.[27] The queen of Spain, according to this version, would adopt the protocol of the queen of France. Anticipating his master's instructions, Gourville advised not to press for better treatment, as this might incite *Monsieur* to create new distinctions. Condé, in reply, reaffirmed his willingness to settle for stools as long as the Granddaughters of France received the same treatment. He instructed his agent to ensure the matter well before the Conti brothers paid their visit to the bride: 'please do not leave before the *affaire des sièges* is over'.[28]

THE CRITICAL PHASE (31 AUGUST–2 SEPTEMBER)

The affair reached its critical phase in the next couple of days, marked by intense negotiations among the king, Gourville, Condé and Henri-Jules, *Monsieur*, and the Spanish ambassador. Eight of the letters in our corpus deal with this phase: three by Gourville, four autographs of Condé, and one of Henri-Jules. The earliest two offer particularly precious insights into status interaction and negotiation. The first is a sixteen-page-long letter by Gourville, detailing two private audiences with Louis XIV. It was sent on the night of 31 August, with instructions to rouse the *Grand Condé* by 5 a.m. so that he could read and respond immediately. Condé replied the next morning, elaborating the position of the Princes of the Blood in a memorandum to the king in the guise of a letter to Gourville.[29] The remaining exchanges are fragmentary and do not fully account for the outcome of the crisis. For this reason, and due to the complexity of the negotiations, the discussion from now on will be divided into several thematic threads. This section focuses on the immediate problem of seats, leaving the analysis of other aspects to the following two sections.

The main priority of the Princes of the Blood, we have seen, was to secure equal footing with the Granddaughters of France. Bourbon politics trumped international considerations, and the Condés were willing to set aside Carignan's precedent and to accept any type of seat from the queen of Spain, provided that the Granddaughters received the same treatment. The latest news seemed promising, as the Orléans appeared to have opted for stools. Entering the first audience with

---

[27] Condé-Gourville, no. 56. They also practised irreciprocal address: the infant, Mademoiselle de Chartres, addressed her now royal sister (more precisely, half-sister) 'Madame', receiving the kinship term 'ma soeur' in return (see Chapter Six, esp. pp. 137–8). On Gourville's espionage skills, see Lecestre, 'La mission de Gourville en Espagne', esp. pp. 128–34.

[28] Condé-Gourville, no. 38.

[29] The first is no. 39 (it is unpaginated like the others, but, given its length, I cite it with sequential page numbers in square brackets). Written shortly after the audiences, it combines direct and indirect quotations. The second is nos. 42 and 47 (erroneously marked separately). The others are nos. 41, 40, 50, 51, 37, and 53. See Appendix II and Figure 2.2.

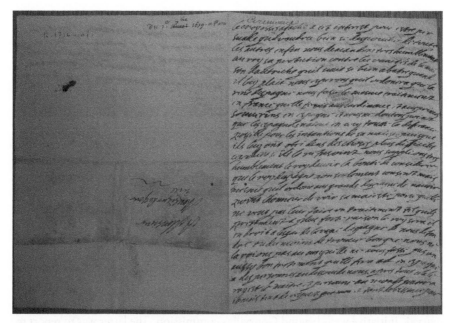

Fig. 2.2 Cover and page of text from the letter/memorandum of the *Grand Condé*, 1 September 1679. AN, K 1712, no. 47. Document conserved at the Archives nationales, Paris; reproduced by kind permission.

the king on the afternoon of 31 August, Gourville learned that this was no longer the case. The Orléans princesses had refused the settlement, and *Monsieur* had been told that (even) cardinals received armchairs in Madrid.[30] Gourville was quick to seize on the last point, arguing that if these princes of the Church were to receive armchairs in France, it would surely resolve the affair. The king agreed that in such a scenario he himself would insist on arm-chaired visits for the Conti brothers too (as this would have a bearing on the international status of the house of France). He added, though, that 'if my brother is happy that the queen of Spain treat everyone as before [her marriage], I could not maintain the contrary'.[31]

This scenario, of treating the bride according to her birth rank rather than her marital rank, pushed Gourville into an uncomfortable bargaining position. It confronted the Princes of the Blood with the reality of their place within the Bourbon hierarchy, a reality which they had so far tried to evade—perhaps even modify surreptitiously—via the constructive ambiguity of bridal status. In this position, Gourville could only express dismay at the prospect of distinctions between *Mesdemoiselles* and the Princes of the Blood 'in a public ceremony... as Your Majesty

---

[30] cf. Coniez, *Le Cérémonial de la Cour d'Espagne*, p. 204; Antonio Álvarez-Ossorio Alvariño, 'La chapelle royale dans l'Alcázar de Madrid: un espace courtisan', in Sabatier and Torrione (eds), *¿Louis XIV espagnol?*, p. 167.

[31] Condé-Gourville, no. 39, [p. 3], the only exception to this rule of pre-nuptial treatment being Louis's own person, courteous as ever in his wish to treat his niece as a royal guest.

has always ruled for complete equality in all the other ceremonies'.[32] The king called this bluff on the spot, noting that his sentiments were different, as he had already told Condé (presumably, apropos the *plume*). Gourville subsequently tried to put up a couple of weak lines of defence,[33] and finally fell back on the last resort in his brief, namely avoidance: if equality was not possible, the Princes of the Blood would like to refrain from seeing the queen of Spain. Louis found this resort 'a bit harsh, because if I agree to it, my brother will be angry [*fasché*] with me, and if I do not agree, it would have another *air* which would not be good'.[34] He suggested in any case that he discuss matters with *Monsieur* and that they reconvene later that evening.

Gourville was summoned back earlier than expected. Apparently convinced that past precedent favoured the Orléans, Louis repeatedly attempted in this second audience to press Gourville into admitting that the Princes of the Blood had received back-chairs from *Mesdemoiselles*. Gourville did his best to dodge these challenges, pleading ignorance and creating diversions. Finally, the two began exploring a new line of negotiation: that the Condés accept defeat on this occasion in return for a guarantee that the next generation of Orléans will not receive pref-erential treatment. The king raised the possibility of issuing a regulation (*règle-ment*) to that effect, but adjourned the meeting when it became clear that such a dynastic initiative went beyond Gourville's commission. The latter was to report to his masters, while the king talked to *Monsieur*.[35]

After duly reporting the two audiences in the sixteen-page-long letter, Gourville 'dared to take the liberty' of offering his view of the situation. It would be impos-sible, he believed, to persuade the king to support the equality of seats. Implicitly questioning Condé's instructions, he added that the avoidance tactic would make it clear to everyone 'that one has lost one's case'.[36] In such circumstances, would it not be more worthwhile to pursue the regulation initiative, the alternative line that he has begun to explore with the king? Concerned about public image, Gourville advocated a swift resolution to the crisis, to forestall discussion at court. If the Conti brothers did not see the queen of Spain the following day, 'this will arouse attention and awaken an affair that seemed completely dormant'.[37]

Condé responded the next morning by trying to reframe the negotiations entirely. The crucial turning-point had occurred in the first audience, when the king had declared that he would not intervene if *Monsieur* insisted on pre-nuptial treatment. Given Louis's sentiments and past precedent, the Condés could not

---

[32] Condé-Gourville, no. 39, [pp. 3–4].

[33] The first line of defence involved the distinction between Royal House and Royal Family (see next section). In the second, Gourville claimed that equal armchair treatment among Granddaughters of France was 'like the bishops, who all address each other *Monseigneur*, but nobody [else] treats them so' (Condé-Gourville, no. 39, [pp. 6–7]; cf. Chapter Six, p. 135): this was more of a diversion than an argument.

[34] Condé-Gourville, no. 39, [pp. 7–8].

[35] Condé-Gourville, no. 39, [pp. 8–13]. Having employed Gourville as a diplomat in the past, Louis XIV was perhaps aware of the former's tendency to overstep his commission.

[36] Condé-Gourville, no. 39, [p. 14].

[37] Condé-Gourville, no. 39, [p. 16].

succeed within this Bourbon framework. The international framework, on the other hand, seemed more promising. Before the turning-point, Gourville had even managed to commit the king into declaring that under certain international circumstances he himself would insist that the Princes of the Blood receive armchairs, namely if cardinals receive this seat-type in France as they did in Spain. What Condé set out to achieve, then, was to widen the crack, by convincing Louis XIV that it was in the sovereign's own interest—a classic rhetorical strategy—that the bride be treated according to her marital rank.

The affair, Condé argued in the autograph letter/memorandum, has become a matter between the king's house and the 'house of Austria': a dynastic affair between Bourbons and Habsburgs. The princes of the royal blood of France represented the international reputation of the king and of his dynasty in the Society of Princes, whereas the bride has now passed over to their Spanish rivals. She could not hold the stick at both ends: 'when princesses marry a person whose rank they wish to hold, as *Mademoiselle* now does, then they must give up that of France [...] she cannot make distinctions here which she would not make in Madrid'.[38] Europe would not recognize the rank of *Mademoiselle*; maintaining it now would only establish that the queen of Spain, in plain sight of the king of France, treated the princes of his house worse than she would their international near-equals: cardinals, German electors, and sub-royal sovereigns like the duke of Savoy.[39] To support his claim, Condé specified not only the Carignan precedent, but also cases where other European monarchs had treated the Princes of the Blood equally or preferentially to foreign princes who received armchairs in Spain.

Targeting a notorious soft spot of Louis, Condé claimed that the grandeur of the king's house was inseparable from the king's own. He invoked past and present status rivalries between the two dynasties—notably the ongoing dispute with Don Juan—and asked the king 'very humbly for his protection against the vanities of the house of Austria which he knows so well to beat when it pleases him'.[40] *Monsieur*, too, should remember where his loyalties ultimately lay and support the grandeur of the house of France against 'les estrangers', casting off other interests. After the marriage, it was the Spanish ambassador, not the bride's father, who should speak for her interests. Condé, in return, expressed willingness to declare that the Princes of the Blood will not hold the queen of Spain's treatment as a future claim against *Mesdemoiselles*. He thus revealed the weak hand of the Condés: having probably hoped, at the outset, to take advantage of the ambiguity of bridal

---

[38] Condé-Gourville, no. 42. But cf. AAE, MD, France 1851, fo. 26v.

[39] The Condés thus tried to play on rivalries with other European dynasties too. Such deep and comparative concern with seat-type was equally shared by these international parties: witness the constant vigilance of Sophie of Hanover, who was visiting the French court at the time of the marriage, about the seats that she received from her hosts and how they compared with her treatment in Germany (Sophie de Hanovre, *Mémoires et lettres de voyage*, pp. 142, 149, 151–2, 153, 156, 161, 250, 257).

[40] Condé-Gourville, no. 47. The case of Don Juan was particularly pertinent, as there the king had instructed the Princes of the Blood to stand their particular ground for the broader interest of the house of France (see previous chapter, pp. 34–5).

rank in order to establish a precedent against their rivals, they were now willing to disambiguate it in order to prevent a precedent against themselves.

Condé also drew on the international framework in order to buttress his fallback position of avoidance, a position which Louis, as we have seen, had found 'a bit harsh' during the first audience. The Prince of the Blood noted that the king of Spain 'not only allows, but even orders' Spanish grandees to refrain from seeing the French king because the latter would not award them the treatment that they claim.[41] All the more reason for the king of France 'to forbid us or at least to agree that we do not see [the queen of Spain] in case she does not award us as good a treatment as she will award in Spain to persons beneath us'.[42] Avoidance, then, still remained a viable option for the Condés, Gourville's arguments notwithstanding. The long memorandum, moreover, contains no reference to the regulation initiative. In what was probably a covering letter, Condé wrote to his agent that he had nothing to add, and that the 'other matters of your letter' were best sorted out in person between himself, his son, and the king.[43]

Gourville did not present the letter/memorandum to the king until the next day (2 September). In the meantime, however, there was an important development 'on the ground': the Granddaughters of France visited their former colleague in the afternoon of 1 September. Generally laconic, the newspaper accounts nevertheless note that the visitors received armchairs.[44] More details and nuances appear in Gourville's reports of this development, based on two sources: the cardinal of Bonzi and 'the only person who was present'.[45] According to both, the queen of Spain received the Granddaughters while in bed. According to the second, she then rose and sat at her *toilette*, giving her guests stools. Nobody entered the room during this private visit, except one or two of the Legitimated Princesses.[46]

As usual, the inside version of the other camp is missing, because of the nature of surviving documentation. In retrospective accounts, members of the Orléans clan claimed that the Spanish ambassador had approved the armchair.[47] The Orléans may have used the most recent position of their Condé rivals to argue that such treatment should not be viewed as controversial. For the *Grand Condé's*

[41] Condé-Gourville, no. 47. Was he referring to the famous grandee privilege of keeping hats on in the presence of royalty? In any case, he instructed Gourville in a postscript to request that the Conti brothers 'se couurent vn moment' during their visit.

[42] Condé-Gourville, no. 47.

[43] Condé-Gourville, no. 50. More later, on the question of regulation and on the micro-politics of negotiation.

[44] The *Gazette* (1679, p. 430) significantly adds that the queen of Spain returned the visit; the *Mercure Galant* (September 1679, p. 274) repeats the same information. For Sainctot's account, see later.

[45] Condé-Gourville, nos. 41, 40. On Bonzi's relations with Gourville and with his masters, see *Mémoires de Gourville*, ed. Lecestre, *passim*; Béguin, *Les princes de Condé*, p. 403. Is the second source the same member of *Monsieur's* household who had passed on the earlier intelligence?

[46] According to Bonzi, Mademoiselle de Blois and the duchess of Verneuil received a back-chair. According to the second source, only the latter entered, receiving a stool (possibly during the *toilette*).

[47] *Mémoires de Mlle de Montpensier*, ed. Chéruel, iv, 406; 'Correspondance de Louis XIV et du duc d'Orléans (1707)', ed. C. Pallu de Lessert, *Mélanges publiés par la société des bibliophiles françois*, pt 1 (1903), p. 9 (where Orléans invokes the precedent thirty years later, when visiting another Spanish queen).

memorandum did not deny the Granddaughters the armchair; it only demanded the same for the Princes of the Blood. Furthermore, the Orléans seem to have choreographed the event cleverly, achieving their main goal while keeping the occasion private and ambiguous enough. Armchairs were given—and hence could be publicly reported; the host, however, was in bed, avoiding a clear-cut equality of seats; later, during the *toilette*, she resorted to the stool expedient. Marie-Louise was, after all, a Spanish queen.[48]

Despite its private nature, the visit became public knowledge at court that same evening, putting pressure on the Princes of the Blood as Gourville feared. Other news concerned the international dimension of the affair. The cardinals of Bouillon and Bonzi, 'answerable to Rome', inquired with *Monsieur* about their own treatment. Gourville learned that they had expected to receive back-chairs 'as before', and that *Monsieur* expressed willingness to give them the same treatment as the Princes of the Blood.[49] Such a solution would undermine Condé's argument on Spanish treatment: if the princes of the Roman Church—firmly entitled to armchairs in Madrid—settled for back-chairs in France, the same treatment to the Princes of the Blood would not really upset the position of the Bourbon dynasty in the international status regime.

Evidence on the final stages of negotiation is fragmentary. Gourville met with Louis XIV at least one more time, on the morning of 2 September. In this meeting, the agent summed up the arguments for armchairs to the Princes of the Blood, adding another international precedent, from Christina of Sweden's stay in France during the 1650s: having awarded armchairs to Gaston's daughters, the Swedish queen had initially given the princess of Conti a stool only; even though Christina had taken the same type of seat herself and had taken care to remove all armchairs from the room beforehand, the Princess of the Blood had complained and had won a repeat, arm-chaired visit. This precedent failed to impress the king, who attributed it to the credit of Cardinal Mazarin, the uncle of the princess.[50] More generally, he added that these arguments better suited the case of a Spanish queen passing through France than that of a member of the house of Bourbon. Again, Louis could not force his brother to have the queen of Spain give an armchair to the Princes of the Blood, when she had previously given them armless chairs only.

On the other hand, the king proved more forthcoming than before regarding the possibility of avoidance, and even suggested a face-saving pretext, based on the incongruity between the two regimes: 'I could accept what the Spanish ambassador says, that men do not visit [*vojent*] their queen'.[51] He thus offered the Condés the

---

[48] On the use of beds for seating exceptions, see Brocher, *À la cour de Louis XIV*, p. 32.

[49] Condé-Gourville, nos. 41, 40.

[50] Christina's status was problematic anyway because of her abdication. The king's suspicion about Mazarin's involvement is vindicated in Gourville's own account of this incident in his *Mémoires*, ed. Lecestre, i, 119–21. See also *Mémoires de Mlle de Montpensier*, ed. Chéruel, ii, 456.

[51] Condé-Gourville, no. 40. Another notable gender-based incongruity which does not come up here is the fact that, on similar occasions in Spain, women generally did not sit on legged furniture at all, but rather on the floor or on cushions (*almohadas*). See e.g. *Mémoires de la cour d'Espagne*, ed. M.A. Morel-Fatio (Paris, 1893), p. 104; SSB, ix, esp. 201–2, 332, 453.

choice between back-chairs and avoidance. Gourville, however, curiously insisted on leaving the decision to the monarch, and alluded to the regulation initiative. Louis continued to show support for the initiative, and concluded that he would announce his decision after dinner. That morning, the king also joined other members of the Royal House at the queen of Spain's apartment. No Grandchild of France or Prince of the Blood was present, but *Monsieur* received an armchair, and the Legitimated Princes and Princesses—back-chairs.[52]

In the last thread of the surviving corpus, Condé expressed disappointment with his agent's performance. Given that the king had offered them a choice without showing a clear preference, Gourville should have followed his instructions and have opted for avoidance. He should still do so, if the matter has not yet reached the point of no return and the Princes of the Blood were offered a choice again. 'Above all,' Condé concluded, 'do not speak anymore of the regulation, *ny en blanc ni en noir*'.[53] It is now time for a more thorough discussion and analysis of these two recurring themes, of dynastic politics and of status negotiation, before we return to the problem of seats and to the final outcome of the affair.

DYNASTIC POLITICS: REGULATION OR AVOIDANCE?

In a dynastic context based on the principle of primogeniture, a procreative main line entails the increasing marginalization of cadet lines. At the beginning of the seventeenth century, Henri II of Bourbon-Condé had been heir to the throne. By 1679, his son and successor, the *Grand Condé*, dropped to fourth in line, not to mention the six female native Bourbons who preceded him in proximity to the monarch. Three decades later, his grandson Louis III would already be eighth in line, shortly before the dynastic catastrophe of the final years of the reign would bring the Condés closer to the throne once again. As the main line burgeoned, so did internal distinctions, in substance and in terminology. Terms such as 'Family of the King' or 'Royal Family' designated the more immediate family of current or of former kings, setting them apart from the 'Royal House' in general. More controversially, members of the third generation of the Royal Family sought to carve themselves a new rank of 'Grandchildren of France' in order to differentiate themselves from the rest of the Royal House, and in particular from the Princes of the Blood. The *affaire des sièges* turned on the struggle over this novel Bourbon rank.

---

[52] Somewhat inconsistent, the narrative accounts of this dynamic gathering demonstrate the complexity of the 'musical chairs' game of the seating code, as each successive entry of a higher-ranking visitor caused changes in seat allocation. Complex to begin with, the situation was exacerbated by the uncertainties of the bride's rank. According to Sainctot (fos. 38v–39r), *Monsieur*'s armchair derived from the one that the queen of England (wife of Charles I, also French by birth) had given to Gaston in 1644. In the queen of Spain's apartment, moreover, Louis XIV was his guest's guest, and therefore occupied the best position spatially; cf. *Gazette* (1679), pp. 430–1.
[53] Condé-Gourville, no. 37.

Dynastic politics, we have seen, came up during the audiences of 31 August. When Gourville tried to claim that there had always been total equality in public ceremonies between *Mesdemoiselles* and the Princes of the Blood, the king denied it and said that 'there had been differences between the Royal House [*Maison Royale*] and the Princes of the Blood'.[54] This statement set Gourville off in a terminological digression, explaining to Louis XIV the difference between *maison* and *famille*. All descendants of Saint Louis were members of Louis XIV's house, but only one of them—the dauphin—also belonged to his family. *Monsieur* and his offspring, according to this terminology, could only have belonged to the Royal Family while Louis XIII was alive; Gaston's daughters never belonged to it, strictly speaking, since they were all born after Henri IV's death.[55] This was not simply an exercise in labelling. Gourville thereby challenged the divisional line that increasingly excluded the Condés, pointing out that the Orléans were as much a cadet branch as their more distant cousins (and faced the same fate in the future).

The Condé opposition to divisional lines within the Bourbon dynasty, it should be noted, extended to the junior lines of their own branch too. Thus, Henri-Jules emphasized that in the event of the Conti brothers having to see the queen of Spain, Gourville should not use the 'smallpox air' as a pretext for him and for his father not to see her:

> we will have no problem in doing what *Messieurs* the princes of Conti will have done. On the contrary, it is not in our interest to distinguish ourselves from them. The bad air is the business of *Monsieur* and of *Mademoiselle*. So do not think of using this reason as a pretext in case the king has decided that the princes of Conti see her.

Henri-Jules added that the princess of Carignan should do the same.[56] Marginalizing the Contis would not be in the interest of the senior line: the Condés had probably realized that they would be next in line for demotion if they encouraged intra-Bourbon divisions.[57]

Returning to the main divisional line, Louis declared in the second audience of 31 August that, even if he agreed with Gourville's definitions of 'family' and 'house', he still believed in 'some differences' between the 'Grandsons of Royalty' (*Petits filz de Roy*) and the Princes of the Blood.[58] Gourville, in reply, asked what was precisely

---

[54] Condé-Gourville, no. 39, [p. 4].

[55] Condé-Gourville, no. 39, [pp. 4–5]. Struggling with the same problem, Sainctot differentiated between 'famille du Roy' (denoting the concept put forward by Gourville here, of the current monarch and his descendants) and 'famille Royalle' (including the first two generations of descendants of previous monarchs): AN, K 1712, no. 6/3. As noted in the Introduction, I use 'Royal Family' in the latter, inclusive sense.

[56] Condé-Gourville, no. 53. This did leave open the possibility of *de facto* distinction, but only as a result of an Orléans fear of contagion, not of a Condé excuse.

[57] Perhaps they had learned a lesson from the *plume* and come to the conclusion that Conti presence voided their own avoidance. Note also Henri-Jules's use of the idiom of 'interest' rather than of blood ties or of solidarity in referring to his young first-degree cousins; cf. an earlier incident, where the Orléans reportedly tried to drive a wedge between the two lines, claiming that the Contis are 'trop cadets', 'mais n'y deuant pas auoir de distinction entre les Princes du Sang, Monsieur le Prince et Monsieur le Duc ne crûrent pas pouuoir abandonner leurs jnterests': AC, MS 1131, fos. 8v, 19v.

[58] Condé-Gourville, no. 39, [p. 11].

meant by 'Grandson of Royalty' and how far down it would extend. For, in a way, all Princes of the Blood were the grandchildren of Saint Louis, but, strictly speaking, a future son of the duke of Chartres (*Monsieur*'s son) would no longer be a king's grandson. Louis explained that he meant the latter, stricter sense, and offered—'if I [Gourville] thought that this would satisfy YMSHH'—to issue a regulation, that the children of the duke of Chartres would receive the same treatment as the Condé princes. When he realized that the agent did not have the power to authorize such a regulation, the king ended the audience, forbad Gourville 'to speak of this conversation to anyone', and ordered him to report to his masters while Louis discussed the matter with *Monsieur*.[59]

The matter came up again in their last reported audience, on 2 September. Leaving the decision on seats to the monarch (see earlier), Gourville told Louis 'that YMSHH were entirely convinced that their submission to all [the king's] wishes would better maintain their rights than anything they could gain while causing him the slightest pain, and that I did not doubt that when all this is over, [the king] would agree to save all the interests of YMSHH, either by a general regulation, or by restoring the rights that they enjoyed before this ceremony'. Louis replied that he had spoken with *Monsieur*, and was ready to issue 'a regulation that would surely satisfy YMSHH by regulating a difference for the Grandchildren of Royalty only'. Gourville again voiced terminological reservations, but noted that the matter exceeded his commission anyway, and that his masters wished to discuss it directly with the monarch.[60]

Yet this late disclosure of the limits of his powers hardly nullified the effect of the linkage just made between the decision on seats and a future dynastic regulation. Had Gourville been following his commission to the letter and to the spirit, he would not have referred to the matter at all. Ever since it had first come up, Condé repeatedly instructed his agent to drop it:

> I say nothing to you about the other matters of your letter. On such affairs, my son and I should have the honour of talking to the king. Many of them require a lot of explanation that cannot be done by letter, and we have long wished to expound them to His Majesty and to receive his orders.[61]

The 'ny en blanc ni en noir' reaction to the report of 2 September illustrates Condé's exasperation with Gourville's meddling. While a dynastic regulation would rein in the future ambitions of the Orléans, it would at the same time amount to *de jure*—and hence more binding—recognition of the *de facto* gains of the Grandchildren of France, gains that the Condés have been fighting against for decades. The logic of regulation was diametrically opposed to the logic of avoidance. Such a paradigm shift called for direct, face-to-face negotiation with the monarch, rather than for the delegation of powers to an independent-minded agent.

---

[59] Condé-Gourville, no. 39, [pp. 11–13].   [60] Condé-Gourville, no. 40.
[61] Condé-Gourville, no. 50, reiterated in no. 51.

THE MICRO-POLITICS OF STATUS NEGOTIATION

What, then, can the affair tell us about status negotiation at the court of Louis XIV? The Condé-Gourville correspondence is invaluable because such real-time inside evidence is hard to find. The special communicational setting of this exchange is almost ideal for the historian. On the one hand, physical separation between agent-on-the-spot and absent masters gave rise to written, and hence documented, communication. On the other, the relatively short distance between the parties facilitated frequent exchange, and involved the Condés in the almost hour-by-hour tactics of negotiation, in a way that pre-electronic diplomatic correspondence normally does not. For the same reasons, though, one must be cautious in generalizing from a single case, however rich. The Condé-Gourville correspondence has come about due to an unusual turn of events—the absence of key courtiers from a ceremonial highlight. Delegation of delicate matters like status and rank was not necessarily the rule at the court of Louis XIV, where aristocrats normally attended the person of the king and were thus available for face-to-face negotiation. In 1679, the question of Condé presence at court, during and after the ceremonies, was part of the problem.

Indeed, the question of parties and their representation illuminates the nature of power relationships, within the Royal House and beyond. Though the affair turned on the seating protocol of the queen of Spain, née *Mademoiselle*, no one seems to have consulted the bride herself. When Condé contested *Monsieur*'s right to speak for her interests after the marriage, the alternative party he had in mind was the Spanish ambassador, not the queen.[62] While these assumptions certainly fit our notion of a patriarchal seventeenth-century social order, they should not lead us into drawing gender lines too simplistically. The Conti brothers, the bride's most immediate interactants in the *affaire des sièges*, were similarly disregarded. Despite their presence on the spot, it was Gourville who conducted negotiations on their behalf. The *Grand Condé* repeatedly employs the patronizing first-person plural, certainly encompassing his own line, and probably often his Conti protégés too. Conversely, Gaston's daughters—older than the under-age bride and Contis, with no father, husband, or guardian to account to—may have played a more active role.[63] Agency, then, was also a question of age.

The main protagonists in our sources are the patriarchs of the two rival clans: the *Grand Condé* (and his heir Henri-Jules) on the one hand, *Monsieur* on the other. The bad blood between the two sides, however, hindered direct communication. Before the beginning of negotiations, Gourville feared that too direct an approach might suggest lines of action to *Monsieur*; afterwards, he kept contact with informers in the Orléans household. Towards the end, Henri-Jules warned the agent

---

[62] Condé-Gourville, no. 42. Not to mention *Mademoiselle*'s opposition to the match in the first place.

[63] As we have seen, in the first audience the king noted that they had refused to settle for stools. Though technically married, the grand-duchess of Tuscany lived separately from her husband. For explicit examples of female agency, see subsequent chapters, esp. Chapter Three.

against establishing direct communication with the rival patriarch: 'if you have not spoken to *Monsieur*, do not speak to him; reread my letter, you will see that I told you to speak to the king, not to *Monsieur*'.[64] Instead of sorting out their differences among themselves, the Condés and the Orléans negotiated with the king.

Louis XIV acted in multiple, and not always compatible, capacities: mediator between his brother and his distant cousin; party to the negotiations, as grand patriarch of the house of Bourbon, responsible for its internal order and its international prestige; and supreme arbiter in affairs of status, as 'master of the ranks' in France. The extent of his personal involvement in the *affaire des sièges* is remarkable, enough to dispel any lingering doubts about the significance of status interaction in early modern France.[65] This rare close view of the monarch in action—albeit partial—also offers a further corrective to the simplistic perceptions of Louis XIV as manipulative 'divider and ruler' or as authoritarian stage-manager. Gourville describes a sovereign more reactive than proactive; patiently seeking a compromise acceptable to both sides rather than laying down the law; defusing tensions rather than fanning the flames.

Gourville, on the other hand, proved more proactive than one might expect—that is, if one were not familiar with his character. In status diplomacy as in diplomacy proper, the Condé agent pursued independent lines of negotiation and deviated from his script, in style as in substance.[66] Substantially, Gourville raised and continued to explore the issue that his masters wished least to delegate—the dynastic initiative. His style also elicited their criticism:

> I fear that you have not read my [letter] carefully, or that you have not really taken in its meaning. If you read it carefully, you will have noticed that we mention all the reasons that can make the king take on our interests in this affair, as being his own [interests], but also at the same time we show him total devotion and perfect obedience [...] Please understand then that it is in our interest to have our reasons asserted, but no less than that to demonstrate well our submission and our obedience, and that we prefer the advantage of pleasing to all our greatest interests, by explaining them and arguing them in a manner that could not cause chagrin[67]

---

[64] Condé-Gourville, no. 52. The letter Henri-Jules refers to is probably no. 53, and in particular the claim that the 'bad air' is *Monsieur*'s business (see previous section). This is apparently in response to yet another independent line of negotiation, announced by Gourville in another letter, now lost.

[65] The king, as we have seen, gave Gourville at least four slots of royal attention in the space of two days (at a time, moreover, when he was not only busy with the festivities surrounding the marriage, but was also concluding a peace treaty with Denmark, signed at Fontainebleau on 2 September). The first slot took place during the wedding procession on the morning of 31 August (Condé-Gourville, no. 54; an interesting use of ceremonial time to transact business). This possibly improvised exchange was followed by two audiences later that day (no. 39). In the first, the king summoned Gourville to his *chambre*, where Seignelay, Secretary of State in charge of the royal household, was also present. They were then supposed to speak in the *cabinet* at the time of Louis's *coucher*, but the king re-summoned the agent earlier than expected. He then scheduled another meeting for the next morning, 1 September, at the *lever* (not reported; the last couple of days are under-covered in the surviving corpus). The last reported meeting took place on the morning of 2 September (no. 40), and the king expected to announce his final decision to Gourville and to Conti after his *diner* that day.

[66] See esp. Lecestre, 'La mission de Gourville en Espagne'.

[67] Condé-Gourville, no. 51. This letter too responds to an apparently lost communication by Gourville.

In his enthusiasm to get results, the agent conducted negotiations in a manner that threatened to jeopardize his masters' relationship with the king. Perhaps these admonitions explain why Gourville kept leaving the final decision to the monarch on 2 September (a case of hyper-correction?). His allusion to the dynastic regulation on the same occasion, on the other hand, suggests continued self-will. Condé, as we have seen, criticized both.

It is always tricky, of course, to find the golden mean of effective advocacy, between 'a manner that could cause chagrin' and excessive complaisance. Gourville's reported interactions with the king do include many examples of what modern readers may view as an 'obsequious mode', not least in the openings, endings, and strategic moments of the meetings. For example, at the end of the second audience of 31 August, Gourville told the king that 'if YMSH had heard what His Majesty had had the goodness of saying to me, and the manner in which he had done me the honour of speaking to me about [Condé], YMSH would live another ten years; and I spoke to him further of the *attachement*, of the *respect*, and, if I dared say so, of the *tendresse* that YMSHH had for the person of His Majesty'. Earlier in this audience, when the king had driven him into a corner (concerning the seats that the Granddaughters had given the Princes of the Blood in the past), Gourville said that he would have to check the matter with his masters, and then 'elaborated a bit on the sentiments that YMSHH had for His Majesty'.[68] We would need a better grasp of the implicit code of such interactions, though, before we can determine with confidence the likelihood of any given 'move' to cause pleasure or chagrin.[69]

We should also not take instances of the obsequious mode in Condé's letters at their face value. The *Grand Condé* of 1679 certainly recognized the limits of his power vis-à-vis the sovereign. At the same time, he used language strategically to further his interests. Blatantly obsequious passages appear only in letters that were, in all likelihood, written to be shown.[70] In another letter, Condé implicitly contrasts obsequiousness and sincerity: 'thank the king very much for the extreme kindness which he has shown in talking to you, and express to him well our gratitude for it, but frankly [*mais pour vous parler franchement*] …'[71]

The letter/memorandum of 1 September is a particularly interesting example of strategic writing in status diplomacy. As we have seen, this long text detailed 'all the reasons that can make the king take on our interests in this affair, as being his own [interests]'. In form a letter to Gourville like the others, this text was also meant, in fact, to be presented to the king as a memorandum. Accordingly, it abounds with obsequious turns of phrase. Its putative covering letter, in contrast,

---

[68] Condé-Gourville, no. 39, [pp. 10, 13].

[69] Bearing in mind that even conventional or transparent sycophancy sometimes works. The nature of our source obviously calls for further caution: a recording of the meeting would have been more reliable for decoding. Chapter Six attempts a systematic reconstruction of another linguistic code, overriding the problem of re-presentation by investigating a medium where interaction was written in the first place.

[70] Condé-Gourville, no. 43, and the letter/memorandum.

[71] Condé-Gourville, no. 37. He then moves on to criticize Gourville's indecision in the audience of 2 September.

is characterized by a matter-of-fact tone, intended for Gourville only. The covering letter explains that the Condés purposely did not address 'the other things of your letter' (the dynastic regulation), and ends by instructing Gourville on the tactics of presentation:

> You can give the king the attached letter which I write to you, and talk to him exactly accordingly. [...] What we write are our real sentiments, to which I have nothing to add.
> Louis de Bourbon
> Try to have our letter read in your presence[72]

In status diplomacy as in regular diplomacy, the gesture of showing one's instructions added a semblance of authenticity and authority to the message. It also ensured its accurate rendering, especially important in the case of independent-minded envoys.

Gourville, accordingly, tried to stage a showing in his last reported audience:

> I have just told His Majesty that I could not express to him how much YMSHH had been touched by all his kindness, and that he could see this in YMSH's letter, which I held in my hand, unfolding it, and [that he could see there] all the reasons that could demonstrate that the queen of Spain should give armchairs to *Messieurs* the Princes of the Blood. As I wanted to present [the letter] to him, he told me that it seemed a bit long, and that I should instead tell him what it contained.[73]

Gourville began the session in the obsequious mode, and tried to hand in the memorandum, but Louis preferred an 'executive summary'.

RESOLUTION?

Our real-time coverage of the *affaire des sièges* unfortunately dwindles and ends at the beginning of September. The Condé-Gourville correspondence does not shed light on the final outcome, and we must make do with the standard post-facto narrative sources. The *Gazette* report is again laconic: on 3 September, the prince of Conti and the prince of La Roche-sur-Yon visited the queen of Spain in Fontainebleau and received back-chairs; a few days later, she gave the same treatment to the prince of Condé and to the duke of Enghien at the Palais Royal in Paris. Interestingly, this report couples each of the two princely encounters with a back-chaired visit by cardinals on the same day.[74] The Condé ceremonial register too

---

[72] Condé-Gourville, no. 50. As we have seen, the material evidence supports the covering letter hypothesis. Note again the implied potential contrast between a letter intended for the king's eyes and 'real sentiments'.

[73] Condé-Gourville, no. 40. It is very likely that the letter in question is the letter/memorandum of 1 September. Its cover looks quite smudged (see Figure 2.2)—has it preserved the traces of Gourville's sweaty hands, as he held it in the Sun King's presence?

[74] The cardinals of Bouillon and Bonzi on 3 September: *Gazette* (1679), p. 431; the cardinal d'Estrées on 5 September: *Gazette* (1679), p. 432. The register attributed to Bonneuil remarks here, moreover, that 'on dit qu'en Espagne deuant la Reyne les Cardinaux ont un fauteüil': AAE, MD, France 2192, p. 89.

offers a brief account of the princely visits. It explains that the bride 'gave them a back-chair, because before her marriage she had given them a back-chair only'. On the other hand, the register recounts favourable past precedents in the international arena, notably including Carignan's armchair in Madrid, and elaborates on the Spanish ambassador's respectful treatment of Conti.[75]

In the end, then, the Princes of the Blood, Condés as well as Contis, lost the ceremonial battle. In accounting for it, the Condé register posited the pre-nuptial Bourbon precedent as the deciding factor.[76] Having lost out in the home front, the Princes of the Blood wanted to ensure at least that their international prestige remained intact. In this context, it is somewhat surprising that their register does not mention the visits by cardinals. While these back-chaired visits answered the expectations of the princes of the Church to equate themselves with the Princes of the Blood, they also provided the Condés with counter-precedents in the event of future arm-chaired visits by cardinals in Spain.

More surprising is Sainctot's report of these events, or rather—the lack of it. For he makes no mention of the Princes of the Blood in his otherwise detailed account of the queen of Spain's schedule after the wedding.[77] What is more, in explaining the seats allocated to other Bourbons, the Master of Ceremonies remarked that

> With regard to the Granddaughters of Royalty one used the example of the queen of Sweden, who in 1657 had an armchair given to Madame the princess of Conti.
>
> On the authority of this last example, the Princesses of the Blood could claim the same, all the more so since cardinals in Spain have armchairs in the presence of queens. But the Granddaughters of Royalty did not have armchairs in the *cercle* of the queen of Spain, and they only had them in private [*en particulier*] in her chamber.[78]

This remark practically embraces the position of the Princes of the Blood. It acknowledges the international precedents that they put forward during the negotiations and thus equates the validity of their claim with the Granddaughters of France's. Furthermore, it qualifies the actual achievement of the latter, by underscoring the private nature of their arm-chaired visit.[79] The Master of Ceremonies may not have turned a deaf ear, after all, to the recording requests of the Grand

---

[75] AC, MS 1217, pp. 38–9 (dating the second visit to 8 September).

[76] The final wording stressed the causal link to the pre-nuptial precedent, compared with an earlier version (AC, MS 1218, fos. 56–57).

[77] This is true for all versions consulted, including the certified copy of Desgranges, with the notable exception of BM, MS 2285, which mentions a back-chaired visit by the Contis (p. 52, apparently dated to 2 September), but not by the Condés. All versions note the back-chaired visit of the cardinal d'Estrées (e.g. BM, MS 2285, p. 54; BM, MS 2741, fo. 39v); this too presumably served the interests of the Bourbon princes.

[78] Sainctot, fo. 39r.

[79] Private occasions could indeed suspend seating protocol, or rather reframe it. *Monsieur*, who as Son of France had the right to a stool only in the presence of the king, would occupy an armchair during the private gatherings of the royal family that took place every evening after supper. Philippe, Saint-Simon explains, 'dans le particulier vivoit avec le Roi en frère'. Moreover, the dauphin and his children, superior in rank to the king's brother but inferior in age, would remain standing during these regular familial occasions (which, incidentally, refute the common notion that Louis XIV spent his entire daily schedule in public). SSB, xxviii, 346–7, 360, 363.

Master of the Household. Sainctot's account of the *affaire des sièges* thus seems to balance his harshness on the *plume*.[80]

In the absence of evidence, one can only speculate about the denouement of the affair. The most probable explanation would be that the king ended it, as expected, by announcing his decision on the afternoon of 2 September. In their last reported audience in the morning, as we have seen, Gourville had deferred the decision to the monarch, hinting at a package deal of back-chaired visits in return for a Bourbon regulation, to which Louis appeared favourable. It is therefore likely that he ruled for back-chairs, while promising to continue negotiations on the regulation with the Condés in person. The *Grand Condé*'s last letter, preferring avoidance to back-chairs, probably arrived too late. Once the Contis were forced to visit the queen of Spain in Fontainebleau, the Condés, as promised, did the same in Paris.

From the start, Louis XIV expressed support for 'some differences' between the Grandchildren of France and the Princes of the Blood, and he ruled accordingly in the end. While a greater sympathy with his brother may have influenced his conduct as mediator, the outcome probably reflects a more general belief, as patriarch and arbiter, in the need for internal gradations within the Royal House. Condé's eloquent letter/memorandum failed to convince the king about the possible international ramifications of the decision. This was probably because Louis XIV—like the Condés—saw internal Bourbon considerations as a higher priority. That said, he may also have hoped that the special circumstances of the bride—reinforced, moreover, by the back-chaired visits by cardinals—would dissuade other European princes from trying to challenge the house of France as a result of the visits by the Princes of the Blood. France, after all, occupied a strong position internationally in 1679. The alternative explanations—that Louis simply disregarded the international arena, or merely wished to mortify his cousins—are less likely.

Our disappointment at being denied hard evidence about the denouement of the *affaire des sièges* underscores the otherwise rare quality of the Condé-Gourville correspondence and the privileged insight that it has offered into aspects of court society that are usually denied to outsiders. Indeed, without this corpus, one would hardly have suspected that behind a few laconic sentences in the standard sources lay such an intensity of negotiations, such complexity and subtlety of argumentation, or such heavy involvement of king and princes. The secrets of status interaction and negotiation, conducted face-to-face behind closed doors, could escape contemporaries too, including those with a personal or a professional interest.[81] One wonders how many other *affaires* have been similarly swept under the historical carpet. The under-representation of status interaction in

---

[80] See previous chapter, pp. 37–8, 45–7. Here, on the other hand, the Condés failed (by oversight?) to 'censor' the newspapers.

[81] I have found no mention of the affair in the standard correspondences of the period, like those of Sévigné or Bussy-Rabutin, nor in the detailed synthesis of various diplomatic and ceremonial sources on the marriage, prepared at the French foreign ministry in the first half of the eighteenth century (AAE, MD, Espagne 73). Even Saint-Simon was probably ignorant of the controversy (see his claim, apropos a discussion of armchairs and Spain, that the *Grand Condé* had no pretensions in his status interactions with royalty: SSB, xiv, 413–14).

surviving sources could not but have contributed to its undervaluation in subsequent historiography.

What about the aftermath of this *affaire des sièges*? There is some indication of continued negotiation. Following the affair, the Condés drafted a memorandum to the monarch, detailing their status grievances and requests.[82] It deals primarily with the Grandchildren of France, but also touches on interactions with various other French and European parties, including Foreign Princes, Dukes and Peers, cardinals, sub-royal sovereigns, and Spanish grandees. The rank of Grandchildren of France, the memorandum argues, has grown out of a gradual, sometimes surreptitious accumulation of distinctions. Apparently resigned now to some difference, the Condés focus on limiting its extent and its scope—not least by expressing support, finally, for dynastic regulation.[83] What is more, if they could not undo the gains of their superiors, the Princes of the Blood could try to establish similar advantages—seat-wise and otherwise—vis-à-vis their inferiors, according to the same logic of increased gradations.[84] They also enlist the support of the French king against their international near-equals.

The Condés would have to wait two generations to receive a favourable regulation on the great-Grandchildren of France.[85] The last years of the reign would also formalize the most dynamic of Bourbon ranks: the Legitimated Princes. Yet before—and after—formal regulation, status interaction would continue to play a key role in shaping these and other social positions. The range of themes and codes in the memorandum is remarkable: from high ceremonies to everyday life, from dress to address, from religious rites to table service. Each of these themes has its own history, each code its own grammar. The following chapters single out some of the more prominent ones, reconstructing and analysing their logic, workings, and evolution.

---

[82] AC, MS 1131, fos. 2–4, 6–10, 14–24.

[83] 'on espere que le Roy aura la bonté de regler *ainsy quil a este pratique de tout temps &* comme il auoit fait l'honneur de le dire au S.ᵣ de Gouruille a fontainebleau, qu'ils [the grandchildren of *Monsieur*] n'auront d'autre rang que celuy des Princes du Sang': AC, MS 1131, fo. 16v (the emphasized phrase appears in the margin, probably added by Henri-Jules himself).

[84] In the matter of seats, 'c'est vne chose bien contr[aire] a la grandeur de la Maison Royale, qu'y ayant cette grande distinction entre les Petites filles de france et les Princes du Sang, Jl n'y en ayt point là dessus entre eux et les Princes estrangers qui ont aussy bien [que] les Ducs des chaises a bras deuant les Princes du Sang': AC, MS 1131, fo. 14v.

[85] See the Conclusion, p. 163.

3

The Battles of the Mantles: Ceremonial Gear and Status Conflict

On 24 June 1701, Henri-Jules, now prince of Condé, sent an express packet to his cousin François-Louis, now prince of Conti.[1] The packet contained two folders and a covering letter, which began as follows:

> I am sending you, *Monsieur*, the extracts of everything that happened at the ceremonies since the death of the late *Monsieur* Gaston [...] The first envelope contains the extracts from Sainctot which I took care to obtain as the ceremonies were made. Please make sure, however, that nobody finds out—not even he—that I have shown them to you. The separate notebook is the extract from what I have had written.[2]

After pointing out the main results of his findings, Condé asked Conti to complement the covert intelligence operation by approaching the marquis of Blainville, who had just stepped down from the post of Grand Master of Ceremonies:

> It would be very important to see what Monsieur de Blainville has written [...] As Monsieur de Blainville is a friend of ours, and no longer has an interest in his post, I am sure that he would communicate his registers to us with pleasure. Please talk to him about it, the sooner the better, for once things are decided, there is no return[3]

What prompted the operation? Why the urgency? And what did the secret dossier contain?

A fortnight earlier, Louis XIV's brother *Monsieur* had died unexpectedly. For the Princes of the Blood, the removal of their ceremonial arch-rival opened up risks as well as opportunities. It was imperative to act before the king made up his mind; after that, 'there is no return'. *Monsieur*'s death had immediate ceremonial implications: a series of rites, culminating in a solemn funeral at the abbey of Saint-Denis. The two folders—one of them based on a secret copy of the registers of the king's Master of Ceremonies, the other on Condé's own record—surveyed status distinctions at analogous occasions over the previous four decades.[4]

---

[1] Following the deaths of Louis-Armand of Bourbon in 1685 and the *Grand Condé* in 1686 (see Appendix I).

[2] AN, K 121, no. 35¹, pp. 1–2.

[3] AN, K 121, no. 35¹, pp. 7–9. Henri-Jules also asked his cousin to involve his wife in the affair.

[4] This dossier—like the whole of the 'K' series at the Archives nationales of which it forms part—offers an illuminating example of the perils of archival 'rationalization'. It no longer exists as such: having originally spanned forty years of ceremonies in two folders, the extracts were subsequently disassembled and distributed by date across the boxes of the 'Cartons des Rois', from K 118 to K 121. The Condé-Conti correspondence is in K 121, no. 35, among documents of other provenance relating to *Monsieur*'s

These distinctions concern, above all, the quintessential item of pre-modern ceremonial gear: the mantle. We have already caught a glimpse of this multiform garment on the occasion of the Spanish marriage. Involving diverse and subtle distinctions of cut, bearing, and occasion, mantles provide an excellent case-study of an early modern status code. The second and the third sections analyse the vocabulary and the grammar of these distinctions, focusing on the most contested area of the garment: its end, or train. The final section—like the secret dossier—examines the dynamics of status interaction and rivalry by tracing the evolution of train-related distinctions and struggles throughout the long reign of Louis XIV. Let us begin, though, by a brief overview of garment and ceremonies: who wore what, when, and where?

A MANTLE FOR EACH SEASON

Over-garments trailing backwards and downwards, early modern mantles varied widely in shape and in terminology: from everyday coats, through the official garb that gave its name to a part of the nobility, to the lavish ermined objects that European monarchs wore for coronations.[5] The robes of magistrates, in the periphery as in the centre, operated as a badge of authority and as an object of hierarchical and jurisdictional strife.[6] Ecclesiastical over-garments were similarly rich in social and hierarchical signification: from the cope donned by officiating clergy, through the surplice, rochet, and *camail*, to the notorious mantlet of subordination (see next chapter). In this chapter I focus on the high stakes involved in the over-garments that French aristocrats, male and female, wore for life-cycle ceremonies, and in particular for obsequies and for nuptials.

Obsequies were the most intricate of these life-cycle ceremonies. They consisted of multiple phases, each with its own elaborate ceremonial, culminating in solemn funerary services.[7] These included the burial service, or funeral, and memorial services

---

death. The extracts refer back by page number to two sets of manuscripts currently held in Chantilly: a full copy of Sainctot's registers and the Condés' own ceremonial registers, respectively. For details on this and on other aspects of the Condé knowledge-base, see Sternberg, 'Manipulating Information'.

[5] See the superbly-illustrated Arizzoli-Clémentel and Gorguet-Ballesteros (eds), *Fastes de cour*, bringing together objects and images from many European countries. On garment and nomenclature, with special reference to the medieval period, see Odile Blanc, 'Le manteau, vêtement de l'autorité', in Christine Aribaud and Sylvie Mouysset (eds), *Vêture et pouvoir: XIIIe–XXe siècle* (Toulouse, 2003), pp. 53–66.

[6] See e.g. Sylvie Mouysset, ' "Pensan d'esse creniat, lou capairou sul col…": jeux et enjeux de la robe consulaire dans le Sud-Ouest de la France (XVIe–XVIIIe siècle)', and Antoine Coutelle, 'La robe rouge comme enjeu: l'exemple du présidial de Poitiers au XVIIe siècle', both in Aribaud and Mouysset (eds), *Vêture et pouvoir*. At the royal court, on the other hand, *robins* sometimes sought to eliminate the sartorial traces of their origins.

[7] I focus here on background details essential for the understanding of what follows, occasionally smoothing over diachronic variation that is elaborated later. On Bourbon funerary rites, see the recent and detailed (though not always precise) Leferme-Falguières, *Les courtisans*, chs. 1 and 3. The classic work on the earlier period is Giesey, *The Royal Funeral Ceremony*; for newer critical approaches, see e.g. Alain Boureau, *Le simple corps du roi: l'impossible sacralité des souverains français, XVe–XVIIIe siècle* (Paris, 1988); Balsamo, *Les funérailles à la Renaissance*. See also Cosandey, *La reine de France*, pp. 206–56.

held in other venues. The French royal necropolis at Saint-Denis served as the stage for the funerals of Bourbon monarchs, of their children, and of their grandchildren. In addition, the cathedral of Notre Dame in Paris would hold a supplementary service at the death of French monarchs or of their heirs, and occasional memorial services for others, especially those allied to the house of Bourbon. Here as elsewhere, relatives would represent the state of deep mourning (*représenter le grand deuil*). The monarch would usually pick three persons for this role, of the same gender as the deceased and slightly inferior in rank.[8] These representatives would process solemnly to the choir, take their place at the high seats, and rise at the designated time for the offertory.

The most telling signs of the state of deep mourning were the long-trained black mantles that covered these representatives and other major participants. Specially ordered for the occasion, and different from the regular mourning mantle, the male garment preserved a medieval, clerical appearance, already foreign to observers by the end of the seventeenth century. It consisted of a cloak of Holland cloth, with an attached hood and a long pointed train.[9] The female counterpart, called *mante*, was 'a large black crêpe, all of one piece, which is attached at the head, arms, and waist, and trails a lot'.[10] Like the male hood, its veil was lowered during the ceremony. Women also wore long trains during the initial period of widowhood.[11]

What about nuptial rites? As we have seen in Chapter One, these consisted of two consecutive events: engagement and wedding. For the bride especially, this chain of events functioned as a status rite of passage, creating interesting, and sometimes constructive ambivalences.[12] Grooms wore mantles on these occasions too, but only the female garment was long-trained and symbolically consequential. Most consequential was the *mante* worn during the engagement: typically a narrow strip of gauze, lined with gold or silver, and attached to neck and shoulders.[13] Wedding accounts, by contrast, mostly do not dwell on *mantes*. One notable

---

[8] See Appendix III. When women represented, each was conducted by a man.

[9] Sources, ii, 29, n. 2; xiii, 135; SSB, xvii, 593; xix, 422. Perhaps its relative invariability explains the virtual lack of detailed descriptions. For a rare visual depiction, see Figure 3.1. On medieval antecedents, see Michèle Beaulieu and Jeanne Baylé, *Le costume en Bourgogne de Philippe le Hardi à la mort de Charles le Téméraire (1364–1477)* (Paris, 1956), pp. 119–24.

[10] SSB, i, 512. Saint-Simon typically noted that the crêpe of princesses and duchesses was much thicker than that of other ladies.

[11] See e.g. Dirk Van der Cruysse, *Madame Palatine, princesse européenne* ([Paris], 1988), pp. 421–2; BM, MS 2744, fo. 173. On the regular mantles of deep mourning, see next chapter.

[12] A mantle dramatically signals this transformation in an anecdote about Catherine of Clèves, who became duchess of Guise in 1570. She was born a princess, but her first husband did not hold princely rank at the time of their marriage. As the wedding ended and she was coming out of church, her princely ermined mantle was pulled off her shoulders, 'luy faisant connoistre par là, qu'elle changeoit sa condition en celle de son mary, dont elle pleura'. BN, NAF 9770, fos. 172–173; cf. AN, KK 1430, fo. 583; KK 1448, fo. 107.

[13] SSB, xix, 88. See the colour drawing of the *mante* worn by Mademoiselle de Blois for her engagement to the duke of Chartres in 1692: BN, Estampes, Gaignières 1243, RES OA-18-FOL, fo. 57 (although the caption here refers to her wedding day rather than to that of her engagement, the details of her outfit match the latter rather than the former, as described in BM, MS 2743, fos. 13, 15; *Mercure Galant*, February 1692, pp. 309–10, 318). On the male garment, see Breteuil, *Mémoires*, ed. Lever, p. 290.

Fig. 3.1 The duke of Noailles representing the deep mourning in a mantle carried by three of his gentlemen, at the service in memory of the queen celebrated by the Estates of Languedoc in 1683. Detail from an engraving by Jean Troy. BN, Estampes, DB-14(+)-FOL, fo. 2. Photo: Bibliothèque nationale de France.

exception is royal weddings, where the new queen would wear an ermined and fleur-de-lised velvet mantle, and other princesses long-trained garments.[14]

These *mantes* differed from one marriage to another and from funerary *mantes*, not to mention the male garments. Yet despite the material polymorphism, a similar logic of distinction applied to mantles of all genders and occasions. Precedents acquired by one gender or in one type of ceremony could thus transfer to another. In this intricate grammar of distinction, two aspects of the garment figure above all others: length and bearing.

ON LENGTHS AND MEASURES

Elites have brandished textile tails from time immemorial. By the early 1500s, spectators and recorders were already noting how precise differences in the length of trains signified subtle differences in the status of their wearers.[15] Mantles reached gigantic proportions by the second half of the sixteenth century, reportedly culminating in a twenty-ell train worn by Elisabeth of Austria at her marriage with Charles IX in 1570.[16] In the following centuries, trains of several metres remained standard at ceremonial highlights throughout Europe.[17]

The basic logic of train-length as a form of distinction was simple: the longer the better. In order to understand the code, however, it is not enough to cite a few examples or to marvel at the staggering figures. Absolute numbers taken out of context are a poor guide. If the train-length of the Princesses of the Blood doubled between the sixteenth and the seventeenth centuries, this does not entail that their status did the same. Conversely, the fact that they wore four ells rather than five at the baptism of the dauphin in 1668 does not mean that they suffered a setback then. It merely shows that baptisms did not follow the same scale as marriages or funerals did. On the other hand, a numerically similar shift in 1679, from five ells to six during the Spanish marriage, heralded a decade of train-related manoeuvres.[18]

---

[14] See the tapestry depicting the marriage of Louis XIV in 1660, part of the 'Histoire du Roi' series: Mobilier national, Paris, inv. GMTT 95/4. On the earlier period, see Chatenet, 'Habits de cérémonie'.

[15] Abbé Reure, 'Notes Bourbonnaises: d'après les manuscrits de la Bibliothèque de Lyon', *Bulletin Revue—Société d'Émulation & des Beaux-Arts du Bourbonnais*, ix (1901), 102; Jean-Marie de La Mure, *Histoire des ducs de Bourbon et des comtes de Forez* (4 vols, Paris, 1860–97), iii, 225–6. See also the historical excursus by Père Ménestrier, *Dissertation sur l'usage de se faire porter la queue*, originally published in 1704 and re-edited in *Archives historiques et statistiques du département du Rhone*, x (1829), 246–65.

[16] Chatenet, 'Habits de cérémonie', p. 223; Papirius Masson, *Entier discovrs des choses qvi se sont passees en la reception de la Royne, & mariage du Roy* (Paris, 1570). One should bear in mind, though, that this oft-quoted figure was a rough estimate only ('à veüe d'oeil'), and its interpretation depends on what exactly the author meant by ell (*aulne*). Like other early modern units of measurement, ells varied across time and space. The standard conversion for the Parisian ell in our period is *c*.1.18 metres. Regular mourning mantles (see next chapter) were often measured in feet.

[17] See e.g. Arizzoli-Clémentel and Gorguet-Ballesteros, *Fastes de cour*, figures 114, 116, 127. On the persistence of train-length as status symbol in nineteenth-century Europe, see Philip Mansel, *Dressed to Rule: Royal and Court Dress from Louis XIV to Elizabeth II* (New Haven-London, 2005), pp. 117, 134–5.

[18] AC, MS 1201, pp. 147–50, and later.

To decipher the code successfully, to tell the meaningful from the incidental, it is helpful to focus on specific, well-defined contexts that can be adequately fleshed out on the basis of inside information. As with the *affaire des sièges*, the well-trodden sources prove insufficient for the task. The occasional mentions of train-length there rarely go beyond simple, and often partial, enumerations. Even the better-informed among them are problematic:

> Men only have trains in the *longs manteaux* of mourning. As for women, they have them at funerary ceremonies and at others [...] The ceremonial has regulated them by ells in uneven numbers. Since the regulation that established the rank of Grandsons and Granddaughters of France, the trains of the queen and of the Sons and Daughters of France have augmented. The trains of husbands and wives are of the same length. The queen eleven ells. Sons and Daughters of France nine ells[.] Grandsons and Granddaughters of France seven ells[.] Princes and Princesses of the Blood five ells[.] Dukes and duchesses three ells[.] People of real quality one ell[19]

Characteristically, Saint-Simon got generalities right but particulars wrong. The transferability of gender and occasion, the two-ell jumps, some of the lower figures, and the universal anxiety about size certainly hold. Not so the claim that the Grandchildren of France established a lasting edge over and above the five ells of the Princes and Princesses of the Blood, nor that the queen and the Children of France consequently extended their own trains to eleven and to nine ells, respectively. And such particulars do make a difference. For in fact, as the final section shows, the dogged resistance of the Princes of the Blood to the elongation attempts of the Grandchildren of France successfully denied the novel Bourbon rank this prominent advantage.[20]

Further down the social scale, Saint-Simon's figures underplay or ignore the train-lengths of his rivals. Thus, on several occasions the Foreign Princes displayed a *longueur intermédiaire* of four ells: midway between the five ells of princes of French blood and the three ells of the non-princely aristocracy.[21] This achievement, in turn, facilitated the upgrade of another group of princes, the Bourbon bastards, to five ells in 1679, an upgrade that served their subsequent claim to equality with the legitimate members of the dynasty.[22] Saint-Simon and his fellow dukes also faced challenges from below. 'People of real quality' did not stop at a single ell, and the most senior among them enjoyed three, just like the dukes. Even the Masters of Ceremonies, despite their relatively modest origins, reached up to three ells in the course of the seventeenth century. That they were involved in the preparation

---

[19] Saint-Simon, 'Matériaux pour servir a un mémoire sur l'occurrence présente', p. 255; cf. SSB, xix, 87–8, 422–3.

[20] Saint-Simon's figures are inaccurate even for the period when he was writing this passage, during the following reign. Thus, mantles of deep mourning ordered for the Daughters of France in the mid-eighteenth century were still seven ells long: AN, O¹ 3262, 'Ce qui a été pratiqué au Catafalque de la Reine de Pologne, le 18. Mai 1747.'

[21] BM, MS 2738, fo. 56 (the count of Soissons, of the house of Savoy, at the service for Mazarin in 1661); BM, MS 2740, fo. 65 (the Bouillons at the service for Turenne in 1675). See also BM, MS 2739, fo. 139.

[22] See Chapter One, pp. 42–3 and 47, and later in this chapter.

of provision lists and in post-facto recording surely helped. Lesser participants had shorter trains, but there too length signified relative importance, offering a measure of the status of individuals or of positions.[23]

How did contemporaries gauge these trains? Spectators could presumably make no more than rough estimates; the figures they provide can indeed vary considerably. This probably explains the logic of two-ell jumps between successive ranks—and conversely of *longueurs intermédiaires* that blurred visible differences. As Sainctot once noted, 'distinctions are useless if they are not clearly perceptible'.[24] But how could he or other officials ensure that mantles extended to the prescribed length? On the occasions where the king footed the bill, the crown was often also in charge of provision. The Masters of Ceremonies would then send specifications, train-length included, to the furnishing departments of the royal household.[25] This, however, did not guarantee that participants actually turned up with the garments they had received. On other occasions, moreover, they would provide for themselves in the first place. As we shall see, some actually took advantage of such situations to stretch their right.[26]

If they stretched too far, though, they would risk the danger of reprisal, by the crown or by their rivals. Wearers would thus often negotiate their sartorial demands in advance. In an increasingly textual culture of memory and precedent, moreover, stretching the garment only was not enough. In the long run, what mattered was how train-length was reflected in the written record, for better or for worse. Whereas the actual event allowed for relative comparisons among co-present parties, writing involved absolute numbers that would relate to past and to future occasions. Participants wanted the record, and the official record in particular, to confirm their successes and to invalidate or to overlook those of their rivals. For the funerary and nuptial rites that concern us here, the crucial textual arena was the registers of the Masters of Ceremonies. Following this paper trail is therefore as important as following the trailing mantles themselves.

---

[23] BN, FF 18536, fo. 363; BM, MS 2738, fo. 76; Maral, *La chapelle royale de Versailles*, p. 82. The provision lists for the funeral of Louis XIV list differential train-lengths of five, three, two, one and a half, half, and nil: AN, K 1717, no. 2³; BM, MS 2346, fos. 121ff., 147ff.

[24] BM, MS 2742, fo. 36. For the funeral of the *Grand Dauphin* at Saint-Denis, the accounts of Desgranges, Breteuil, and Sourches diverge significantly in absolute ells, but preserve the same relative gradation: BM, MS 2746, fos. 41r–42r; Breteuil, *Mémoires*, ed. Lever, p. 304; Sourches, xiii, 135.

[25] On these extraordinary occasions, most sartorial furnishings, including the mantles of the representatives of deep mourning, were provided by the Bedchamber (AN, O¹ 3262), but the Grand Equerry was also involved (AN, K 1717–1718; see the jurisdictional dispute and regulation following the obsequies of Louis XIV: BM, MS 2346, fos. 148ff.; AN, O¹ 1042, nos. 137ff.). For specifications by the Masters of Ceremonies, see also BN, FF 18536, fo. 229v; AN, KK 1448, *passim*. Although some participants received fabrics or financial remuneration only, the representatives seem to have regularly received the finished products, complete with the long trains.

[26] See the last section. In the case of obsequies, representatives had to relinquish possession of their mantles to the heralds after the ceremonies. This typical ancien régime custom could theoretically have provided another opportunity for supervision on the part of central authorities (though not a guarantee: witness the King of Arms who complained in 1781 that he was the victim of a switch, probably for economic reasons; AN, O¹ 3262).

TRAIN-BEARING: A MULTI-DIMENSIONAL
INTERACTION

Such long mantles were not easy to carry about. They could take up a significant amount of space and weigh up to many kilogrammes. Contemporaries had to tread carefully if they were to avoid stepping on their own trains or on those of others. Outdoors, trailing garments faced the risks of the proverbial mud of early modern roads. Their bearing was therefore a practical solution as well as a status symbol, and a familiar sight, at court and elsewhere. From the seventeenth century, trains formed an integral part of the female court uniform known as the *grand habit*. Among men, magistrates and prelates had the nether part of their robes carried on a regular basis, and sword aristocrats—on special occasions like coronations and obsequies.[27]

As a status symbol, train-bearing generated complex interactions within and among three categories of persons: wearers, bearers, and other present parties. These categories, though, were not inherent or even mutually exclusive. The same persons could play different roles in different settings. Some bearers, as we shall see, had their own train carried at the same time as they were carrying another's. Settings varied subtly by time, place, and occasion. In funerary services, train-bearing at the procession did not necessarily entail train-bearing at the offertory. Everyday life and high ceremonies, finally, did not necessarily follow the same conventions.

Wearers tended to employ members of their household, such as lackeys or pages, to bear their trains. Some had designated 'tail'-bearers: *caudatarius* for cardinals, *porte-manteau* or *porte-queue* for princesses. In such cases, a social gulf separated bearers from wearers, and the interesting tensions would occur within the two categories or in their relations with other parties. The latter would not necessarily welcome the prospect of train-bearing in their presence, since this could be construed as disrespectful or impolite, and hence appropriate towards inferiors only. In 1670, for example, the ecclesiastical and lay authorities in New Spain clashed as the archbishop of Mexico refused to let his train down before the viceroy.[28] Conversely, the consuls of Aix-en-Provence recorded the moment when members of the *parlement* of Toulouse did *not* have their trains carried as the two groups walked together in 1730.[29] At the French royal palace, most ladies had to let their garments 'sweep the dust' of princely parquets.[30]

---

[27] For illustration, see Arizzoli-Clémentel and Gorguet-Ballesteros, *Fastes de cour*, pp. 50, 63; and contemporary engravings by Le Clerc and Bonnart: ['Le Président à mortier'], BN, Estampes, Hennin, 4251–2, RES QB-201(47)-FOL, p. 11; 'L'habit du Maistre et le Laquais marquent vn Conseiller du Palais', BN, Estampes, Hennin, 4253–4, RES QB-201(47)-FOL, p. 11; 'Abbé en Sotanne', BN, Estampes, Hennin, 4867, RES QB-201(54)-FOL, p. 70. The latter shows the technique of auto-bearing, or 'trousser', the resort of the long-trained who could not rely on others; cf. Figure 3.2.

[28] Cañeque, 'On Cushions and Chairs', pp. 126–7. See also Breteuil, *Mémoires*, ed. Lever, pp. 264 and 268; BN, FF 6679, fo. 334r; BN, 500 Colbert 141, fo. 3r.

[29] AM, Aix-en-Provence, AA 55, fo. 90v; cf. BN, NAF 9770, fo. 191.

[30] Louis Sébastien Mercier, *Tableau de Paris*, ed. Jean-Claude Bonnet (2 vols, Paris, 1994), ii, 766. All but duchesses had to do so already at the entrance to the royal guard-room: AN, K 1712, no. 6/4. See also a regulation from 1746, balancing the rights of bearers too: AN, O¹ 391, p. 128.

Homme en grand deüil .

Ce jeune-homme habillé de deüil ;   Son Epouse nest pas si tost dans le Cercüeil,
Brûle d'vne nouvelle flame ;   Qu'il cherche ailleurs vne autre fême .

Fig. 3.2 Male and female regular dress of deep mourning, engraved by the Bonnarts (late seventeenth century): **a)** BN, Estampes, Hennin, 5090, RES QB-201(58)-FOL, p. 4; **b)** BN, Estampes, Hennin, 5097, RES QB-201(58) –FOL, p. 8. Photo: Bibliothèque nationale de France.

Dame en grand dueil

Cette belle qui vouloit suiure   Dit apresent quil est fort doux
Son Cher quand jl cessa de viure   D'esperer vn nouuel epoux

Fig. 3.2 Continued

Indeed, the thorniest problems of co-presence occurred when contesting wearers walked side by side. This would happen periodically during Bourbon obsequies, where a Prince of the Blood would arrive in the deceased's apartment, in the company of a non-Bourbon duke (or a princess and a duchess, respectively, when the deceased was female), for the performance of key funerary rites. From the beginning of the eighteenth century, a war of attrition raged on between the two ranks, on whether, and where, ducal mantles could be borne in princely presence. Other parties, present in flesh or in spirit, further complicated the problem. First, there was the dead body. Although physically present, it could not, for obvious reasons, prevent train-bearing in the apartment. When it outranked the prince as well as the duke, the couple would become partners in crime. The bereaved but live relatives, on the other hand, could intervene if present. Finally, in one type of rite— the holy water ceremony—the king's body too would be symbolically present, because represented by the prince. In 1723, the matter received a spatial resolution that defined the limits of train-bearing for both parties, but it remained contested in subsequent years.[31]

At high ceremonies, the profile of bearers often rose, making the wearer-bearer axis more germane to our inquiry. The prestige of wearers increased vicariously through that of the bearers that they could enlist for their service. The latter ranged in rank from simple nobles, through 'people of quality', to dukes and even princes. They often came from among the senior members of the wearer's household. Not least, this vicarious rivalry relied on vicarious display: wearers sought bearers who had a right to their own long mantle of deep mourning, and, most prestigiously, who could adorn it with the collar of the Order of the Holy Spirit. In 1664, the memorial service for the duchess of Savoy at Notre Dame was delayed for two hours as Mademoiselle d'Alençon was searching for a Knight of the Holy Spirit who would carry her train. In the end, she had to give up the effort and to let her rivals outshine her, via the collared bearer of the princess of Condé.[32]

Other aspects of bearers also contributed to the prestige of wearers. Of these, number was perhaps the major one. At the top of the scale, the mantles of sixteenth-century kings sometimes branched into several tails, each held by a different aristocrat.[33] Princely wearers too tried to outdo one another in the number of bearers, as we shall see in more detail in the next section. While nearly all of them had to settle with one or two in the end, local elites enjoyed more room for manoeuvre. For example, as commander-in-chief in Languedoc, the duke of Noailles boasted three mantle-bearers at a memorial service for the queen in 1683. At court ceremonies, the duke (or his wife) would not normally have been entitled to train-bearing at all; in the periphery, he could summon more bearers than the

---

[31] For a detailed analysis, see Sternberg, 'The Culture of Orders', pp. 77–80. Desgranges listed most cases in a memorandum prepared at the height of the contestation in the 1720s: AN, O¹ 1042, no. 97.

[32] BM, MS 2738, fo. 119v. This must have been particularly painful to d'Alençon, having already failed in the attempt to obtain advantages over her Condé rivals on this occasion: see next section.

[33] Theodore Godefroy, *Le Ceremonial de France* (Paris, 1619), pp. 422 (five tails), 568 (three tails).

king's niece had on the equivalent occasion in Paris.[34] A decade later, at the funerary convoy of the First President of the *parlement* of Bordeaux, one of the representatives of deep mourning employed no less than six lackeys for the task.[35] Once again, it was context, rather than absolute numbers, that made the difference.

Another intriguing aspect was gender. For women as well as for men, bearers were normally male in France, but select wearers or occasions merited female service. Already in the sixteenth century, queens employed a senior female member of their household during high ceremonies.[36] In 1668, other princesses demanded female bearers on the occasion of the *Grand Dauphin*'s baptism, but were turned down. Only the princess of Conti, who represented the queen of England as godmother, was served by her Lady of Honour. The length of her train, on the other hand, was equal to that of other princesses. Train-length and train-bearing thus finely balanced the act of representation: length indicated the representing princess, bearing—the represented.[37] On one special occasion, however, all princesses—Foreign as well as Capetian—would receive the regular fare of queens. When they married, their nuptial train would be carried by a princess of similar rank, often by a younger sister.[38] Number, though, distinguished true regal treatment from special exception: while ordinary princesses had to make do with one female bearer, no less than three carried the *manteau royal* of queen brides, in the eighteenth as in the sixteenth century.[39]

So far we have considered the wearer-bearer interaction primarily from the former's perspective. What did bearers make of it? As we have seen in the case of the *plume* in Chapter One, and as we shall see in greater detail in Chapter Five, personal service was a double-edged sword. When subordination was not in question, as in the case of household servants, the duty to carry trains would appear perfectly natural. With exalted wearers, it could even become a coveted honour and an object of competition among bearers, a 'prestige fetish' in Norbert Elias's terms. Such jurisdictional contention involved fine points and crude scuffles. In 1691, for example, an officer of the elite Bodyguard and a Master of the Wardrobe tugged at the king's mantle while he was wearing it for the ceremony of the 'royal touch'.[40] In the course of the eighteenth century, the Princes of the Blood listed the

---

[34] *La Pompe Fvnebre faite à l'honnevr de tres-havte tres-excellente et tres-puissante princesse Marie Therese d'Avstriche* (Montpellier, [1683]), p. 23; Figure 3.1. *Mademoiselle* had two bearers only at the queen's services in Saint-Denis and Notre Dame (see Appendix III).

[35] Jules Delpit (ed.), *Bibliothèque municipale de Bordeaux: Catalogue des manuscrits* (Bordeaux, 1880), p. 149; Caroline Le Mao, *Parlement et parlementaires: Bordeaux au Grand Siècle* (Seyssel, 2007), pp. 246–7.

[36] e.g. Godefroy, *Le Ceremonial François*, ii, 15.

[37] AC, MS 1201, pp. 147–9; cf. *Mémoires du duc de Luynes sur la cour de Louis XV (1735–1758)*, ed. L. Dussieux and Eud. Soulié (17 vols, Paris, 1860–5), i, 98–101, and the balance between train-length and train-bearing in 1679 (Chapter One, pp. 42–5). Conversely, the *longueur intermédiaire* of the Foreign Princes was balanced by their limitation to a single train-bearer, at a time when Bourbon princes already obtained a second one (see n. 21).

[38] On the notion of 'queen for a day' in marriage, see pp. 120–1. The tradition has survived to the twenty-first century, when Pippa Middleton carried the train of her princess-to-be sister in 2011.

[39] e.g. Godefroy, *Le Ceremonial François*, ii, 24–5, and *Mercure de France* (1725), p. 2195.

[40] Sourches, iii, 423. The king's reaction is telling. Louis XIV preferred being dragged by the mantle to being dragged into decision: 'Le Roi ne fit pas semblant d'entendre cette dispute, quoiqu'il sentît

right to carry the bridal mantles of the Royal Family as one of their honours. For the Legitimated Princes, moreover, this act of service, like the chemise, was a measure of their assimilation to the Royal House.[41]

But train-bearing was, after all, a menial service. Early modern contemporaries too perceived this interaction as a sign of the bearer's subordination, and even of potential humiliation. Dangeau hints at this tension in commenting on the case of an elder sister who carried the train of her 'cadette'.[42] Sainctot is more explicit in condemning this custom apropos the marriage of 1679: 'Propriety would not have it that princesses equal to *Mademoiselle* render her an honour as considerable as that of bearing the train of her mantle.'[43] Indeed, this act of service appears as the quintessential form of servility, in Saint-Simon's depiction of the duke of Noailles as an abject courtier who used to carry around the train of the king's mistress.[44]

But the best illustration of the darker side of train-bearing is to be found in cases where potential bearers actually refused the dubious honour. In 1660, Mademoiselle d'Alençon and Mademoiselle de Valois, daughters of Gaston, searched in vain for dukes who would agree to bear their trains at the marriage of Louis XIV.[45] In 1666, *Monsieur* failed to enlist a ducal bearer for his wife at the obsequies of the Queen Mother. When he brought up the precedent of the marshal-duke Du Plessis-Choiseul having carried his own train a year earlier, the crown replied that this example did not count, 'because *Monsieur* could have commanded the marshal Du Plessis [who was also] First Gentleman of his Bedchamber to do anything he had wanted'.[46] The subordination implied in train-bearing could not be forced without functional subordination.

When high-ranking aristocrats did bear trains, they became doubly anxious to assert their status at the same time. Bourbon princesses enjoyed the right to their own noble bearer as they carried the train of other princesses or of queens, visibly demonstrating that they were not the weakest link in the 'chain of service'.[47]

---

bien qu'on lui tiroit son manteau'. Finally, 'la chose ayant été portée devant lui, il décida que cette fonction n'appartenoit à personne'; cf. Duindam, *Vienna and Versailles*, p. 213. On the fine points, see e.g. BM, MS 2750, fo. 5; *Mémoires du duc de Luynes*, xii, 122–4.

[41] e.g. Arsenal, MS 5170, p. 212; AN, O¹ 281, no. 103¹.

[42] Dangeau, vi, 369.

[43] BM, MS 2741, fo. 28r (see also AC, MS 1201, p. 149). The bearers, of course, were not equal to the wearer's marital rank (cf. the variant in AC, MS 1176, pp. 65–6), but what matters here for our purposes is the assumption of equality and its implications according to a contemporary's logic, not the specific facts of the case. Sainctot was probably too narrow-minded to appreciate that it was precisely the suspension of ordinary norms that charged the extraordinary gesture with symbolic force.

[44] SSB, xvi, 377, 507; cf. Noailles's royal treatment in Languedoc as wearer (earlier, pp. 82–3). See also Madame de Maintenon's story of the child's play of Louis XIV with a servant's daughter, whose train he carried around 'à la Madame': *'Comment la sagesse vient aux filles': propos d'éducation*, ed. Pierre E. Leroy and Marcel Loyau ([Etrepilly], 1998), pp. 78–9.

[45] *Mémoires de Mᵗˡᵉ de Montpensier*, ed. Chéruel, iii, 467; *Notices littéraires sur le dix-septième siècle*, ed. Léon Aubineau (Paris, 1859), p. 202. This wearer-bearer problem was also compounded with the inter-wearer relations between the *Grande Mademoiselle* and her half-sisters.

[46] BM, MS 2739, fo. 14r. In his account of the earlier ceremony, Sainctot emphasized that Du Plessis carried *Monsieur*'s train 'comme premier gentilhome de sa chambre, et non comme Duc et pair': BM, MS 2738, fo. 158r. Du Plessis became duke on the month of the ceremony; cf. AC, MS 1201, pp. 146–7.

[47] See Chapter Five, pp. 121–3. These princesses could also count on being at the receiving end during their own marriage.

Another source for anxiety was the identity of co-bearers: aristocrats feared that shared service with their inferiors would degrade their own status. The composition of the princely trio that would bear the queen's *manteau royal* in 1660 provides a vivid example of this anxiety and of the multi-layered complexity of status rivalries. The initial trio consisted of the *Grande Mademoiselle*, the princess of Conti, and the princess of Carignan. When Conti was unable to attend, *Mademoiselle* could not bear the thought of a foreign princess stepping into the breach, and asked Mazarin to send for one of her young half-sisters.[48] Both Alençon and Valois arrived at the Spanish border, seemingly ensuring an all-Granddaughter-of-France trio. But then *Mademoiselle* was promoted to a more honourable task, and Carignan was reinstated in her place. Alençon and Valois now refused to bear with Carignan, a Princess of the Blood who had married a Foreign Prince, but finally resigned themselves to the task.[49]

Bearers could also assert their status in space. In 1711, for example, the duke of Beauvillier was nominated to bear the train of the new heir to the throne at the obsequies of the *Grand Dauphin*. The fact that he could participate in shaping European macro-politics at the High Council did not stop Beauvillier from worrying about the micro-politics of status interaction. Like Du Plessis, he was nominated for the task as First Gentleman of the Bedchamber rather than as duke. Like Alençon and Valois, he faced the problem of co-bearing with rank inferiors—in this case, sub-ducal. In holding the mantle, Beauvillier wished to distinguish himself spatially from his co-bearers, and consulted the Master of Ceremonies about the best position to adopt, based on past precedents. Desgranges discovered that usage was inconsistent: in some cases, the highest-ranking bearers had positioned themselves closest to the wearers, in others—at the end of the train. The duke finally held the garment 'at a distance of an ell or so' from the dauphin, followed by the other two, sub-ducal bearers.[50]

In this case, precedence at least was not contested. When it was, bearers might draw lots for the better spatial position, or avoid the event altogether.[51] Even a

---

[48] *Mémoires de Mlle de Montpensier*, ed. Chéruel, iii, 443–4. She even volunteered to pay for their travel expenses, an indication of how important the matter was in her eyes.

[49] According to Sainctot, the Granddaughters of France posited Carignan's marital rank as grounds for rejection, and the king accordingly issued a patent that confirmed her in her birth rank: BN, FF 14119, fo. 176. *Mademoiselle*, by contrast, implies that the internal Bourbon rivalry between Granddaughters and Princesses of the Blood was in fact at stake: *Mémoires de Mlle de Montpensier*, ed. Chéruel, iii, 466. Her account also demonstrates the role of women and of intermediaries in status interaction and negotiation. Madame de Saujon, sent by the dowager duchess of Orléans to accompany the adolescent Alençon and Valois, played a role analogous to Gourville's in 1679—and equally absent from the official accounts (see previous chapters, esp. Chapter Two). To make matters even more multilayered, Louis XIV's marriage also gave rise to a dispute over the right of Foreign Princesses to a train, involving both members of the Royal House (united this time) and non-Bourbon duchesses: *Mémoires de Mlle de Montpensier*, ed. Chéruel, iii, 475–7; *Notices littéraires sur le dix-septième siècle*, ed. Aubineau, pp. 202–3; BM, MS 2738, fos. 11ff. See also earlier, on the failure of Alençon and Valois to enlist ducal bearers.

[50] BM, MS 2746, fo. 41. To illustrate the inconsistency of spatial logic across ceremonial accounts (in each case, positions are listed in descending hierarchical order): 'queüe' (presumably end), 'pan droict', 'pan gauche' (BN, FF 18536, fo. 295v); 'pan droit', 'pan gauche', 'pointe' (BM, MS 2739, fo. 106v); 'pan droit', 'queüe' (BM, MS 2742, fo. 172r); 'bout', 'milieu' (BM, MS 2744, fo. 166).

[51] BM, MS 2746, fo. 131; BN, FF 23315, fos. 161v–162r. See also AN, O¹ 1043, no. 67, fo. 15r.

single ceremonial action, then, is rarely reducible to a single meaning. By token of one and the same posture, a bearer could show superiority over his colleagues as well as subordination to the wearer. Participating in a seemingly humiliating capacity was thus also a potential source of triumph.

'THE EQUALITY OF TRAINS': BOURBON RIVALRY, 1643–1715

How did length and bearing combine to shape concrete social rivalries over time? This section examines the dynamics of train-related struggles in the Royal House throughout the reign of Louis XIV. This diachronic analysis of a status code over three quarters of a century and across several generations complements the more synchronic perspective adopted in the previous two chapters, and helps discern both evolutionary and recurring patterns. The rich, continuous record of the Masters of Ceremonies, where trains are arguably the main bone of princely contention, makes such a serial analysis possible.[52] Of course, as we have seen previously and as we shall see more dramatically later, this record cannot be considered as fully transparent. But its contemporary value as a recognized official authority makes it germane to the inquiry irrespective of its forensic contribution. Precious morsels of other inside information allow us to flesh out this serial backbone from both perspectives: occasionally raising questions about its reliability, while at the same time demonstrating its effective power. The resulting analysis illustrates the cross-generational vitality, adversarial tactics, and dynastic strategies of status interaction.

How many ells and how many bearers? These two measures, we have seen, had already been reflecting and shaping pre-modern status long before Louis XIV ascended the throne. The early years of his reign witnessed fluidity and change in ceremonial idiom. The obsequies of Louis XIII, the first relevant occasion in our time range, differed from previous practice in several important respects, trains included. When Henri IV had died in 1610, five princes had represented the mourning, only two of them of the house of Bourbon, and the others Foreign Princes of the house of Lorraine.[53] From 1643 onwards, by contrast, members of the Royal House monopolized representation in Bourbon obsequies, even when the number of available representatives fell short of the customary minimum. In cases where Foreign Princes did appear, separately, at non-Bourbon events, they did not enjoy the same length and bearing privileges as their own ancestors had or their Bourbon contemporaries did.[54] This was part

---

[52] On the ceremonial record, see the Introduction (pp. 14, 22–3) and Sternberg, 'Manipulating Information'. It becomes strictly continuous from 1660. For the earlier period there are miscellaneous compilations of accounts made by the previous Sainctot generation. Train details are reported most consistently for obsequies (see Appendix III), but they also appear frequently in marriage accounts and occasionally in others.

[53] *Mercure François*, i (1605–10), 468v–469r.

[54] In 1643, a preparatory memorandum (AN, KK 1448, fo. 65v) initially planned for three additional princes, who were to conduct the three Princes of the Blood representing the mourning. It

of the process of growing exaltation of the French ruling dynasty since the late sixteenth century.[55]

In 1643, three Bourbons represented the mourning at Louis XIII's funeral in Saint-Denis: Gaston of Orléans, brother of the deceased and Son of France, and Condé and Conti, Princes of the Blood. Contemporary accounts differ on the question of mantles, but the subsequently accepted official version, based on the records of the Sainctot family, was that Gaston and Condé had an equal number of ells and bearers, and that trains were not carried during the offertory.[56] At this precarious moment in the life-cycle of the dynasty, Condé immediately followed Gaston in the line of succession, third-in-line overall. In later periods, his own successors would bring up this precedent time and again, in an attempt to counter the claims of their Orléans rivals.[57]

The first dynastic clash came shortly thereafter, apropos the service in memory of the queen of Spain in 1644.[58] Gaston's eldest child, known as *Mademoiselle* (later, as the *Grande Mademoiselle*), was summoned to represent the mourning alongside two Condé Princesses. For the first time in centuries, a grandchild of a French king was not a Child of France.[59] The question arose, then, 'of what sort

---

allotted the former four ells as opposed to the latter's five. This entry was erased from the memorandum, and descriptions of the actual ceremonies do not mention these princes. For subsequent cases where Foreign Princes were not called upon despite a shortage of candidates, see BM, MS 2738, fo. 74 (service for Gaston, 1661); BM, MS 2740, fo. 19v (service for Gaston's widow, 1672). See earlier for the length and bearing allowances of the Foreign Princes during the reign. For their previous glories, see e.g. BN, 500 Colbert 142, fos. 261r, 262r.

[55] On the changes in ceremonial idiom, see Giesey, *The Royal Funeral Ceremony*, and Giesey, *Rulership in France*; cf. Cosandey, *La reine de France*, pp. 240–56. For a recent treatment of 1643, see Cédric Coraillon, 'Les deux morts de Louis XIII', *Revue d'histoire moderne et contemporaine*, lv, no. 1 (2008), 50–73.

[56] In several copies of the Sainctot account, the names (and hence the numbers) of train-bearers are left blank (such lacunae are not uncommon and do not necessarily indicate deliberate omission): BN, FF 18536, fo. 267; FF 23315, fo. 134; FF 23939, fo. 134r. In another copy (BN, FF 18538), the blanks were filled later in a different hand: Gaston received two bearers 'comme fils de france', and the Princes of the Blood one each only. All these copies agree that trains were not held during the offertory. Five ells for all princes are recorded in the account and in the instructions for provision kept by the Sainctots: BN, FF 18536, fo. 267; AN, KK 1448, fo. 65v. Accounts from other sources do not concur in all respects: BN, FF 18540, fo. 38r; *Journal d'Olivier Lefèvre d'Ormesson*, ed. Chéruel (2 vols, Paris, 1860–1), i, 73–4.

[57] The memorial service that followed at Notre Dame in 1643 was unusual. The Queen Mother and regent decided to represent the mourning of her late husband herself after the funeral, in a manner reminiscent of marriages or of coronations: three Bourbon princesses carried her nine-ell train, and another assisted her in the offertory. Here a distinction was made between Gaston's wife, who enjoyed two bearers, and the other princesses who had one only; train-length, however, was equal for all of them: seven ells. These peculiarities would not set a model for the future, apart from the inversion and separation of ceremonies: whereas according to the Renaissance tradition, the representatives of deep mourning would attend the service at Notre Dame on their way to the funeral in Saint-Denis, under the Bourbons from now on the service in Notre Dame would follow the funeral at a later date and would not necessarily feature the same representatives. Appendix III sums up train-length and train-bearing at Bourbon obsequies celebrated in Saint-Denis and in Notre Dame during the reign of Louis XIV.

[58] BN, FF 18536, fos. 337–338, 358–369 (Sainctot); *Mémoires de Nicolas Goulas*, ed. Charles Constant (3 vols, Paris, 1879–82), ii, 59–65; *Mémoires de Mme de Motteville*, ed. Riaux, i, 220–2; *Journal d'Olivier Lefèvre d'Ormesson*, ed. Chéruel, i, 235, 237; cf. Vincent J. Pitts, *La Grande Mademoiselle at the Court of France: 1627–1693* (Baltimore, 2000), pp. 33–5.

[59] i.e. grandchildren by Sons of France, since the descendants of Daughters of France did not belong to the dynasty.

should *Mademoiselle* be considered'?[60] A member of the Royal Family or merely the most senior Princess of the Blood? Status symbols initiated her yet vaguely-defined rank; status symbols could still undo it. *Mademoiselle* thus sought further distin-guishing signs, whereas the Condés, championed by the duke of Enghien (future *Grand Condé*), would concede nothing but simple precedence. The regent decided in the latter's favour, and equally allotted the three princesses five ells and a single gentleman bearer each. What is more, when *Mademoiselle* feigned illness, the Queen Mother refused her even the face-saving expedient of avoidance.[61] Messen-gers continued to rush back and forth on the eve of the ceremony, and Gaston finally had to call on his daughter himself in order to force her to attend.[62]

Unabashed, *Mademoiselle* made several attempts to force distinctions on the spot, but these were thwarted by the vigilant Condés. As the group was leaving the church, Gaston's Captain of the Guards took hold of her *mante*, seconding her official, single bearer. In response, Enghien commanded members of his retinue, 'with injurious words', to grasp the trains of the two other princesses.[63] The indig-nant *Mademoiselle* did not let matters rest, and the regent threatened to confine her to a convent. Tension at court escalated as Gaston eventually decided to demand satisfaction for Enghien's behaviour, and angrily retired to the chateau of Limours. There followed attempts at reconciliation, finally achieved after the Queen Mother took responsibility and Enghien made a show of submission. At the end of the day, though, the Condés won the ceremonial battle. They achieved equal treatment with a grandchild of Henri IV—in ruling, in fact, and in register—and would continue to cite this precedent decades later as proof against the rank of Grandchil-dren of France.[64]

During volatile periods like regencies, any tension among the grandees could potentially ignite rebellion. But the battles of the mantles did not cease with the Fronde or with the personal reign of Louis XIV. The royal marriage in 1660, as we have seen, occasioned mantle contestations on several levels, within and beyond the Royal House.[65] Four years later, a memorial service for the duchess of Savoy replicated the dispute of 1644. Between the two events, the Orléans clan expanded to incorporate daughters of Gaston from his second marriage, and changed heads, as the king's brother Philippe replaced the late Gaston. One of the latter's daugh-ters, Mademoiselle d'Alençon, was chosen to represent the mourning in 1664, and the Orléans demanded that she enjoy several advantages over her Condé co-representatives. Mantle-wise, they wanted two more ells for her train and an extra

---

[60]   BN, FF 18536, fo. 338r.

[61]   The regent's resolve against her turbulent niece contrasts with her handling of other status dis-putes that arose on the same occasion but were left without a binding resolution: BN, FF 18536, fo. 352v. Furthermore, the princess of Condé was allowed absence for health reasons. The latter's daughter, married to the duke of Longueville (a descendant of a royal bastard) thus enjoyed the oppor-tunity to assert her own rank on this occasion.

[62]   Gaston did manage to squeeze in a non-mantle-related distinction in favour of his daughter: BN, FF 18536, fo. 360.

[63]   BN, FF 18536, fo. 368v.

[64]   Notably in the memoir prepared after 1679: AC, MS 1131, fos. 6, 14–15. By contrast, the con-testation is conspicuously absent from *Mademoiselle's* memoirs.

[65]   See the previous section.

bearer. '*Monsieur* even went into quite a fit with the king over it', Henri-Jules reported in a private letter to his aunt, 'but [the king] ruled [...] that there be no distinction among the three princesses and [...] gave us entire satisfaction'.[66] Louis XIV thus upheld the precedent of his mother's ruling.

Encouraged by their wins, the Condés raised the stakes and challenged the advantages of *Monsieur* himself. At the death of the king of Spain in 1665, Louis chose as the representatives of deep mourning his own brother, Condé, and Henri-Jules. *Monsieur* demanded various distinctions over the two Princes of the Blood. This time, Louis approved many of them, including a two-ell differential (seven as opposed to five) and an extra bearer (two rather than one). When the Master of Ceremonies informed the princes of the king's orders, the *Grand Condé* respectfully objected, relying on the precedent of 1643:

> [Condé] cited to [Sainctot] the late king's service at Saint-Denis, [noting] that there had been no distinction [there] between the late *Monsieur* and his father, the late prince of Condé; that both of them had had mourning mantles of the same length, whose trains had been carried equally by two gentlemen [...] Sainctot told him that the king had been informed of all this.[67]

Still unsatisfied, Condé told the king that 'he would render to *Monsieur* all the honours that he would order provided that they were not contrary to usage [*pourueu qu'il n'y eust point d'vsage contraire*]'.[68] In the end, Louis allowed Condé and Henri-Jules to retire to their chateau in Chantilly for the weekend, while *Monsieur* alone represented the mourning at Notre Dame.

This is an instructive instance of decision-making in a system of customary law, which illuminates the limitations of royal power on the one hand and the scope for royal intervention on the other. Louis XIV believed that Children of France merited differential treatment; a sovereign's brother, after all, was more than a late king's niece. Recent precedent, however, contradicted royal inclination. Unlike *Mesdemoiselles* in 1644 or in 1664, Condé could cite a directly relevant recent case to support his claim, one that Sainctot did not refute. Armed with such a precedent, the prince felt confident enough to declare conditional obedience only, provided that the sovereign's orders 'were not contrary to usage'.[69] And the king indeed did not force the princes' hand on this occasion, contrary to what he and his mother had done with *Mesdemoiselles*. Rather, he allowed his cousins to avoid the ceremony, to *Monsieur*'s indignation.[70] In the long run, however, avoidance proved

---

[66] *Le Grand Condé et le duc d'Enghien: Lettres inédites à Marie-Louise de Gonzague, reine de Pologne*, ed. Émile Magne (Paris, 1920), p. 24 n. 1. See also p. 29; cf. Sainctot's account, BM, MS 2738, fos. 116ff., which also reports the additional mortification that Alençon suffered with regard to the collar of the Holy Spirit (see earlier, p. 82).

[67] BM, MS 2738, fo. 154v. Condé conceded that the late prince of Conti had had one train-bearer only on that occasion.

[68] BM, MS 2738, fo. 154v.

[69] Although Sainctot's account cannot naturally be considered a verbatim rendering of Condé's words to him, the formulation is still striking.

[70] AC, R ix, fo. 345 (I am grateful to Madame Léa Ferrez-Lenhard for kindly supplying me with a copy of this document). See also *Le Grand Condé et le duc d'Enghien*, ed. Magne, pp. 229–30; *Journal d'Olivier Lefèvre d'Ormesson*, ed. Chéruel, ii, 411.

to be the resort of the weak. In absolute terms, the king's brother now enjoyed a longer train and more bearers than was the custom for the Princes of the Blood.[71] Usage was thus subtly modified, and even a custom-bound ruler would have more room for manoeuvre in the future. The absolute precedent paved the way for relative advantages—the ones that counted most.

Indeed, a few months later, for the obsequies of the Queen Mother in 1666, Louis followed up his earlier decision with a more general ruling that remained a point of reference for decades to come:[72]

> In order to create some distinction between the Daughters of France and the Grand-daughters of Royalty, the king ordered that *Madame* would have the train of her mantle seven ells long, borne by three gentlemen [...] that *Mesdemoiselles* would only have the train of their mantles five ells long, borne by two gentlemen [...]
>
> There were no Princesses of the Blood at the ceremony, but the king did not fail to say that if ever they were present with the Granddaughters of Royalty on such an occasion, his intention was that there would be no distinction between them[73]

This shrewd regulation struck a balance among ranks and among clans. On the one hand, building on the absolute figures of 1665, the king reaffirmed his will to set the Children of France above other members of the Royal House. *Madame*, and hence *Monsieur*, gained personally. On the other hand, the ruling emphasized the differences within the Orléans clan, forcing the granddaughters below the Children, onto an equal footing with the Princesses of the Blood. Gaston's and *Monsieur*'s children stood to lose relative to their parents, a loss somewhat mitigated, though, by an absolute gain in the number of bearers. The Condés, for their part, faced a similarly mixed result—for the opposite reasons. Deepening the absolute losses of 1665, the ruling at the same time consolidated the claim of the Princes of the Blood to equality with the granddaughters, with 'no distinction'. Their losses, besides, were implicit only, since the regulation, strictly speaking, did not address their interactions with the Children of France.

The careful phrasing was matched by careful casting. The king did not choose Condé representatives for several years and ceremonies. It was presumably easier to establish the new ruling and gradation by making the Orléans princesses defer to *Madame*. In the meantime, these granddaughters could also boast an upgrade, in absolute terms and relative to the Princesses of the Blood before the reform.[74] Only in 1670 did the Condés appear again at a major Bourbon service (the obsequies of *Madame*), and they enjoyed there the reformed absolute measures (five ells and

---

[71] And as we have seen in the previous section, one of *Monsieur*'s bearers was a (recently appointed) duke.

[72] Such explicit ceremonial innovation stands in contrast to the decision to regulate other contestations according to the precedents of 1643 (e.g. BM, MS 2739, fo. 26v).

[73] BM, MS 2739, fo. 13v. The regulation also awarded the Daughters a couple of other, non-mantle-related distinctions. In the secret dossier from 1701 (AN, K 118, no. 104), Henri-Jules marked this ruling in his own hand, as he also did *Monsieur*'s failure on this occasion to introduce yet another distinction in favour of the Children of France—duke as train-bearer (see the previous section).

[74] Tellingly, the only detail that the *Grande Mademoiselle* notes about the services of 1666 is that she had two bearers, both of them Knights of the Holy Spirit: *Mémoires de Mlle de Montpensier*, ed. Chéruel, iv, 30.

two bearers).[75] As a further indication of careful casting, for nearly half a century after the ruling the Princesses of the Blood did not co-represent with either the Children or the Grandchildren of France.[76] The crown, it appears, did not want to risk another direct status confrontation and orchestrated preemptive avoidance instead.

However careful, the settlement failed to put an end to the battles of the mantles. In the absence of direct interactions, the parties competed in absolute measures at separate events (where, strictly speaking, the ruling did not apply). This new phase of the conflict initially centred round nuptials. While the special bearing arrangements at such events (see previous section) were not affected by the ruling, train-length remained a contested stake. As we have seen in Chapter One, the marriage of 1679 introduced a *longueur intermédiaire* of six ells. The granddaughters increased their train there by an ell, nearing the seven ells of *Madame* and surpassing the past lengths of the Princesses of the Blood, who were absent.[77] Contrary to 1666, the king did not match this absolute increase with a promise of future relative equality: according to the official record, he 'said nothing' with regard to the Princesses of the Blood. The Condés, through Gourville, could only content themselves with minimizing the publicity damage in the newspaper accounts. Five years later, another daughter of *Monsieur* repeated the six-ell precedent when she married the duke of Savoy.[78]

This decade of marriages also introduced another group of mantle-wearers into the equation. The Legitimated Princesses wore five-ell trains in 1679, one ell less than the granddaughters. Did this merely signify their inferiority vis-à-vis all legitimate members, or did this reflect on the status of the Princes of the Blood too? The dynastic strategy of Louis XIV, of marrying his bastard daughters to legitimate princes, further complicates the question. Besides, there is the problem of liminality: did bridal *mantes* signify pre-marital or marital status? The identity of the bearer princess on these occasions, as we have seen, generally reflected the former. Initially, it appears, so did train-length.[79]

In 1685, however, the Princes of the Blood seized an opportunity to play on these ambiguities in order to even the score with the Granddaughters of France. When Mademoiselle de Nantes, bastard of Louis XIV and of Madame de Montespan,

---

[75] BM, MS 2739, fos. 130–131. On this occasion, Sainctot's register clarified the regulation of 1666, on the one hand re-emphasizing the equality of trains between the granddaughters and the Condés (and noting the precedent of 1643), and on the other mentioning a couple of non-mantle-related differences. In the secret dossier, Henri-Jules marked this passage, adding in the margin: 'voyes tout cet article bien importans' (AN, K 118, no. 104; cf. AN, K 121, no. 35¹, pp. 3–4).

[76] The next occasion of co-representation was the double obsequies of 1712: see Appendix III and later in this section.

[77] See pp. 42–5. From this perspective, the exceptional upgrade in the gender of *Madame's* bearer on this occasion compensated for the erosion of her length advantage relative to *Mesdemoiselles*.

[78] BM, MS 2742, fo. 106.

[79] In addition to the two marriages of granddaughters in 1679 and in 1684, the prince of Conti married the first Mademoiselle de Blois in 1680. The latter had a five-ell mantle, borne by a legitimated half-sister: BM, MS 2741, fos. 76–77. Apparently in most marriages (1679, as a royal union, being the exception) the bride was the only princess wearing a long-trained mantle. On the liminality of bridal status, see Chapter One.

married Henri-Jule's eldest, the duke of Bourbon, the Condés had her wear a six-ell train, equalling the *longueur intermédiaire* of the granddaughters.[80] The king, though, ordered his ceremonial staff to add a reservation in their registers with regard to future occasions. This event illuminates the role of two key factors: the Grand Master of Ceremonies Blainville, appointed a few months earlier, and the ceremonial record in general. For this phase of the conflict we have the accounts of Blainville as well as of Sainctot; strikingly, these two official voices turn out to be divergent rather than redundant.

Sainctot's register presents the six ells of 1685 as an infringement, and has the king order that 'in the future the trains of the *mantes* of the legitimated daughters would be five ells only'.[81] Ignoring the central controversy, the Master of Ceremonies simply attributes the reservation to the pre-marital origins of the bride. The Grand Master's account, on the other hand, does the very opposite:

> The king wanted that the train of [the bride's] dress were of this length [six ells], because one had represented to him that the duchess of Savoy, *Monsieur*'s daughter, had had [a train] of this same length at her marriage. His Majesty ordered the marquis of Blainville, Grand Master of Ceremonies, to note in his registers that [the king] did not want this to be an example for the future, but that his intention was that the trains of the Granddaughters of France as well as [those] of the Princesses of the Blood be henceforth of five ells only, not wanting any difference between them in this matter.[82]

The divergence relates to the liminality, or ambiguity, of bridal status. Blainville juxtaposes the *mantes* of 1684 and 1685, although in the first case the birth rank of *Monsieur*'s daughter was at stake, whereas in the second it was the marital rank of Henri-Jules's daughter-in-law. Such framing served the dynastic strategies of both Princes of the Blood and Legitimated Princes (as did the union in general).[83] For the latter, the resulting ambiguity blurred the distinction between legitimate and legitimated, cementing their assimilation into the Royal House. For the former, it established a counter-precedent against the Granddaughters of France and unequivocally reemphasized the equality of trains. Blainville, like Dangeau, was indeed a friend of the Condés.

The Granddaughters of France, in any case, continued to press for longer trains— now also at obsequies.[84] At the memorial service for the queen of Spain in 1689, Louis tolerated six ells again. In the same breath, he authorized the Princesses of the Blood to enjoy the same train-length on future occasions.[85] Apparently reversing his

---

[80] AN, K 121, no. 35¹, p. 6.   [81] AC, MS 1182, p. 33; cf. AN, K 119, no. 17².

[82] BN, 500 Colbert 141, fo. 17r; cf. BM, MS 2742, fo. 147; AN, KK 600, p. 769.

[83] cf. SSB, xv, 336.

[84] Earlier, in 1683, they had had five ells only for the obsequies of the queen (BM, MS 2742, fo. 64r; AC, MS 1217, p. 235); the (male) Princes of the Blood had the same for those of the *Grand Condé* in 1687 (AC, MS 1182, p. 129).

[85] This is Blainville's account, supported, as we shall see shortly, by later evidence. Here Sainctot's account diverges on the very facts: he records five ells rather than six, without offering an explanation. But Sainctot, who apparently did not attend the event, was probably mistaken. See Sternberg, 'Manipulating Information', pp. 251–2.

policy on absolute ells, the king remained true to his opposition to relative differences between the two ranks. Finally, having wavered for long in face of contradictory pressures and transgressions, a year later Louis returned, for good, to his original ruling from 1666. While the ceremonial record does not provide clarifications this time, a real-time exchange between the Condés and the crown offers partial but precious evidence about the negotiations that went on behind the scenes—in 1690 as in 1689.

The occasion was the obsequies of the dauphine, in spring 1690. At the funeral in Saint-Denis, the Granddaughters of France had represented the mourning wearing six-ell trains again. Now Henri-Jules's wife and other Princesses of the Blood were supposed to appear at the second service in Notre Dame. The equality principle thus faced a crucial test, akin to co-presence. Henri-Jules accordingly wrote in his own hand to the marquis of Seignelay, Secretary of State in charge of the royal household:

> I think that you will be kind enough to remember that you gave me your word at other ceremonies, that the king agreed that on the first occasion the Princesses of the Blood take six-ell trains. Relying entirely [on this promise] [...] I have not made any incident since then when *Mesdemoiselles* began to take possession of their six ells— I think it was at the service of the queen of Spain. I still rest in the word that you gave me and [I hope] that when the Princesses [of the Blood] have six ells, you will be kind enough to note it on the register. Again, they will not brag about anything, and will not talk of their train in any way [...] avoiding like the plague anything which could cause the slightest nuisance to the king, and wishing only not to be blamed now or [in the future] that, with all my attachment to the king's person, I could not merit that he would conserve in my favour everything that he settled before, in so many ceremonies, in favour of the Princes of the Blood regarding the equality of trains.[86]

At the service of the queen of Spain a year earlier the crown had bought the acquiescence of the Condés to the six ells of the granddaughters in exchange for the guarantee that it would award the Princesses of the Blood the same possession 'on the first occasion'.[87] What is more, it transpires that this understanding concerned the record as well as the event. A *de facto* precedent was not enough: the new possession had to be properly registered for posterity. Indeed, the Condés considered the long-term prospects of the official register more important than the short-term gains of public 'bragging'. Such discretion would presumably serve their interests as well as the king's, as it would decrease the likelihood of opposition by their rivals; if the precedent passed unchallenged in this round, the record would stand them in the next. A single event was but one battle in a war that lasted across generations.[88]

---

[86] AN, KK 601, pp. 227–30 (I thank Monsieur Jean-Marc Roger of the Archives nationales for allowing me to inspect the original document).

[87] The Condés were apparently so eager to take possession that they sent ill princesses to the ceremony. With the exception of the unusual arrangement of 1643, this was the only case in our time range where the crown switched the entire cast of representatives between Saint-Denis and Notre Dame.

[88] cf. SSB, xxxiii, 134–7.

Growing weary of this interminable arms race, however, the crown followed the logic of the record to its limit in order to get the warring parties off its back. Texts, after all, were easier to tailor than textiles. On the eve of the second service, Seignelay informed Henri-Jules that 'one will put down five-ell trains only on the registers'. The minister assured the prince that the crown was still committed to the 'no difference' policy, explaining that 'one put down a length of five ells only' for the Granddaughters of France too. 'According to His Majesty's intention', he concluded, 'this will be observed in all types of ceremonies'.[89] The parties could wear whatever they wanted. The official register, in any event, would record five ells only. A quarter of a century after his original ruling, Louis 'did not want to hear about it' anymore.[90]

This striking policy underscores a general methodological problem: can we rely on the official record to reflect the ceremonial past? Luckily, though, even the king's officials did not follow his orders to the letter. Admittedly, from 1690 onwards the controversy receives less coverage and the general rule is five ells. But breach crops up nevertheless. First, and rather inexplicably, in his account of the obsequies in question Sainctot put down six ells for the Granddaughters of France and five for the Princesses of the Blood.[91] Second, his successor Desgranges does record subsequent cases when the Orléans stretched the rules. In 1692, for example, *Monsieur*'s son married another legitimated daughter, whose train extended to five ells and three quarters. The king's brother, Desgranges explains, instructed the person in charge of ordering the outfits that although the train should be five ells only, 'she should have it made between five and six ells, and that one would not actually measure it'.[92]

It was in this climate of continued sartorial and documentary uncertainty that Henri-Jules launched the intelligence operation of 1701. The First Prince of the Blood wanted to make the best case for his rank before 'things are decided' with regard to *Monsieur*'s funeral. Information was an integral part of status interaction, and Condé could draw on a rich ceremonial knowledge-base built over the previous decades. As he reviewed and annotated the secret extracts from Sainctot, the prince found the accounts of 1685 and of 1690 particularly unsatisfying. Accordingly, he asked his cousin Conti to inquire after Blainville's version. The former Grand Master of Ceremonies indeed proved forthcoming to his 'friends', and enlisted additional official resources in their clandestine private venture.[93] In the end, according to the official account of *Monsieur*'s funeral, the train-length of the

---

[89] AN, O¹ 34, fo. 151r.   [90] AN, K 121, no. 35¹, pp. 5–6.

[91] AC, MS 1182, fos. 387, 397; BM, MS 2742, fos. 229v–230r, 236r. Unfortunately, Blainville's version for the actual events is not available this time.

[92] BM, MS 2743, fo. 13. *Monsieur* repeated the trick six years later when he married his own daughter to the duke of Lorraine: the bride's *mante* 'ne deuoit estre que de 5 aulnes de long, mais je crois qu'on l'auoit faite plus longue' (BM, MS 2744, fo. 26). The *Mercure Galant* (October 1698, p. 261), made it six ells and a half, a publicity triumph. At the obsequies of the *Grande Mademoiselle* in 1693, Desgranges's register has five ells only for the Granddaughters of France (BM, MS 2743, fos. 70–71), but cf. BN, 500 Colbert 142, fo. 8v; AN, KK 600, p. 770.

[93] For details see Sternberg, 'Manipulating Information', pp. 253–5.

new duke of Orléans, Grandson of France, was 'five ells only'.[94] While the numerical figures conformed to the crown's general policy, the 'only' may have been Desgranges's way of hinting at what went on behind the scenes.

Towards the end of the reign, an unexpected series of deaths accelerated the pace of obsequies—and of dynastic change. The Legitimated Princes in particular took advantage of these developments to seal their assimilation into the Royal House. In 1709, for the first time in the reign, a Legitimated Prince represented the deep mourning alongside Princes of the Blood. The duke of Maine forced himself at the last minute into the memorial service for Henri-Jules in Notre Dame, and the official record awarded him the same mantle privileges as the legitimate princes.[95] In 1714, the prince of Dombes enjoyed the same at the funeral of the duke of Berry. Saint-Simon saw in this 'novel' parity between the son of a royal bastard and two legitimate Bourbons a calculated move by the king, in order to prepare the ground for the elevation of the Legitimated Princes to the full rank of Princes of the Blood a fortnight later.[96] Status symbols thus functioned as a subtle barometer of dynastic politics.

On other fronts, subtle distinctions in and among the number of ells, the number of bearers, and the rank of bearers reflected both continuity and change.[97] On the most contested front, for the first time since the ruling of 1666 the Condés co-represented with the Children and with the Grandchildren of France. This happened in 1712, at the double obsequies of dauphin and dauphine. Wearing five-ell-long mantles carried by two gentlemen each, the Princes and Princesses of the Blood acknowledged the superiority of the duke and duchess of Berry, who enjoyed seven ells and three bearers. At the same time, these Condés recorded a complete equality of trains with the duke of Orléans, Grandchild of France, also present.[98] Two decades after the resolution of 1690 and nearly half a century since the original ruling, the two clans, it seems, finally buried the hatchet in the graves of *Monsieur* and of Henri-Jules. The king could afford co-presence and would no longer need to 'hear about it'.

This is a hasty impression, however. The duke of Orléans, it turns out, was not resigned to the equality of trains after all. During the preparations for the funeral of Berry two years later, Orléans represented to the king that he 'should have three train-bearers while the Princes of the Blood would have two, or that they should be reduced to one as in the past'. The king refused this demand, and the Grandchild of France did not appear at the funeral.[99] Unlike his father *Monsieur*, the

[94] BM, MS 2744, fo. 166.

[95] AN, K 577, no. 69; BM, MS 2745, fos. 154–155. The legitimate princes retained a small advantage in the size of their retinue. More on the context of 1709 in the next chapter; cf. *Mémoires du duc de Luynes*, iii, 483.

[96] SSB, xxiv, 324–5, 412. Here as in 1709, Desgranges reports equality in the number of bearers, but does not mention train-length: BM, MS 2747, fos. 43v, 47v.

[97] These included differences at the top, among the Children of France: see Sternberg, 'The Culture of Orders', pp. 93–6, and Appendix III.

[98] BM, MS 2746, fos. 130v–131v, 139r. At the second service in Notre Dame, Orléans enjoyed a small advantage in retinue; cf. SSB, xxiii, 52, 415.

[99] BM, MS 2747, fo. 48.

second Philippe of Orléans is not known for ceremonial punctiliousness; he was also about to become the most powerful person in France. But status interaction was not a pastime or a matter of personal inclination. While protagonists and generations may change, the importance of symbolic markers for mediating social positions and tensions remained.

When Louis XIV died a year later, Orléans, made regent and heir to the throne, was at last in a position to overturn the regulation. If he ended the equality of trains, though, he would risk alienating the Princes of the Blood at the precarious start of a regency period. A shrewd politician, Orléans subtly manipulated the mantle code in a way that avoided such potential alienation without unduly compromising his own status pretensions. He decided that neither his mantle nor those of the Princes of the Blood who represented the mourning at his side would be carried during the services for the late king. This decision relied, Desgranges explained, on the precedent of 1643: 'at the service of Louis XIII, the train of Monsieur the duke of Orléans, Son of France, trailed, as did those of Monsieur the prince of Condé and of Monsieur the prince of Conti'. The regent, accordingly, prescribed the same treatment for himself and for the Princes of the Blood, 'rather than use his authority to establish his right'.[100]

The train has come full circle: the obsequies of Louis XIV saw the reintroduction of the mantle code employed for Louis XIII's funeral.[101] This solution maintained the equality of trains between Grandchildren of France and Princes of the Blood, but established it on radically different premises. The parity of the Louis XIV era demoted both groups below the Children of France. Louis XIII's funeral, by contrast, had seen an equality of trains with Gaston of Orléans, Son of France. The regent could afford a tie mantle-wise, since by now other codes had set him above the Princes of the Blood. Paradoxically, he gained in status by cutting down on his own status symbols—by *not* having his train carried. For what ultimately mattered in status interaction was relative position, not absolute measures. To gauge this position, parties compared themselves to others present, but also to those absent—sometimes far away in space or in time. Thus, a ceremonial event involving a Grandchild of France and two Princes of the Blood in 1715, when the era of Louis XIV was finally over, derived its meaning from the bearing of a Son of France seventy-two years earlier, when the reign began.

---

[100] BM, MS 2346, fos. 35v–36r. Train-length is not mentioned in the accounts of the services, but the preparatory memoranda for both allot five ells equally to the three princes, as in 1643: BM, MS 2346, fos. 121, 147. More generally, see Robert N. Nicolich, 'Sunset: The Spectacle of the Royal Funeral and Memorial Services at the End of the Reign of Louis XIV', in David Lee Rubin (ed.), *Sun King: The Ascendancy of French Culture during the Reign of Louis XIV* (Cranbury-London-Washington, 1991), pp. 45–72.

[101] At least the subsequently accepted official version of what had happened in 1643: contemporary reports, as we have seen, were contradictory.

4

To Wear or Not To Wear? Mantled Visits in the Early Eighteenth Century

Vestments of authority and status, early modern mantles of diverse names and forms normally carried a positive social value from the wearer's perspective. Judicial and municipal officers, from the Parisian *parlementaires* to the syndics of small provincial towns, used their robes to assert their social position and to command obedience in the streets.[1] Prelates took pride in the right to wear the *camail* and the rochet as signs of their ecclesiastical jurisdiction.[2] Nobles and courtiers, as the previous chapter has shown, eagerly sought the privilege of long-trained mantles at ceremonies. In these and other cases, the corollary of the positive value associated with the garment can be seen in the attempts to restrict its wearing to an exclusive group, through the various forms—more or less codified—of sumptuary law so prevalent in the early modern period.

However, if we consider wearing not as an absolute or static attribute of wearer identity, but as a dynamic interaction involving multiple protagonists, a more complicated—and more interesting—picture emerges. The signification of dress did not depend on wearer or on occasion only, but also on other parties to the interaction, whose own interests were at stake. We have already seen one example in the case of train-bearing, which simultaneously involved wearers, bearers, and others present.[3] In the case of complimentary visits that concerns us here, the garment highlighted the relations between visitors and hosts, the protagonists—or antagonists—of these social duels.[4] What is more, this interactional aspect could reverse the positive value normally associated with mantle-wearing itself. For in the code of mantled visits, dress in fact honoured the other party, becoming a duty, and sometimes even a liability, for its wearer.

Wearers did not award all their interactants the full sartorial treatment. Municipal authorities, for example, honoured the most distinguished ones by wearing robes and chaperons, others by chaperons only, while the least fortunate received neither. In 1719, the *échevins* of Marseille denounced one of their colleagues for

---

[1] See e.g. Aribaud and Mouysset (eds), *Vêture et pouvoir*; Turrel, 'L'identité par la distinction'.
[2] See e.g. *Recueil des actes, titres et memoires concernant les affaires du clergé de France* (12 vols, Paris, 1716–50), iv, 1234–5.
[3] See the previous chapter, esp. pp. 79–86.   [4] On visits as social duels, see Chapter Two.

wearing his chaperon in greeting a naval commander.[5] Ecclesiastics, in France and elsewhere, showed similar reluctance to wear the *camail* and the rochet for courtesy calls.[6] Most humiliating from their perspective was the injunction to cover these items with another over-garment, the mantlet, in the presence of a supposedly higher authority. French prelates repeatedly protested against the requirement to wear mantlets before papal legates, arguing that the liberties of the Gallican Church were at stake.[7] But whereas the mantlet as a distinguishing sign subordinated its wearer by definition, the other examples are especially interesting because of their duality: that they could be prestigious in an absolute sense but humiliating relative to the interaction.[8]

This chapter examines mantled visits in the context of the courtesy calls that followed deaths. Like the visits examined in Chapter Two, these interactions occupy a middle ground between high ceremony and everyday life. This was reflected in the cut of the garments themselves: regular mourning mantles were more uniform in length and generally shorter than the over-garments worn by the representatives of deep mourning at funerary services.[9] Another feature common to mantled and to seated visits is their directionality. The *Grande Mademoiselle* defined these mantles as 'the garment of respect, when one is in mourning, the first time one sees the people to whom one owes it'.[10] From a modern perspective of mourning duties, one might associate the dress with the bereaved and the visit with other parties. But in this early modern context, the determining factor was the directionality of respect: in most cases, the duty to wear as well as the duty to visit fell on the inferior party, whether or not it was the active mourner.

In these cases, mantled visits, like train-bearing, were asymmetrical interactions that necessitated the cooperation of inferiors. Unlike the relation between wearers and bearers, however, visits regularly pitted parties close to one another on the social ladder. While the king would not force a duke to bear the train of a Child of France, junior Bourbons could demand mantled visits from princes.

---

[5] AM, Marseille, AA 68, fo. 85v; cf. Tillet, *Chronique bordeloise*, pp. 11–12, 65, 223; Mouysset, 'Jeux et enjeux de la robe consulaire', pp. 43–4; BM, MS 2740, fo. 93.

[6] *Mémoires de Mlle de Montpensier*, ed. Chéruel, iii, 567–9; De Wicquefort, *L'ambassadeur et ses fonctions* (2 vols, The Hague, 1681), i, 667–8.

[7] Pierre Blet, *Richelieu et l'Église* (Versailles, 2007), p. 34; BM, MS 2739, fos. 55–56. See also BN, FF 14117, pp. 459, 466–7; Philipp Zitzlsperger, *Gianlorenzo Bernini Die Papst- und Herrscherporträts: Zum Verhältnis von Bildnis und Macht* (Munich, 2002), pp. 50–2 and figure 48, which shows Scipione Borghese's rochet peeping from under his mantlet in the presence of his uncle, Pope Paul V.

[8] Train-bearing was the opposite: subordinating by definition, but potentially a relative honour (see the previous chapter).

[9] The male garment was known as *manteau long* or *grand manteau*, and its train was often measured in feet rather than in ells. Here too, the female garment was known as *mante*. See Sternberg, 'The Culture of Orders', pp. 69–70, and Figure 3.2. On funerary services and their mantles, see the previous chapter, pp. 73–5.

[10] *Mémoires de Mlle de Montpensier*, ed. Chéruel, iii, 468. As we shall see shortly, the first 'one' in the quote did not always coincide with the second. Formal court dress in general could be viewed as a garment of respect: Wilhelm Ludwig Holland (ed.), *Briefe der Herzogin Elisabeth Charlotte von Orléans* (6 vols, Stuttgart, 1867–81), [i], 306; cf. Hannah Greig, 'Faction and Fashion: The Politics of Court Dress in Eighteenth-century England', in Paresys and Coquery (eds), *Se vêtir à la cour en Europe*, pp. 67–89.

After all, the right to wear the garment was theoretically limited to aristocrats in the first place. The duty, on the other hand, did not derive automatically from simple precedence, but rather was a question of degree: visitors did not have to challenge the superiority of hosts to deny them mantled visits. From the perspective of the superior party, finally, the question also transcended the immediate interaction, and played a part in their rivalries with third parties who claimed the same honour.

Who visited whom, and when? In the most frequent and least documented scenario, those who suffered death in their family would put on their mourning mantles and do reverence (*faire la réverence*) to the king and to other members of the Royal House. How far down the ladder of Bourbons or how far up the ladder of mourners? That was the first question. When the mourners were Bourbons themselves, they would follow up their mantled visits to the Royal House with the reception of visitors in their own place of residence. Would the latter appear mantled or unmantled? Finally, when the king too was close kin of the deceased, the phases and the questions converged. With the rapid succession of Bourbon deaths in the early eighteenth century, mantled visits became a familiar sight in court society. The evolution of their code in these years reflected and shaped contemporary changes across this social spectrum: from the dynastic upheavals within the ruling house, through the evolution of its relations with the rest of the aristocracy, to the climbing attempts of those in the margins.

PRECEDENT-MAKING: COLLUSION, EQUIVOCATION, COERCION

Since mantled visits did not belong to the realm of high ceremony, they do not receive the same serial coverage as mantled services do in the registers of the Masters of Ceremonies. Instead, we are often left with irregular or partisan accounts, and even these are rather sporadic until the end of the seventeenth century. It is therefore more difficult in this case to flesh out the contours of the code or to trace its initial evolution. Perhaps it gained in importance with the expansion of the Royal Family and with the sedentarization of court life in Versailles. Whatever the case, mantled visits clearly became a bone of contention by the beginning of the eighteenth century.[11]

By then, the Grandchildren of France seem to have adopted (or usurped) the honour of receiving mantled visits on the occasions that the king received them. As in other aspects of ceremony and etiquette, they followed in the footsteps of the previous Bourbon generation. The fact that they grew up with their parents and often continued to live under the same roof in adulthood facilitated the creation of precedents: courtiers arriving to compliment the Children of France would find

---

[11] Foreign diplomats at court also participated in mantled visits, on occasions of deaths in France or in their own country, and these are described by the Introductors of Ambassadors. See e.g. Breteuil, *Mémoires*, ed. Lever, pp. 264, 282–5.

the Grandchildren there as secondary hosts.[12] As in other aspects again, the Princes of the Blood did not wish to fall behind.[13] Here, however, success depended on the cooperation of independent interactants, high-ranking in their own right, not simply on tailors or on household members.[14] To achieve it, the Bourbon princes adopted a multi-phased strategy, gradually augmenting the occasions for visits and the ranks of visitors.

This began, according to Saint-Simon, with the courtiers who did reverence to the king on the occasion of deaths in their own family. Allowing for the duke's typical inaccuracies and exaggerations, his detailed description of the adversarial tactics of these status interactions nonetheless illuminates the subtle manoeuvres of precedent-making that laid the ground for subsequent change and the multi-layered rivalries involved.[15]

To establish the precedent, the Princes of the Blood first targeted 'persons of quality who agreed to please them out of attachment'. Friendship and obligation thus continue to play their part. A second target group consisted of the social climbers who sought to establish their own right to the prestigious garment.[16] When such climbers paid a visit to the Princes of the Blood, clad in their arguable mourning mantles, both sides stood to gain from the precedent. Status interaction was not always a zero-sum game, and the larger the gap between interactants, the greater the potential for collusion. Novelty subsequently turned into fashion and insinuations into demands, as the Princes of the Blood made it clear to others that they would not regard refusal favourably. They obliged more and higher-ranking people into seeing them in mantles.

The non-Bourbon aristocracy thus felt threatened from both directions: its inferiors were usurping its sumptuary privilege, while its superiors were extending their advantages at its expense. What was once a distinction was turning into a liability. Accordingly, mourners asked the king to dispense them from wearing the garment. This counter-measure, however, exacerbated their predicament rather than solved it. Those dispensed by the king were expected to inform the Children and Grandchildren of France of the dispensation. Many saw no harm in extending the notification to the Princes of the Blood too: 'it is a courtesy, they said, which

---

[12] *Mémoires de Mlle de Montpensier*, ed. Chéruel, iv, 28, 154 (including visits to the one-year-old Mademoiselle de Valois); Dangeau, ii, 339; AC, MS 1217, p. 60. By 1690, the *Grande Mademoiselle* received mantled visits while living away from court and from the Children of France: *Correspondance de Bussy*, ed. Lalanne, iv, 330. Sainctot notes the same mechanism for the mantlet and for other ambassadorial garb: BN, FF 14119, fo. 284r.

[13] In parallel, the Condés minimized their own mantled respects to the Orléans in order to prove that it was not 'trop vn deuoir': AC, MS 1217, p. 354; cf. p. 269.

[14] cf. the case of ministers and the *plume* (Chapter One, pp. 37–8).

[15] The following two paragraphs summarize and cite SSB, xv, 333–5, 504; cf. Saint-Simon, *Hiérarchie et mutations*, ed. Coirault, pp. 107–10 (written by 1711).

[16] Saint-Simon specifically mentions ministers in this context of the 'prostitution' of mantles (see also SSB, xii, 344–5). Secretary of State Pontchartrain indeed did reverence to the king in mantle when his wife died in 1708: Sourches, xi, 117. More generally, see Thierry Sarmant, 'Quand le noir est couleur: costume et portrait des ministres en France du XVIIe au XXe siècle', in Bernard Barbiche, Jean-Pierre Poussou, and Alain Tallon (eds), *Pouvoirs, contestations et comportements dans l'Europe moderne: mélanges en l'honneur du professeur Yves-Marie Bercé* (Paris, 2005), pp. 513–27.

costs nothing'. In so doing, though, they were playing right into the hands of the latter, since this amounted to recognition of the original obligation. The Princes of the Blood were happy to exchange the garment with the notification; either would serve their combined agenda: to eliminate the edge of their superiors within the Royal House, while increasing the subordination of their inferiors outside it. As veteran practitioners of salami tactics, they could expect the full obligation to follow.

The opportunity arose with the death of the countess of Armagnac in December 1707.[17] Encouraged by recent success in an analogous dispute, and aided by the assimilation of the influential royal bastards into their ranks, the Princes of the Blood openly challenged the last bastion of resistance. When the Armagnacs initially refused to pay them a mantled visit, the junior Bourbons brought their case before the king. Louis spoke with the count and ruled that the bereaved go with their mantles to the Princes of the Blood. For the latter's purposes, Armagnac was the ideal victim: as a member of the house of Lorraine, he was a Foreign Prince of the highest 'quality'; as Grand Equerry and assiduous courtier, he could hardly evade a royal command.[18] And indeed, two days later, the bereaved princes and princesses of Lorraine had to undergo the ordeal in their *mantes* and *manteaux*.

From then on, says Saint-Simon, the right of the Princes of the Blood was established. Even the titled nobility, the pinnacle of the non-Bourbon aristocracy, had to swallow its subordination. As a result, most resorted to the notification expedient, but this, the duke sadly remarks, 'only freed from the bother of the garment'.[19] The decision of the monarch, master of the ranks, was binding. Like other forms of royal decision-making, though, it was the culmination of a long process of interactions and precedent-making, which began outside the king's orbit, and most likely also without his knowledge.

ALL FOOLS' DAY: THE DEATH OF HENRI-JULES

If they could not disobey a direct command of their sovereign, the Foreign Princes and the Dukes and Peers could nevertheless interpret it in the narrowest possible sense. In the case of Armagnac, titled nobility did reverence to junior Bourbons on the occasion of its own mourning. What would happen when the Princes of the Blood were the mourners? Then, their pool of potential visitors—and hence antagonists—would include the entire aristocracy, not an isolated family. According to Saint-Simon, they made an initial attempt to secure such mantled visits on the death of the prince of Conti in February 1709, but had to resort to the avoidance tactic after realizing that the titled nobility would not acquiesce and that the king

---

[17] SSB, xv, 335–6. Contrary to the Boislisle note (SSB, xv, 336 n. 1), Dangeau does report the facts: xii, 37, 69–70, 71.

[18] For the same mechanism with a different code, see BM, MS 2745, fo. 58; Maral, *La chapelle royale de Versailles*, pp. 128, 278.

[19] For the continued use of this expedient later in the eighteenth century, see the memoirs of Luynes.

would not intervene.[20] Soon afterwards, however, the death of Henri-Jules, on 1 April, triggered the decisive showdown.

This status crisis is noted in the major narrative sources: journals, memoirs, and ceremonial registers.[21] In addition, we fortunately have a remarkable, extremely detailed account of ceremonial developments that the duke of Maine, the king's eldest legitimated son, composed shortly after the event for his own personal use.[22] Son-in-law of the deceased, Maine was involved in the funerary rites as close kin. Furthermore, the death of Henri-Jules marked a turning point in the relations between the royal bastards and the Princes of the Blood. As alliance turned into animosity, Maine's attempts to buttress the status of the Legitimated Princes would meet with growing opposition from the younger Condé generation, culminating in the 'affaire des princes' during the Orléans regency. From 1709 onwards, therefore, the question of mantled visits would test the dynastic realignment of legitimate and legitimated in the final years of Louis XIV's reign as well as the relations of both groups with the rest of the aristocracy.

The new leader of the Condés was the duke of Bourbon, Henri-Jules's son and successor and the king's son-in-law since his marriage with a Legitimated Princess in 1685.[23] Maine tried to coordinate policy on mantled visits, but Bourbon did not share the least notion of his plans. Bourbon's wife thought that one should either receive no visits on this occasion, or receive them in mantles. Maine therefore decided to refrain from seeing anyone until his brother-in-law arrived in Versailles, 'for fear of making some mistake which might have consequences' and 'to do everything as he did'.[24] The Legitimated Prince wanted no differences between himself and the legitimate Bourbons and followed their example religiously as the funerary rites unfolded.[25] If the bastards were to become Princes of the Blood, they had to act like ones.

On 5 April, Bourbon, his son the duke of Enghien, the prince of Conti (grandson of the deceased), and Maine, all in mantles, did reverence to the king and to other members of the Royal House and began receiving visits themselves. Courtiers who arrived at their door without mantles were refused admittance. As a result, very few visits were held that day. Even after the king instructed Maine's brother, the count of Toulouse, to pay his respects in mantle, the titled nobility still refused to budge.[26] Bourbon complained vociferously, and, the next morning, the king

---

[20] SSB, xvii, 259; cf. SSB, xvii, 147, 149, 153.

[21] Dangeau, xii, 380–3; SSB, xvii, 258–62; Sources, xi, 310; BM, MS 2745, fo. 140v (Desgranges); Arsenal, MS 3863, pp. 385–6 (Breteuil, who considered the matter noteworthy even though it did not directly concern him as Introductor of Ambassadors).

[22] Transcribed in SSB, xvii, 585–98. On the documentary angle of Maine's dynastic campaign, see Sternberg, 'Manipulating Information', pp. 255–61.

[23] Maine and Bourbon were thus brothers-in-law on both sides. Animosity would subsequently feed off a long-drawn-out lawsuit over Henri-Jules's succession.

[24] SSB, xvii, 586.

[25] A few months later, he would insist on representing the mourning at Notre Dame, together with Bourbon and two other Princes of the Blood: see the previous chapter, p. 95.

[26] They even claimed, Maine heard, that they had not paid mantled visits to the duke of Orléans, Grandson of France, when *Monsieur* had died: SSB, xvii, 589. One of the leaders of the ducal party, according to this report, was the duke of Chevreuse. As in the case of Beauvillier, the macro-political influence of Chevreuse did not stop him from actively engaging in the micro-politics of status interaction.

spoke to the duke of Beauvillier, First Gentleman of the Bedchamber. Louis told Beauvillier, as the Master of Ceremonies recorded, that his fellow dukes should make no difficulty, considering Toulouse's instructions.[27] Desgranges nevertheless added a critique in the margin of his register:

> I must observe that it would have been enough for the king to make his intention known in order to be obeyed, for the example of the count of Toulouse, scrupulously examined, would not be sufficient, because *Monsieur le Duc* [Bourbon] and the two other princes repaid him [Toulouse] the visit in mantles.
>
> These three Princes of the Blood and the two Legitimated also exchanged a mantled visit.[28]

Striking in its 'scrupulous' audacity—in the claim that, while the king's authority is absolute, his argument was lacking—this critique also supplies the key for a more precise definition of the conditions for subordination in mantled visits: the question of reciprocity.[29]

A mantled visit, a single event, was not necessarily sufficient to determine subordination of visitor to host. A return visit in the same attire could offset it. Maine's account of the compliments within the Royal House indeed details return visits too. In these, the Princes of the Blood and the Legitimated Princes are generally mantled.[30] What is more, Maine insisted on exchanging mantled visits even among the close kin of the deceased:

> in the belief that I should handle my proceedings with *Monsieur le Duc* more exactly than would seem necessary among brothers, brothers-in-law, nephews, *and people of equal rank*, I went mantled [...] to *Monsieur le Duc*'s apartment, where the duke of Enghien was also receiving his visits. This surprised them: they were without mantles; but they apologized to me about it, and, after a brief moment of courtesies, led me to *Madame la Duchesse*'s apartment. She was at her *toilette* and teased me about my stringency. I found the prince of Conti there, and told him that I would go to see him in form. He wanted to exempt me; but I refused.[31]

These Princes of the Blood paid back his visits, in mantles, the same day.[32] Thanks to his stringency, Maine secured further proof that they were all 'people of equal rank'. This opportunity would have been lost otherwise, since virtually all the Princes of the Blood were among the bereaved. From the perspective of the status relations between legitimate and legitimated, such direct, reciprocal exchange gave

[27] This royal message is corroborated in Dangeau, xvii, 382.

[28] 'se sont aussy fait mutuellement visite en manteau': BM, MS 2745, fo. 140v.

[29] See also Saint-Simon, *Hiérarchie et mutations*, ed. Coirault, p. 110; SSB, xvii, 260. On Desgranges's independent spirit, see Sternberg, 'Manipulating Information'.

[30] SSB, xvii, 588ff. Interestingly, Maine also wore his mantle for his return visit to the duke of Vendôme, grandson of Henri IV's bastard (SSB, xvii, 591–2). The latter did not normally enjoy the same rank as first-generation Legitimated Princes; was Maine preparing the ground for his own progeny?

[31] SSB, xvii, 588 (my emphasis). The bereaved generally wore the garment in receiving visits, including those that they did not reciprocate.

[32] SSB, xvii, 589.

the latter stronger proof of equality than did the indirect sharing of honours received from third parties.

These third parties—the rest of the aristocracy—could not expect to receive mantled visits in return. The titled nobility, and the dukes in particular, refused to pay this irreciprocal honour without an order from the king. This illuminates another subtle and somewhat paradoxical feature of status negotiation and of pre-cedent- and decision-making. If the monarch was seen to use his authority, this very fact would detract from the cause he supported, because it would imply that the outcome was not self-evident. The king's reaction, moreover, underscores that the arbiter of ranks was reluctant to use arbitrary power. Literally, he may have avoided an imperative in his conversation with Beauvillier; the pragmatics of his speech-act, though, qualified its semantics.[33] His own Master of Ceremonies called the bluff by exposing the shaky premises of the royal argument. Interestingly again, as with Armagnac, Louis chose to convey the difficult decision through a house-hold officer who owed him personal allegiance.

But the king had spoken, and the titled nobility gave ground at last: the men went mantled the same day, the women on the morrow. Even then, though, they expressed their resentment through transgressions and discourtesies in related codes. In a celebrated passage, Saint-Simon described the ridiculous 'masquerade' of dress and gestures, highly inappropriate for the solemn mourning occasion.[34] Maine admitted that some visitors made him walk all the way to the entrance to his apartment as he saw them off, without 'the slightest courtesy'.[35] Like the insist-ence on an express order, questionable execution set a price for obedience and prepared the ground for future appeal. Eager to take possession of the honour, however, the hosts stomached the insults and piled up mantles at their door to forestall excuses.[36]

Among other parties that stood to lose from developments, the Children and Grandchildren of France do not seem to have registered any active protest at the continued erosion of their once-exclusive honours. The Children could at least still assert their superior status on this occasion by not reciprocating: they visited the bereaved junior Bourbons 'without mantles'. The Grandchildren, by contrast, appear to have avoided the ceremonial scene altogether.[37] Initiative remained at the hands of the Princes of the Blood and of the Legitimated Princes, the most dynamic elements in the Royal House in the early eighteenth century.

---

[33] Saint-Simon and Maine differ on whether or not the king's words constituted an order: contrast Saint-Simon, *Hiérarchie et mutations*, ed. Coirault, p. 108; SSB, xvii, 260, 502 with SSB, xvii, 590. See also Arsenal, MS 3863, pp. 385–6.

[34] SSB, xvii, 260–2, discussed, inter alia, in Brocher, *À la cour de Louis XIV*, pp. 129–31; Solnon, *La Cour de France*, pp. 366–7; Dirk Van der Cruysse, *La mort dans les Mémoires de Saint-Simon: Clio au Jardin de Thanatos* (Paris, 1981), pp. 285–9.

[35] SSB, xvii, 590. It was customary to dispense the host from this duty, itself a status interaction. Not to dispense was particularly cruel in the case of Maine, who suffered from a limp.

[36] SSB, xvii, 261–2. Bourbon later retaliated against the dukes: SSB, xvii, 265; BM, MS 2745, fo. 143; Arsenal, MS 3863, p. 386. The expedient of piling mantles in the antechambre is recorded still in 1720, at the death of the princess of Condé: Dangeau, xviii, 259.

[37] SSB, xvii, 501, 588–9, 594–5; cf. SSB, xvii, 145, n. 7; SSB, xv, 239.

A year later, the sudden death of the duke of Bourbon precipitated a repeat round. Maine then impressed on the widow the need that her orphaned son receive the complimentary visits 'en manteau', in order to 'maintain the possession of the ceremonial' observed at the death of Henri-Jules.[38] The son received mantled visits a few days after the death, and the widow at the end of the first period of mourning. The official register of Desgranges specifically includes 'the dukes and Foreign Princes and the other people of quality' among these visitors. Although one or two accounts suggest repeated transgressions and discourtesies, none report anything resembling the crisis situation of the previous, precedent-making year.[39]

Ironically, Maine himself received mantle-less visits on this occasion. To blame was the dowager princess of Conti, another legitimated child of Louis XIV and hence sister-in-law of the deceased. Some family members, Maine explains, had already begun to receive visits informally, and the princess thought that there was no need to recommence them in form.[40] Register Nine of Desgranges, however, had recorded the facts but not the circumstances, having simply noted that the visitors of Maine and of Toulouse went 'not in mantle [*non en manteau*]'. The year before, the same register had failed to mention Maine among those receiving mantled visits.[41] Was this partial reporting a result of partiality?[42] Whatever the cause, the Legitimated Princes would subsequently have to deal with the consequences.

THE FINAL SCENARIO: MANOEUVRES AT MARLY

What happened when the king was among the bereaved? In these cases, the range and the number of visitors would augment considerably. As the barrister Barbier noted in 1752, 'all the Princes of the Blood, the ambassadors, and all the *seigneurs* and other court people or those who want to appear as such' would present themselves in *grand manteau* to pay their compliments. The king would hardly notice most of them, but they could put on 'court airs in the *grande galerie* in this gear'

---

[38] Maine composed a detailed account on this occasion too: 'Trois mémoires du duc du Maine', ed. A. de Boislisle, *Annuaire-Bulletin de la Société de l'Histoire de France* (1895), p. 223.

[39] BM, MS 2745, fos. 176–178, 187–189; SSB, xix, 88–9; Dangeau, xiii, 134. Sourches notes a 'multitude' of courtiers in the first round of visits, and makes a cryptic comment on how the widow closed her doors early on in the second: xii, 167–8, 191.

[40] 'Trois mémoires du duc du Maine', ed. Boislisle, p. 224. On the other hand, Maine noted, the orphan visited him and his brother Toulouse. See also BM, MS 2745, fos. 188–189. Unlike the previous year, Toulouse was close kin, as brother-in-law of the deceased. Among the other exchanges within the Royal House, the Orléans, Grandchildren of France and also close kin, do appear on the scene this time as receiving visits from the other bereaved (BM, MS 2745, fos. 177–178); it is not clear if they paid visits, and if so, in what dress. Finally, the dowager duchess of Orléans, Daughter of France, raised objections about the visits to the widow. BM, MS 2745, fo. 188; *Lettres de Madame de Maintenon* (7 vols, Paris, 2009–), iv, 790; *Lettres du maréchal de Tessé au prince Antoine Ier de Monaco*, ed. André Le Glay (Monaco-Paris, 1917), p. 73.

[41] BM, MS 2745, fos. 140v, 178. Dangeau, xii, 382, corroborates Maine's claim that he had received mantled visits in 1709.

[42] In the same account, Desgranges again criticized the king's judgement and made a striking sneer at illegitimacy: BM, MS 2745, fo. 188.

and be seen by the ministers.[43] For social climbers, death at the top was a moment of opportunity. Not all could count on it, though, as the sumptuary restrictions on the garment were sometimes enforced on these occasions.[44] To appear mantled at centre stage would thus be a marker of social success as well as a chance to meet the high and the influential.

At the death of the *Grand Dauphin* from smallpox in 1711, the multitude invaded the country resort of Marly. Normally out of bounds even for the average courtier, the small royal residence was not built for mass reverences. All the accounts note the great crowds on this occasion.[45] One can imagine that the rare opportunity to penetrate the inner sanctum augmented the ranks of the curious even more than was usual in such extraordinary circumstances. A good number of those who came, Desgranges noted, should not have been there.[46] For Saint-Simon, it offered another occasion to denounce the 'prostitution' of *mantes* and *manteaux*:

> there were quite a few people [whom nobody at court knew]. *Robe* people also min-gled with the crowd, which seemed very peculiar too. The variety of faces and the jumbled apparel of many persons ill-fitted to wear it could hardly fail to supply some object of ridicule, of the sort that can undo the most concerted gravity. It happened on this occasion, where the king sometimes could barely control himself, and even succumbed once, with all those attending, [to laughter] at the passage of some bump-kin half out of his gear.[47]

Powerless to prevent parvenus from usurping sartorial distinctions, aristocratic participants—and, subsequently, narrators—could instead engage in the symbolic violence of snobbery. Posture and reputation were harder to acquire than garments, and hence more effective as social barriers. Clothes alone did not always make the man—or, at least, the 'man of quality'.

For Saint-Simon and for other regulars of the court, the reverences of 1711 brought inside challenges too. While all saw the reverences to the monarch as an honourable duty, other interactions did not cease to create problems, within the Royal House and in relation to the rest of the aristocracy. With such an exalted cadaver, one might have expected all close kin to be of unquestionable rank, and, accordingly, the contentious rights of the junior Bourbons to remain out of the question. Two factors complicated the picture, however. First, *Madame la Princesse* (Henri-Jules's widow) claimed the right to mantled visits based on a precedent from the queen's obsequies in 1683.[48] Having established their right on the deaths of individual courtiers and on the deaths of their own close kin, the Princes of the

---

[43] Barbier, *Chronique de la régence et du règne de Louis XV* (8 vols, Paris, 1857), v, 170–1.
[44] e.g. *Mémoires du duc de Luynes*, vii, 369–70.
[45] Vol. xxi of the Boislisle edition of Saint-Simon conveniently assembles several key accounts, by Breteuil, Desgranges, and Maine (pp. 412–31), besides the memoirs themselves (esp. pp. 120–7) and the earlier *addition* to Dangeau's journal (p. 400). See also Sourches, xiii, 96.
[46] SSB, xxi, 422.
[47] SSB, xxi, 124–5.
[48] SSB, xxi, 429. The Condé ceremonial register indeed recorded such a precedent: AC, MS 1217, p. 79. But cf. p. 280.

Blood now extended their claim to a third scenario, that of mass reverences paid to a bereaved king.

The second factor concerned the implications of the extra-marital adventures of the king and of his subsequent endogamous marriage policy on the definition of close kin. If we add 'natural' bonds to the equation, then the *Grand Dauphin* left three half-sisters who married into the legitimate line and two half-brothers: a Granddaughter of France, two widowed Princesses of the Blood, and two Legitimated Princes.[49] At a time when the Legitimated stock was on the rise, recognition that their birth entitled them to share honours with the very top of the dynasty would prove significant.[50] Their marriage ties lower down the legitimate hierarchy created further ambiguity, which, combined with the fear of smallpox and with the logistics of the small residence, could be fruitfully exploited in the interest of junior members of the dynasty.

When Maine arrived in Marly on the eve of the reverences, he discovered that the issue of mantled visits had not yet been resolved and accordingly 'put the wheels in motion'. The next day, natural half-siblings were included in the host list, together with the senior Bourbons. As in 1709, the king evaded a clear-cut order but signalled his support for his close family through the channel of a titled office-holder. Saint-Simon blames Maine's machinations and the ineptitude of the duke of Tresmes, in charge that year as First Gentleman of the Bedchamber. The latter tried, at least, to undercut the general pretension of the Princes of the Blood by arguing that the duty to visit on this occasion stemmed from the specific degree of consanguinity rather than from the rank of the hosts.[51] Given the multivalence of identity, the same event could have very different consequences depending on its framing. Ambiguity nonetheless remained, reinforced, moreover, by the absence from Marly of most junior members who were not close kin. Fear of contagion was the official cause of absence, but the practical consequence was that virtually all Bourbons on the spot would receive mantled visits in one form or another.

The identity of the hosts settled, they now deliberated the question of reciprocity among themselves. Here, thanks to Maine's diligent recording, the stakes of the Grandchildren of France at last surface. When he inquired with his sister, the duchess of Orléans, whether she would like her siblings to visit her 'en cérémonie', she replied negatively, explaining that kin of the same degree were exempt from this duty and that the obligation of repaying the visit would be a 'grand embarras' to her and to her husband.[52] Maine did not insist this time, as opposed to his conduct with the Princes of the Blood two years earlier. Although the exemption applied to close kin only, *Madame la Princesse* unilaterally decided to extend it to herself: she had nowhere to receive return visits in Marly, and could not afford irreciprocity with

[49] The duchess of Orléans (the younger, not *Madame*), the duchess of Bourbon, the princess of Conti (the elder dowager), the duke of Maine, and the count of Toulouse. See Appendix I.
[50] A few weeks later, the crown would issue two pieces of legislation advancing their formal status: see the Conclusion, p. 167.
[51] cf. SSB, xxi, 120–2, 400, and 427–8. Desgranges again singles out Maine and Toulouse, here as questionable hosts: SSB, xxi, 422.
[52] SSB, xxi, 428.

the Orléans 'without great consequences'.[53] Maine implies that his mediation in this matter only just managed to put off an incident.

Madame la Princesse also turned the logistics to her advantage vis-à-vis her inferiors. She cunningly installed herself in a separate room of the Marly apartment of her daughter, the duchess of Bourbon, in a way that all mantled visitors had to pass by as they were doing the rounds. Saint-Simon claims that many failed to notice her, and that many more pretended not to have noticed. The implication, however, is that some did pay their respects in passing.[54] This probably involved again collusion between transgressors; the less informed among the illicit visitors must have been happy to bow before anyone with a Bourbon aura. The lack of independent lodgings in Marly, normally a disadvantage, enabled the senior Princess of the Blood to receive mantled visits without receiving express permission.

This was the stuff that precedents were made of. A year later, following the premature double death of dauphin and dauphine, a mantle-clad titled nobility shuffled 'like sheep' through the Versailles apartments of the Princes of the Blood as well as those of the Legitimated Princes.[55] There is no indication of argument or resistance. Perhaps the titled nobility was disheartened by its successive failures, or hesitant to approach the king at such a difficult moment. Champions of ducal rank like Chevreuse and Saint-Simon were devastated by the sudden disappearance of their great hope, the young dauphin. The fruitfully ambiguous precedent of 1711, in the makeshift circumstances of Marly, had thus prepared the ground for the clear-cut example of 1712, where all members of the Royal House received visits in their proper apartments, regardless of rank or of degree of consanguinity.

* * *

Precedent by precedent, combining cunning tricks with formal demands, the junior Bourbons established their right to mantled visits in all scenarios. A distinction between them and the senior members was abolished; and their inferiors, dukes and princes included, had to perform subordination in public, in person, and in garment. For other mantle-wearers lower down the social scale, the advantages of the prestigious garment itself offset the drawbacks of interactional subordination. Among the junior Bourbons, finally, the Legitimated Princes used their position of influence to promote shared honours for all, while at the same time establishing their particular claim to equality—in the period leading up to their inclusion in the line of succession.

This dramatic decision to raise the bastards to the full rank and title of Princes of the Blood turned decades of accumulated precedents, in mantles and in other codes, into positive *de jure* legislation. Conversely, the *lit de justice* of 1718 formally deprived Maine of all Bourbon honours, irrespective of earlier *de facto* possessions. The patents of April 1723, by contrast, revived the logic of custom

---

[53] SSB, xxi, 429.
[54] SSB, xxi, 125–6; cf. Dangeau, xiii, 390. Among the Grandchildren of France, the grand-duchess of Tuscany went to the apartment of the duchess of Orléans. As noted at the beginning, logistics may similarly have aided the earlier extension of mantled visits from Children to Grandchildren of France.
[55] SSB, xxii, 348. See also Dangeau, xiv, 106–7; BM, MS 2746, fo. 118. Breteuil, *Mémoires*, ed. Lever, p. 311, notes a great disorder on this occasion.

and precedent: they restored all court honours enjoyed 'before 1710'.[56] Denied the honours en masse of the late legislation of Louis XIV, Maine would need to prove *de facto* possession of each honour separately in order to rehabilitate his position. The significance of the mantled visits earlier in the century would now resurface.

As the keeper of the official ceremonial record, Desgranges was instructed to consult his registers in order to determine the precise implications of the new patents. In early May 1723, he sent Maine a copy of a memorandum that he was about to deliver to court, summarizing honours enjoyed by the Legitimated Princes up to 1710.[57] It ended by citing Register Nine, which claimed, as we have seen, that Maine and Toulouse had been visited 'non en manteau' during Bourbon's obsequies in 1710, in contrast with the treatment of the orphaned Prince of the Blood. The official ceremonial record thus undermined the claim for *de facto* equality at a critical juncture for the Legitimated Princes.

Maine scribbled 'I don't believe *this* to be true' in the margin of the memorandum, and sent one of his men to sort out the problem with Desgranges. The latter produced his records and wrote an explanatory letter to Maine, where he referred also to his accounts of 1709 and 1711, again unfavourable to the bastards. The visits of 1709, the Master asserted, concerned the Princes of the Blood only; 'I do not doubt, however', he added, 'that all those who were attached to you, *Monseigneur*, gave you marks of their respect on this occasion'. The Master of Ceremonies thus insinuated the usurpation tactics outlined by Saint-Simon.[58]

The resolution of this conflict of versions appears in a signed statement by Desgranges, dated 12 May 1723, and pasted on top of his original account in Register Nine.[59] 'What I have marked here "without mantle" is true', stated the Master of Ceremonies, 'but it calls for clarification'. Since writing the original version, he explained, he has seen Maine's accounts of 1709 and of 1710, 'which are very rigorous and in great detail'. He then recounted Maine's explanation for the event in question, namely the dispensation from mantled visits at the request of the princess of Conti.[60] Finally, Desgranges noted the difference between this turnout and what happened in 1709 and in 1711, 'where the same persons who had seen the Princes of the Blood in mantles saw the Legitimated Princes too in the same form'. He thus in effect also corrected his factual account of the obsequies of Henri-Jules.

Desgranges's prejudice against the royal bastards may have affected—consciously or unconsciously—the penning of the original version. Faced, however, with the 'rigorous and detailed' accounts of Maine, the Master of Ceremonies had to 'clarify' this version in the official register. During the final years of Louis XIV's reign, the question of mantled visits had formed part of the Legitimated Prince's drive for status and power. In the following reign, his diligence in keeping record of these precedents proved vital, when, once again, every distinction counted.

---

[56] AN, O¹ 67, pp. 255–6.
[57] AN, K 577, nos. 104–5 (memorandum and letter of Desgranges to Maine).
[58] AN, K 577, no. 106; on usurpation, see the first section.
[59] Desgranges's original Register Nine is now BM, MS 2745. The statement is pasted on fo. 178.
[60] See earlier, p. 105.

5

The Duality of Service: Between Honour and Humiliation, between Primary and Secondary Functions

In a key passage of his classic work on court society, Norbert Elias illustrated the 'symbolic function' of etiquette at the French court through a detailed description of the *lever*, the public rising of the king at his bedchamber each morning. This daily routine culminated in the moment when a courtier would hand the king his chemise. In this social context, Elias argued, a 'necessary procedure' was 'invested with a different meaning'. Each act had an 'exactly graded prestige-value that was imparted to those involved'. The Grand Chamberlain had the prerogative to hand the chemise, a prerogative that he would cede to a prince and to no one else. It became a 'prestige fetish', an indicator of the position of an individual within the balance of power, 'a balance controlled by the king and extremely unstable'. After Louis XIV, in contrast, etiquette and ceremony became 'a ghostly *perpetuum mobile* that continued to operate regardless of any direct use-value'. This is demonstrated through an example of the *lever* of Marie-Antoinette, where the chemise kept changing hands as higher-ranking participants entered the bedchamber while the queen had to stand it out in a state of nature. 'Surely', Elias concluded, 'Louis XIV would never have tolerated such overriding of the main purpose by etiquette'.[1]

Elias insisted in this context on the importance of a 'step by step' description, just as one would describe a work-process at a modern factory or 'the royal ritual of a simple tribe'.[2] This worthy and inspiring ethnographic agenda, however, has hardly been realized—there or since. Elias drew the above examples from secondary sources, misquoting or mistranslating them in the process, and thus exacerbated what were anyway partial or inaccurate renderings of primary accounts readily accessible in printed editions.[3] In the final analysis, moreover, he was not really interested in the tribesmen or in the details of their ritual. Ironically, the pioneer who argued so convincingly for the significance of etiquette could not

---

[1] 'eine solche Überwältigung des Hauptzweckes durch die Etikette': *Gesammelte Schriften*, ii, 149. The English translation transformed the meaning into 'such subordination of the main purpose *of* etiquette' (my emphasis): *The Collected Works of Norbert Elias*, ii, 95. For the other quotes, see *Gesammelte Schriften*, ii, 146–7; *The Collected Works of Norbert Elias*, ii, 93–4.

[2] *Gesammelte Schriften*, ii, 142; *The Collected Works of Norbert Elias*, ii, 91.

[3] For details, see Sternberg, 'The Culture of Orders', pp. 112–14. On Elias and on his questionable methodology in general, see the Introduction, pp. 4–5.

bring himself to consider it as a 'main purpose'. For him, the prestige-function remained secondary to other functions, and the courtiers' perspective—to the monarch's. When the 'secondary' took over—allegedly in the post-Louis XIV era—it signalled the impending collapse of the entire system.

This chapter revisits the question by re-contextualizing the handing of the chemise thematically, socially, chronologically, and functionally. This key gesture occurred in a variety of settings and belonged to a wider category of 'honourable service' in pre-modern Europe, notably including also the closely analogous handing of the serviette at table. In non-royal settings, these fetishes of apparent prestige could in fact become a source of humiliation. Furthermore, if one actually takes pains to reconstruct the gesture 'step by step', it turns out that the regular trajectory of the chemise in Louis XIV's bedchamber was not significantly shorter than the one depicted in the Marie-Antoinette anecdote. Secondary service and extra-royal agendas were thus already subverting the so-called 'main purpose' in the heyday of the Sun King's system. Finally, the social trajectory of the Legitimated Princes provides a novel link between the prestige-function of honourable service and the macro-political 'power-function'.

HONOURABLE SERVICE AND THE DAILY ROUTINES OF CHEMISE AND SERVIETTE

Often viewed as peculiar to the solar system of Louis XIV's Versailles, the ceremonial handing of the chemise appears less singular once examined in its broader context in time, in place, and in repertoire. Honourable service by noblemen dates back to medieval traditions, if not earlier. The specific routines of chemise and serviette were already current by the reign of Francis I in the early sixteenth century, codified by Henri III later in that century, and continued under their Bourbon successors.[4] The Sun King's court may have been extreme in the degree, and in the combination, of publicity, corporeality, and rank. Few monarchs dressed and undressed in the presence of so many people, or enjoyed the daily assiduity of such high-ranking servers in the process. But one need only relax these parameters slightly to find many more parallels, across early modern Europe, of personal domestic service as status interaction.

At table, for example, even the Habsburgs—often considered the ceremonial negative of the Bourbons—received the serviette in public from the hands of aristocrats and princes. Bedchambers closed to outsiders nonetheless saw graded scales of service, where higher-ranking attendants competed over the handling of garments. Furthermore, since the Sun King's court set an example, by the eighteenth

---

[4] Gerd Althoff and Christiane Witthöft, 'Les services symboliques entre dignité et contrainte', *Annales HSS*, lviii (2003), 1293–318; Chatenet, *La cour de France*, ch. 4; R.J. Knecht, *Renaissance Warrior and Patron: The Reign of Francis I* (Cambridge, 1996), pp. 128, 545; David Potter and P.R. Roberts, 'An Englishman's View of the Court of Henri III, 1584–1585: "Richard Cook's Description of the Court of France"', *French History*, ii (1988), 323, 334, 339, 340; Duindam, *Vienna and Versailles*, pp. 203–5.

century its particular ceremonial idiom was imitated elsewhere in Europe.[5] The codes of honourable service also extended to the international arena, to the relations among sovereigns and states. Francis I famously handed Henry VIII the chemise during the Field of Cloth of Gold. Visiting sovereigns or crown princes gave—or chose not to give—the chemise at the royal bedchamber. In 1717, the audience at the Paris opera observed as the regent Orléans passed a glass and a serviette to Peter the Great.[6]

Honourable service involved a wide range of occasions and objects: from the ceremonial duties of German Electors at Imperial coronations, through the offering of candles at religious services, to the daily routines of table and bedchamber. In all their diversity, these acts nevertheless followed a similar logic. Contemporaries explicitly drew analogies among them, in function and in terminology. In 1636, the rank of those who were to serve *Mademoiselle* during her baptism was inferred from the routines of the chemise in her bedchamber.[7] In this context, liturgical candles and everyday handkerchiefs belonged to the same category of objects, called 'honneurs' and handed by aristocrats to yet higher-ranking aristocrats.[8]

The two paradigmatic 'services honorables' in French court society were the daily routines of chemise and serviette.[9] The analysis of their code continues our journey across the ceremonial spectrum: having so far focused on high ceremonies and on protocolar social occasions, we now move to the status interactions of everyday life at court. Such a move entails two significant shifts: in the household officers in charge and in the documentation available. First, domestic space and daily activities lay outside the official scope of the Grand Masters and Masters of Ceremonies. Instead, the persons involved were heavyweight protagonists in their own right—often of ducal or of princely rank. In fact, some of the household posts in question conferred court rank by definition, as Grand Offices of the Crown.[10]

The corresponding shift in documentation introduces a methodological challenge, one that generally faces the ethnography of everyday practices in past societies. The surviving manuscript papers of the officials in charge do not follow the routines of the bedchamber or of the table to the same extent that Desgranges or Sainctot account for high ceremony. This is hardly surprising: why—indeed, how—would they make a detailed record of activities that recurred on a daily basis? Those most versed in the intricacies of the code would normally have no reason to describe or to explain it in real time. The few comprehensive accounts at our disposal are retrospective, normative, or written by outsiders—

[5] Coniez, *Le Cérémonial de la Cour d'Espagne*, pp. 64, 104, 190; Samuel John Klingensmith, *The Utility of Splendor: Ceremony, Social Life, and Architecture at the Court of Bavaria, 1600–1800* (Chicago, 1993), pp. 156–7, 162; Mansel, *Dressed to Rule*, p. 3 n. 21.

[6] Knecht, *Renaissance Warrior and Patron*, p. 175; AC, MS 1194, fo. 382; Dangeau, iv, 227; xvii, 81, 86–7; SSB, xxxi, 373–4.

[7] Godefroy, *Le Ceremonial François*, i, 206.

[8] In the marriage of 1679, for example, the bride's sister, Mademoiselle de Valois, and the duke of Crussol handed the *honneurs* during the offertory to the bride and to Conti, respectively: *Gazette* (1679), pp. 446–7. For a list of everyday *honneurs*, see SSB, xi, 404–5; see also Cosandey, 'Les préséances à la cour des reines de France', p. 272.

[9] AN, K 577, no. 72, fo. 1v.   [10] See the Introduction, pp. 14, 19–20.

and hence insufficient for the reconstruction of the actual practices and perceptions of contemporaries. On the other hand, the rare occasions when the chemise or its counterparts do crop up in the better-informed inside sources call for special attention. However laconic or seemingly incidental, these mentions often indicate moments of contention or of change, revealing the high stakes latent in everyday routines.[11]

The handing of the chemise took place in the monarch's bedchamber every morning and every evening, as part of the multi-step ceremonial routines of *lever* and *coucher*.[12] The staff of the Bedchamber and of the Wardrobe would dress the king up (or down), while a multitude of relatives, household members, courtiers, visitors, and foreigners watched by according to a graded right of entry (*entrées*). The moment when dayshirt replaced nightshirt, or vice versa, was arguably the highlight of the event.[13] The senior officer present, usually either the Grand Chamberlain or the First Gentleman of the Bedchamber, had the honour of giving the king the new chemise.[14] However, if Bourbon princes were present, the highest-ranking among them would 'oust' the officer (*ôter le service*). Officer or prince, the privileged server of the day enjoyed a moment of intimacy with the naked body of the sovereign, screened from the rest of the attendance by two valets holding up the royal dressing gown.[15]

The serviette routine operated according to the same principles. The paradigmatic scenario involved the serviette given at table (half-moist, half-dry, so that the king could use the same object for washing and wiping his hands). He also used a serviette to wipe his mouth on other occasions, for example at the light breakfast served during the *lever* or when he was taking his medicine.[16] As in the case of the chemise, the senior officer in charge would hand the serviette by default. In the Bedchamber, this would be the same person who would hand the chemise. When the king ate *en grand couvert*, the Grand Master of the Household or the *maîtres d'hôtel* would perform the task. And again, if Bourbon princes were

---

[11] Among our inside reporters, Dangeau held a special patent that granted him privileged entry to the king's bedchamber, enabling him to follow domestic routines closely: Mathieu Da Vinha, *Les valets de chambre de Louis XIV* (Paris, 2004), pp. 47–8; SSB, iii, 185 n. 1. He was also a senior member of the household of both dauphines. Saint-Simon's wife was Lady of Honour of the duchess of Berry.

[12] Recent general discussions of these routines include Da Vinha, *Les valets de chambre*, pp. 45–58; David M. Gallo, 'Royal Bodies, Royal Bedrooms: The *Lever du Roy* and Louis XIV's Versailles', *Cahiers du dix-septième*, xii (2008), 99–118; Leferme-Falguières, *Les courtisans*, pp. 232–9, 252–3. Two famous accounts are Ézéchiel Spanheim, *Relation de la cour de France en 1690*, ed. Émile Bourgeois (Paris-Lyon 1900), pp. 277–82, and SSB, xxviii, 335–41, 361–4. Since 1687, the periodical publication *L'État de la France* included a detailed section describing the daily routines of the king.

[13] The objects in question were long undergarments worn by both genders: see Madeleine Delpierre, *Se vêtir au XVIIIᵉ siècle* (Paris, 1996), pp. 48–9. I generally use 'chemise' to avoid confusion with other meanings of 'shirt'.

[14] On the members and hierarchy of Bedchamber and Wardrobe, see Da Vinha, *Les valets de chambre*, esp. pp. 44–65; Georges Lizerand, *Le duc de Beauvillier, 1648–1714* (Paris, 1933), ch. 3; Leferme-Falguières, 'Le monde des courtisans', ch. 6; William Ritchey Newton, *La petite cour: services et serviteurs à la Cour de Versailles au XVIIIᵉ siècle* (Paris, 2006), pp. 53–104.

[15] The act of honourable service may have included putting the garment on the sovereign body: *Briefe der Herzogin Elisabeth Charlotte von Orléans*, ed. Holland, [v], 68–9; Dangeau, i, 75–6.

[16] AN, K 577, no. 72, fo. 1v.

in attendance, the highest-ranking among them would oust the non-Bourbon household staff.[17]

How often did aristocrats perform these tasks in practice? It is difficult to tell in the absence of serial coverage of court routines. One assumes that attendance varied within as well as between reigns. According to Sainctot, when Louis XIV was 'very young', senior officers and princes often neglected to show up at the Bedchamber. After the king's majority in 1651, Gaston reportedly exploited the routine strategically: though boycotting the royal council, the Son of France nevertheless 'used to go often to the *lever* of His Majesty in order to give him his chemise, and show [Gaston's] attachment to his person'. In all likelihood, the greater assiduity of princes and courtiers during much of the personal reign led to higher levels of senior attendance. According to Saint-Simon, *Monsieur* handed the lunch serviette to his brother 'very often'. Referring in retrospect to the occasions when she gave the chemise to the queen, *Madame* noted, in her typically refined manner, that 'I have seen her naked a hundred times'.[18]

BETWEEN HONOUR AND HUMILIATION

How honourable were the 'services honorables'? From our perspective, it may seem inconceivable that such menial tasks could be considered respectable, let alone desirable. In the eyes of the *Grand Condé*, however, giving the chemise or the serviette to the monarch in lieu of the household staff was the functional equivalent of receiving a military guard of honour.[19] Within the household, the honour of serving generated numerous jurisdictional disputes. In principle, the Grand Chamberlain's ceremonial primacy over the First Gentleman of the Bedchamber was unproblematic. But what happened if the former entered the room after the latter had already started to perform his duties? And did this primacy extend to the dauphin's service too?[20] The fact that Grand Chamberlains invariably came of princely stock, while First Gentlemen of the Bedchamber were usually dukes or dukes-to-be naturally did not help.

An analogous tension disrupted the smooth running of the queen's household. In 1661, it erupted into open conflict when the duchess of Navailles, Lady of Honour, refused to accept the primacy of the newly appointed Superintendent, the countess of Soissons. After examining the arguments and supporting documents presented by both sides, the king awarded Soissons the main advantages, including

---

[17] See *L'État de la France* and the compilation of household regulations in AN, O¹ 756, pp. 19, 34–5, 52–3, 95–6. See also AN, O¹ 822, pp. 9, 14; Da Vinha, *Les valets de chambre*, p. 57. Under the Bourbons, the *grand maître* was almost invariably a member of the dynasty himself; whether or not higher-ranking members present would oust him was controversial: Godefroy, *Le Ceremonial François*, ii, 177. On table routines in general, see Duindam, *Vienna and Versailles*, pp. 170–9.

[18] AC, MS 1194, fo. 382; *Nouvelle collection des mémoires pour servir à l'histoire de France*, ed. Michaud and Poujoulat (32 vols, Paris, 1836–9), 3rd ser., v, 255; SSB, xxviii, 346; *Briefe der Herzogin Elisabeth Charlotte von Orléans*, ed. Holland, [v], 68.

[19] SHD/DAT, A¹ 3779, no. 447. See also AN, K 577, no. 72.

[20] AN, O¹ 822, pp. 6–7; BM, MS 2746, fo. 75v.

the chemise and the serviette.[21] Navailles reportedly considered quitting her post as a result. When the queen asked her to stay, the duchess requested to be dispensed from performing her duties, claiming that she could not serve at table without giving the serviette.[22] The king then 'explained' his ruling, in effect modifying it in favour of Navailles. He decided, *inter alia*, that the Lady of Honour would hand the serviette when waiting at table, and that, once the chemise reached her hands, she would not have to cede it to the Superintendent.[23] The countess felt slighted, and her husband challenged the duke of Navailles to a duel; the latter declined, and the king exiled the count from court.[24]

When present, titled nobles who did not serve permanently also sought to perform the 'services honorables'. This naturally gave rise to rivalry among potential ousters.[25] When more than one server was called for, the dynamics of co-service operated in a manner similar to the dynamics of co-bearing; mantle-bearing, after all, was a form of service.[26] Such cases again underscore the complexity and multilayered nature of the quest for prestige. When a visiting duchess handed the chemise to a senior Bourbon princess, the significance of the act lay not only in that direct, subordinating interaction, but also in its implications on other status relationships: on the non-present junior Bourbons whose honour, as ouster, the duchess shared, and on the untitled yet senior officer whose honour she ousted.[27]

Indeed, the titled nobility, to Saint-Simon's chagrin, faced more resistance from the regular household staff than Bourbon ousters did. He cites a particularly interesting case—instructive about the subtle dynamics of status interaction in general—from the bedchamber of *Monsieur*'s daughter-in-law, the duchess of Chartres. Madame de Rochefort, Lady of Honour, refused to cede the service to the visiting duchess of Chevreuse. Although technically untitled, Rochefort believed that her rank as *maréchale* protected her from titled ousters. On a subsequent occasion, the chemise was handed to Chevreuse in Rochefort's absence. This time, though, Chevreuse declined the honour on the pretext that she could not take off her gloves. Paradoxically, in order to defend the claim to hand the chemise in the *maréchale*'s presence, the duchess had to avoid the chemise in the *maréchale*'s absence.[28]

---

[21] BN, Clairmbault 814, pp. 675–6.   [22] *Mémoires de Mme de Motteville*, ed. Riaux, iv, 266.

[23] *Mémoires de Mme de Motteville*, ed. Riaux, iv, 266; BN, Clairmbault 814, pp. 677–8.

[24] *Mémoriaux du Conseil de 1661*, ed. J. de Boislisle (3 vols, Paris, 1905–7), i, 296–8; *Archives de la Bastille: documents inédits*, ed. François Ravaisson (19 vols, Paris, 1866–1904), i, pp. 275ff. See also M-L. Fracard, *Philippe de Montaut-Benac, duc de Navailles, maréchal de France (1619–1684)* (Niort, 1970), pp. 61–76. Analogous jurisdiction disputes existed elsewhere on the social spectrum (Da Vinha, *Les valets de chambre*, p. 63; AN, O¹ 756, pp. 320–1), and well into the eighteenth century (Newton, *La petite cour*, pp. 253–6).

[25] See Sévigné's malicious account of the duchesses of Gesvres and of Arpajon in the bedchamber of the *Grande Mademoiselle* (*Correspondance*, ed. Duchêne, i, 204). For a sixteenth-century example, see Nicolas Le Roux, 'La cour dans l'espace du palais: l'exemple de Henri III', in Marie-France Auzépy and Joël Cornette (eds), *Palais et pouvoir: de Constantinople à Versailles* (Saint-Denis, 2003), p. 252.

[26] BM, MS 2739, fo. 54v; AN, KK 1448, fo. 109r. On bearing and co-bearing, see Chapter Three, esp. pp. 83–6.

[27] SSB, xi, 292–3; Saint-Simon, 'Estat des changements', pp. 198–9.

[28] Saint-Simon, 'Estat des changements', pp. 198–9. In yet another illustration of the polysemy of these interactions, *Monsieur* initially took offence when he thought that Chevreuse's avoidance was targeted at his daughter-in-law. On the latter type of avoidance, see later in this section.

Complexity and subtlety aside, the preceding examples seem to confirm Elias's notions of the chemise as a prestige fetish and, more generally, of a fundamental difference between early modern and modern conceptions of the relation between honour and subordination.[29] As a first qualifier to these notions, one should note that not all service was considered honourable. The status symbols of service were precisely that—symbolic. Ousters did not take on all duties of the bedchamber or of the table. On each occasion, they performed one or two hardly cumbersome tasks, elevated above many others.[30] The case of Navailles refusing to serve at table without handing the serviette illustrates the difference between regular service and honourable service.[31] Why did some aspects of domestic service become more honourable than others? Ease of performance and intimacy with the superior served seem plausible as general criteria, but ultimately the specifics are probably a child of circumstance.

Second, contemporaries themselves clearly perceived the acts of service as subordinating interactions. When the governor of the *Grand Dauphin*'s sons thought that the younger ones should give the chemise to the duke of Burgundy, eldest and presumptive heir after his father, the king decided otherwise, ruling 'that all these princes be treated equally'.[32] Service, like train-bearing, and unlike mantled visits, was irreciprocal by definition, and would not normally occur among status equals. That some recipients initially refused the honour and would accept it after 'repeated compliments' only also hints at the duality of service. This occurred especially in cases where subordination was not obvious, notably in international encounters.[33] Sainctot, finally, puts it bluntly again: giving the chemise 'is a lowly function in itself despite usage, one that properly belongs to a *valet de chambre* only, and perhaps the princes abase themselves when they make it some kind of honour to render this service to the king'.[34]

The menial, then, already seemed demeaning in the *Grand Siècle*. What the Bourbons themselves really felt about the service of their patriarch is moot, but when we move our focus from the royal apartment to other arenas, it turns out that

---

[29] See also Solnon, *La Cour de France*, pp. 408–14. On this duality in the medieval Holy Roman Empire, see Althoff and Witthöft, 'Les services symboliques entre dignité et contrainte'.

[30] Nor did they have to perform these tasks in all instances. The king used several serviettes at each meal and often changed his chemise informally during the day: AN, O¹ 822, p. 12; Sourches, i, 361; xi, 39; SSB, xxviii, 349, 357. Indeed, he used to change sweaty nightshirts in the morning, before the multitude entered the bedchamber for the *lever*: SSB, xxviii, 335–6; another indication of the private dimension of the royal body that allegedly exposed itself to permanent public representation.

[31] cf. the distinction between 'noble' and 'subaltern' tasks in Da Vinha, *Les valets de chambre*, p. 58.

[32] AN, KK 1424, fo. 299. The mirror gesture, often contrasted with the subordination of service, was to share the same serviette: *Mémoires de Mⁿᵉ de Montpensier*, ed. Chéruel, iii, 123; AC, MS 1131, fos. 8, 18–19; SSB, xix, 501.

[33] *Mémoires de Mᵐᵉ de Motteville*, ed. Riaux, iv, 61. In 1717, commentators were divided on whether the Czar received the regent's service (see earlier, p. 112) graciously enough. See also *Mercure François*, xi (1625), 361; SSB, xxviii, 347; and cf. the anecdote about the five-year-old Louis XV putting his hands behind his back and refusing to accept the serviette (and other signs of subordination) from the duke of Bourbon, Grand Master of the Household: Mathieu Marais, *Journal de Paris*, ed. Henri Duranton and Robert Granderoute (2 vols, Saint Etienne, 2004), i, 57.

[34] BM, MS 2738, fo. 111v; cf. p. 84 for his similar verdict on princely train-bearing.

some of them shared Sainctot's sentiments. For the monarch and his consort were not the only recipients of honourable service. Aristocrats regularly handed chemises, serviettes, and *honneurs* to other members of the Royal House (and beyond). This pluricentral regime of service existed since the early seventeenth century, if not before.[35] What is more, service—this time like mantled visits and unlike train-bearing—regularly pitted near-equals in direct status interaction. In particular, sub-royal Bourbons regularly expected the chemise or the serviette from other members of the dynasty. Among rivals and near-equals, such an irreciprocal sign of subordination was bound to generate tension and resistance, turning Elias's prestige fetish into a fetish of humiliation.[36]

The Children of France provide a first case in point. The *Grand Dauphin*'s sons, we have seen, grew up as status-equals despite the seniority of the duke of Burgundy as eldest. The death of their father on 14 April 1711 disrupted this equality, however: the duke of Burgundy and his wife became dauphin and dauphine, elevated in rank above the duke and the duchess of Berry. The widening status-gap between the two couples would manifest itself in a variety of codes, not least in the numbers of ells and bearers at the obsequies, several weeks later.[37] But the code of service called for an immediate, direct, and more dramatic demonstration of the transformation: the duke and the duchess of Berry were expected to enact their subordination by giving the chemise, respectively, to the new dauphin and to the new dauphine.

What do our sources tell us about this occasion (and conversely, what does this occasion tell us about our sources)? On 17 April, Dangeau noted that the duke of Berry will give the chemise to the new dauphin, and that the duchess of Berry will give the chemise and the *honneurs* to the new dauphine. In the next day's entry, he added that the duke of Berry wanted to give the chemise to his brother, but that the latter insisted that they wait until they have seen the king. On the morning of 19 April, he reported, the duchess gave the chemise to the dauphine, and the latter embraced her; 'two days earlier, they had had a long conversation on the matter, at the end of which they had been very pleased with one another'. Finally, both Dangeau and Sources briefly report the equivalent session in the dauphin's bedchamber, complete with chemise-giving and tender embraces.[38] On the face of it, this all seems rather unexciting. However, if we bear in mind the assumptions, constraints, and communicational strategies of the two texts, a few questions arise. Why did these two telegraphic writers consider the matter noteworthy?[39] Why did Dangeau

[35] Godefroy, *Le Ceremonial François*, ii, 206; *Mémoires de Daniel de Cosnac*, ed. Le comte Jules de Cosnac (2 vols, Paris, 1852), i, 158; ii, 206; Tallemant des Réaux, *Historiettes*, ed. Antoine Adam (2 vols, Paris, 1960–1), ii, 368.

[36] See Brocher, *À la cour de Louis XIV*, p. 41.

[37] Compare the services of 1701 and 1711 in Appendix III. For details, Sternberg, 'The Culture of Orders', p. 93.

[38] Dangeau, xiii, 385, 387, 388, 390; Sources, xiii, 97. According to Dangeau, the setting was the dauphin's *coucher* on 20 April; Sources reports it on 21 April, pointing out that this was 'pour la première fois'.

[39] So did Tessé: *Lettres du maréchal de Tessé*, ed. Le Glay, p. 119.

devote four separate consecutive entries to it? What happened at the long conversation between the two princesses, and why was its amicable end also noteworthy?[40]

For answers, we must turn to the more forthcoming Saint-Simon. Though generally less reliable, in this case the memoirist could draw on direct personal channels to both parties, especially through his wife's position as Lady of Honour to the duchess of Berry. Saint-Simon places the episode in the context of a rivalry between the two princesses, which had resulted in alienation between the two couples over the preceding year.[41] The princesses then agreed to turn over a new leaf in a long private conversation on 16 April. The duchess of Saint-Simon subsequently hinted that the Berrys should follow up the reconciliation with chemise-givings. This enraged the duchess of Berry. She claimed that such service was not due among brothers, called it 'valetage', and heaped abuse on her husband when he tried to persuade her to yield. The matter became public knowledge, and the ladies of the dauphine protested against the vilification of their service tasks. Berry's father, the duke of Orléans, joined forces with her husband, and they finally convinced her to yield rather than risk a direct order and reprimand from the king.[42]

In cases of contested subordination, then, service might be a dreaded valetage rather than a coveted honour. True to form, the Orléans-Condé rivalry supplies several such cases—with a variety of outcomes. Already in the early seventeenth century, the question arose with regard to the service of Gaston's daughter. Although the princess of Condé allowed her unmarried daughter to serve *Mademoiselle*, the princess of Conti denied the obligation. Louis XIII ruled that she indeed did not owe such 'deference'.[43] A couple of decades later, according to Saint-Simon, the *Grand Condé* took advantage of the Orléans's need for his alliance during the Fronde to extract from them the agreement to dispense with the service obligation. Micro-political status symbols thus became macro-political currency (and vice versa).[44]

The Condés' aversion to serve the Orléans, moreover, did not stop at the level of *Mademoiselle*. It extended to the head of the branch, although Son of France and brother to the sovereign. A first hint appears in an account of the prince of Condé's predicament at Gaston's apartment in 1644.[45] When already present on the spot, Condé could not refuse service to a Son of France without a direct affront. He could, however, have resorted to the avoidance tactic in the first place.

---

[40] Like the proverbial sailor who noted on his ship-log that 'the captain was not drunk today'. Dangeau may have been even more circumspect than usual here, given that he was *chevalier d'honneur* of the duchess of Burgundy.

[41] SSB, xxi, 79–84; 98–106.

[42] SSB, xxi, 106–10.

[43] Godefroy, *Le Ceremonial François*, ii, 206. This precedent was cited as evidence in the early eighteenth century: BN, Clairambault 515, pp. 699–700.

[44] SSB, xix, 501; *Grimoires de Saint-Simon*, ed. Coirault, p. 308. For analogous concessions in epistolary ceremonial 'du temps de la guerre', see AAE, MD, France 304, fo. 147v, and more generally the next chapter.

[45] 'On luy donna la chemise, qu'il [Condé] tint longtemps, et enfin il la donna à Monsieur et après s'en alla': *Journal d'Olivier Lefèvre d'Ormesson*, ed. Chéruel, i, 210. Just a few months later, the two branches openly quarrelled over the question of mantle trains: see Chapter Three, pp. 87–8.

The status interaction in question entirely depended on the presence of the subordinate party. Yet this presence was not called for on any specific occasion, all the more so since sub-royal bedchambers did not command the same level of attendance as the royal one did or as was customary in high ceremonies.[46] The Condés could therefore get away with avoidance almost imperceptibly and with relative impunity.

Condé's great-grandson, the duke of Bourbon, thus reportedly evaded the service of the following *Monsieur*, Philippe. But adding insult to injury, he also bragged about it. The furious *Monsieur* could have fallen back on his royal brother's authority in order to coerce Bourbon into subordination. This, however, would have detracted from his cause, by implying that his claim was not self-evident.[47] Instead, he awaited the right opportunity to exact retribution himself:

> One morning, as [*Monsieur*] was rising at Marly, where he used to lodge in one of the four apartments on the ground floor, he saw, through the [French] window, *Monsieur le Duc* [Bourbon] in the garden. He opens it quickly and calls to him. *Monsieur le Duc* comes up. *Monsieur* goes backwards, asks him where he is headed to, obliges him, [by] constantly going backwards, to enter and to advance in order to reply. As one remark was leading to another, [*Monsieur*] slips off his dressing-gown. At once, the First Valet of the Bedchamber presents the chemise to *Monsieur le Duc* at the beckoning of the First Gentleman of the Bedchamber of *Monsieur*, while the latter was undoing his own [the nightshirt]. *Monsieur le Duc*, caught thus in a trap, did not dare to make the slightest difficulty at giving it to *Monsieur*. As soon as *Monsieur* had received it, he laughed and said: 'Good-bye, my cousin; go along, I do not want to delay you longer'. *Monsieur le Duc* felt all the malice, and went away very angry. He became angrier still afterwards by the high tone that *Monsieur* kept up on the subject.[48]

To avoid, one did not have to do anything; by contrast, to break the avoidance tactic without resorting to overt force required ingenuity. When the opportunity arose, *Monsieur* used his interactional skills to lure his cousin into his apartment. Once on his home turf, he could call the bluff at last. Stripped of the avoidance defence, Bourbon had to react to the offer of the chemise—and gave, as expected. *Monsieur* received his *honneur*; Bourbon was left with the humiliation.[49]

---

[46] In 1706, the younger duchess of Orléans reportedly gave the chemise for the first time to the duchess of Burgundy—a decade after the latter's arrival at court: Dangeau, xi, 15.

[47] cf. the same logic of precedent-making in the case of mantled visits in the previous chapter.

[48] SSB, viii, 347–8; cf. the earlier version in SSB, viii, 400–1. As usual, one should treat the details of a Saint-Simon story with caution (while enjoying their literary quality). The crucial part for our purposes, at any rate, is his assumptions about the general positions of the two parties with regard to the honour—and humiliation—of service, and there is no reason to doubt his reliability on that score. Far from superfluous, the detail about the beckoning of the First Gentleman is in fact germane to the humiliation: see later, on secondary service.

[49] *Monsieur*'s granddaughter, the duchess of Berry, similarly entrapped Princesses of the Blood into giving her the chemise: SSB, xxi, 398; *Grimoires de Saint-Simon*, ed. Coirault, p. 309. Those who lacked the authority to coerce subordination might end up humiliated themselves: Tallemant, *Historiettes*, ii, 368.

NUPTIAL INVERSIONS: THE CHEMISE TURNED
UPSIDE DOWN?

On one special occasion the normal relations of subordination inherent in honourable service were suspended. During marriage ceremonies, we have seen, princesses replaced domestic servants in carrying the trains of princess brides. Thus, near-equals rather than marked inferiors performed this personal service, eliminating the regular social gap between wearers and bearers.[50] The solemn act of chemise-giving in the bedchamber on the night of the wedding took this spirit of social inversion to its logical conclusion. Instead of receiving the chemise from their inferiors, bride and groom were served at this special nuptial *coucher* by their superiors. In Bourbon marriages, the most high-ranking man at court—normally the king—handed the night-chemise to the groom, while the most high-ranking woman—queen, dauphine, or Daughter of France—served the bride.[51] As he gave the chemise to the duke of Berry in 1710, Louis XIV said to his newly-wed grandson that 'he was paying him back [*rendoit la pareille*], since he [Berry] had given it to him [the king] many times'.[52]

Sainctot characteristically disapproved: the custom of marital chemise-giving was 'ill-fitting [*peut seante*] for royal majesty'.[53] As in his censure of mantle-bearing by princesses on these occasions, the ceremonial bureaucrat seems to have missed the point. The power of the symbolic gesture derived precisely from the inversion of everyday norms. On their marriage, the bride and the groom were 'queen and king for a day'. The perpetuation of the social cycle, as it were, momentarily suspended social hierarchies. Sainctot could rest assured, though. As was the case in 'mardi gras' rituals in general, the temporary inversion of the social order did not fool anyone. Dangeau's terminology on these occasions leaves no doubt as to the real relations of subordination. The superior would 'do the honour' (*faire l'honneur*) of giving the chemise to the newly-wed, an expression never used to denote actions performed by a subordinate.[54]

Indeed, the nuptial giving of the chemise formed a visible act of patronage by superiors, similar in function to two other gestures more current in the historiography as measures of social networks: signature on the marriage contract or presence at the wedding. At the time, such marks of favour did not pass unnoticed. When Louis XIV gave the chemise to the count of Ayen at his marriage with a niece of Madame de Maintenon in 1698, 'this seemed very novel to most courtiers, who did not know that the king had done the same honour to the marquis of Roure'; the latter had married a companion of Mademoiselle de La Vallière, 'His

---

[50] See Chapters One and Three, esp. pp. 43, 83–5.

[51] In the years that followed the arrival of the exiled Stuarts in France, the Bourbons ceded the honour to them (when present), thus effecting a twofold inversion of status. See e.g. BM, MS 2743, fos. 19v, 28; SSB, iv, 314; and more generally Corp, *A Court in Exile*, ch. 6.

[52] Sourches, xii, 258.

[53] BM, MS 2738, fo. 111v.

[54] e.g. Dangeau, x, 275; xvii, 85. On this and on other aspects of the 'ceremonial of expression', see Chapter Six, pp. 144–7.

Majesty's mistress at the time'.[55] Service *by* the king, as a mark of favour, allowed more room for manoeuvre than the service *of* the king, which was largely governed by precedence.[56]

Just as he was not the only receiver on regular occasions, the king was not the only giver on nuptial ones. Other Bourbons gave the chemise to household members or to other persons they wished to honour. Despite the inversion of hierarchies and the relative room for manoeuvre, the rank of the giver does seem to have varied according to the rank of the receiver.[57] Furthermore, such ceremonies took place outside the court too. On the night of the Parisian wedding of the duke of Saint-Simon, the bride and the groom received their chemises from their respective 'in-laws'. The generational inversion of deference was thus complemented by the familial inversion that symbolically sealed the union.[58] In regency Paris, the duke of Orléans honoured marriages by making a late appearance and giving the chemise to the groom. He thus asserted his own position at the fountain of patronage as well as that of the receiver and of his family.[59]

Analogous inversions took place when princesses married God, so to speak. As Mademoiselle de Soubise received the habit in 1679, the superior of the convent—also a princess of the house of Rohan—passed the veil to the queen who handed it herself to the young novice. In what was doubtless meant to echo the other special nuptial act of service, Soubise's sister had carried the train of a 'large *mante* of silver gauze' that the novice had worn at the beginning of the ceremony, before receiving the religious habit.[60] Such cases are also part of a larger tradition of pious inversion of service acts, practised throughout Europe. In the Maundy ceremony (*coene/cène*), for example, princes washed the feet of the poor and served them at table. The entire Royal House participated in the French variant, expending more than a token effort.[61]

THE GREAT CHAIN OF SERVING: SECONDARY SERVICE AND PRIMARY FUNCTIONS

The nuptial presentation of the chemise to the duke of Berry in 1710 gave rise to a contestation between the duke of Bouillon, Grand Chamberlain (and Foreign Prince), and the duke of Beauvillier, First Gentleman of the king's Bedchamber

---

[55] Sourches, vi, 22, n. 1. See also BM, MS 2744, fo. 17v. On another occasion, the duchess of Burgundy gave the chemise to a graduate of Saint-Cyr, again to please Maintenon: SSB, xii, 424.

[56] cf. Duindam, *Vienna and Versailles*, pp. 212–16, and the non-nuptial inversion in *Mémoires de Mme de Motteville*, ed. Riaux, i, 126.

[57] When Bourbons married, the senior lady of the court was expected to give the chemise irrespective of her feelings towards the bride: SSB, xxiv, 41. For the variability on other occasions, see e.g. Dangeau, i, 142; xiii, 326; Sourches, vi, 48; x, 4, 12.

[58] *Mercure Galant*, April 1695, p. 237. See also SSB, xii, 436.

[59] Dangeau, xvi, 325; xvii, 85.

[60] *Mercure Galant*, November 1679, pp. 280, 352. For other examples, see *Mercure Galant*, January 1680, p. 221 (queen to Mademoiselle d'Elbeuf); *Mercure Galant*, June 1692, pp. 42–3 (duchess of Verneuil to Mademoiselle de Sully).

[61] Duindam, *Vienna and Versailles*, p. 139; Maral, *La chapelle royale de Versailles*, pp. 374–6.

and senior officer of the *Grand Dauphin*'s children. As we have seen, Louis XIV was to give the chemise to his grandson on that wedding night. Clearly, though, the king would not simply pick up the garment himself; someone had to give it to him. But who would it be? In the king's apartment, the Grand Chamberlain enjoyed precedence over the First Gentlemen of the Bedchamber. The bedchamber in question, however, was the groom's. There, Beauvillier could be regarded as the most senior officer in his other capacity, as Berry's governor. The king indeed decided to rule in his favour.[62]

This contestation touches on the important question of secondary service. Just as princesses had their own mantles born at the same time as they bore other trains, so did the *honneurs* pass from hand to hand before reaching their ultimate recipient. This 'chain of service' could easily involve multiple links. During the offertory at the marriage of 1679, for example, the liturgical candle changed hands no less than four times.[63] In the paradigmatic case of chemise-giving to the monarch or to his wife, a subaltern officer would hand the garment to the senior officer present: usually the First Gentleman of the Bedchamber at the king's *lever*, and the Lady of Honour in the queen's. The latter officer, in turn, would give the chemise to Their Majesties.

When Bourbon princes or princesses were present, secondary service varied according to the rank of the primary server. As *Madame* explained to her half-sister Louise:

> the First Woman of the Bedchamber gives the chemise to the Lady of Honour, the Lady of Honour to me, I to the queen; but if I am not there [...] and only a Princess of the Blood [is there], then the First Woman of the Bedchamber gives her the chemise to put on the queen, and not to the Lady of Honour.[64]

Whereas the Princes and Princesses of the Blood received the chemise from the hands of the subaltern officer, the Children of France enjoyed the mediation of the senior one. This established differences in both the rank and the number of secondary servers. As Saint-Simon's story of the duke of Bourbon and *Monsieur* illustrates, the Princes of the Blood had to suffer the same disadvantage at the Children's own apartment. The humiliation of serving there was thus crowned with the humiliation of receiving subaltern secondary service.[65]

How did the Grandchildren of France fit into this scheme? Dangeau's entry on 13 February 1686 notes the following:

---

[62] Saint-Simon noted in surprise that Bouillon 'saw that chemise given' despite the ruling against him, i.e. that he did not resort to the avoidance tactic: SSB, xix, 355. See also Dangeau, xiii, 199, 201; cf. Dangeau, iv, 32; BM, MS 2746, fo. 75v.

[63] King-of-Arms to Grand Master of Ceremonies, to Mademoiselle de Valois, to queen of Spain, to officiating cardinal: *Gazette* (1679), p. 447. In reporting the equivalent chain of the groom, Sainctot omitted himself—probably by accident—and Desgranges rectified this in his own hand, maintaining the honour of the Masters of Ceremonies as secondary (or tertiary, to be precise) servers: BM, MS 2741, fo. 35r.

[64] *Briefe der Herzogin Elisabeth Charlotte von Orléans*, ed. Holland, [v], 68–9.

[65] See earlier (p. 119) and Saint-Simon, 'Estat des changements', p. 216; *Grimoires de Saint-Simon*, ed. Coirault, p. 310.

M. the duke of Chartres came to the king's *lever*: the duke of Aumont gave him the chemise. The Grand Almoner gives him the holy bread at mass, and the Secretaries of State the *plume*, for signing marriage contracts. These are honours that the Princes of the Blood do not receive.[66]

The Grandson of France thus received the chemise from the king's First Gentleman of the Bedchamber, just as a Son of France would have done. For Dangeau, this honour of secondary service was functionally equivalent to other interactions where Chartres was the primary recipient, such as the holy bread and the *plume*. In all these cases, the Grandson of France received service from higher-ranking persons than the Princes of the Blood would have received.[67] Focusing on Chartres's honours, this entry almost makes us forget that that the ultimate recipient of the honour in question was the monarch. Indeed, readers unfamiliar with the unfolding of the *lever* might miss this point altogether. It is secondary service that receives primary attention, overshadowing the 'main purpose' at the height of the Sun King's reign.

Secondary service expands the scope, and thereby transforms the meaning, of the monarch's domestic routines. Givers were also receivers. When aristocrats served the king, they were served at the same time by the king's officers. These officers, moreover, would render primary as well as secondary service: they would keep the hat and the gloves of Bourbon princes while the latter attended to the monarch.[68] In cases where these chains of service included additional links, primary servers stood almost at the receiving end, enjoying a secondary chain of their own. In the case of the Children or the Grandchildren of France, this secondary chain culminated in personal service from the king's senior officers, members of the highest echelon of the non-Bourbon aristocracy—Foreign Princes or Dukes and Peers.

The multiple givers and receivers along these chains harboured distinct perspectives and agendas—sometimes coinciding, sometimes conflicting. As was the case in mantled visits and in other status codes, the highest-ranking Bourbons had a shared interest with the highest-ranking non-Bourbons: to deny the Princes of the Blood, who ranked between them, the right to secondary service from the titled officers of the king. If successful, the senior Bourbons would maintain the exclusivity of their right, while the non-Bourbons would avoid a humiliating enactment of subordination to the junior Bourbons who ousted their direct service to the sovereign.[69] Reducing this complex series of interactions to its final act results in a blinkered account of what went on in the king's bedchamber. Though holding the most privileged position at the top, Louis XIV was but one link in the great chain of serving.

---

[66] Dangeau, i, 295. See also Dangeau, xi, 15.

[67] Sainctot claims that Chartres had not enjoyed this honour of secondary service from the start: BN, FF 14119, fo. 282v; AC, MS 1194, fo. 382. But cf. *Mémoires de Mlle de Montpensier*, ed. Chéruel, iii, 123. On the holy bread, see AC, MS 1131, fo. 20v; on the *plume*, see Chapter One, esp. pp. 37–8.

[68] *L'État de la France* (1687), pp. 206–7. See also AN, K 1712, no. 25.

[69] What is more, the humbler links were no less contentious: see the contestations over secondary service in Da Vinha, *Les valets de chambre*, p. 63.

GESTURING AT THE THRONE: SERVICE ROUTINES
AND THE ROYAL BASTARDS

The honourable service of the king did not just serve a general 'prestige-function' common to all status symbols. It also came to serve a specific macro-political function of far-reaching ramifications. By the reign of Louis XIV, the right to oust the king's senior officers from primary service had become practically exclusive to members of the ruling dynasty, and hence symbolically synonymous with Bourbon rank. As such, it played a key role in the struggle of the Legitimated Princes to integrate fully into the Royal House, up to and including the right to inherit the throne. If a bastard handed the king the chemise or the serviette, this would—arguably more than other status symbols—indicate his parity with the legitimate princes of royal blood. Honourable service thus surfaces in many important crossroads along the ambitious drive of the Legitimated Princes for status and power: from its beginnings early in the personal reign, through the dynastic upheavals of the late reign and the regency, to later in the eighteenth century.[70]

A rare glimpse of early policy-making reveals the significance of honourable service—and of status interaction in general—in this dynastic drive. During the initial phase of the process, Louis XIV's bastard progeny gradually adopted—or usurped—the honours of the Princes and Princesses of the Blood. Although it is more associated with the children of Madame de Montespan, who lived to see the constitutional revolution of the end of the reign, the process began decades earlier with the count of Vermandois, son of Madame de La Vallière. Away on campaign in the summer of 1675, Louis XIV wrote to Colbert in his own hand:

> I have informed M. de Montausier that I did not want any distinction made at my son's between the princes of Conti and the count of Vermandois. There are things which must be avoided, such as presence at the *lever* and at the *coucher*, unless the princes of Conti are there.[71]

A few days later, in response to a memorandum that the Colberts devoted to the subject, the king reiterated and explained his intentions and his tactics:

> There is nothing more to be said, for I have ordered that [Vermandois] be treated like the princes of Conti. One must only avoid his presence at overly marked [*trop marquées*] occasions, like the chemise or the serviette. [...] All this should happen naturally [*Tout cela se doit faire naturellement*], and this order should remain between you and me. For when it will not be possible to avoid what I am telling you, he must do as the princes of Conti [would].[72]

Vermandois was less than eight years old at the time, but the king was already working to equate him with the princes of Conti, the most junior of the legitimate Bourbon princes. The arena in question was the apartment of Louis's legitimate

---

[70] For an outline of the juridical landmarks of this process, see the Introduction, pp. 18–19.
[71] *Lettres, mémoires et instructions de Colbert*, ed. Clément, vi, 329.
[72] *Lettres, mémoires et instructions de Colbert*, ed. Clément, vi, 329 n. 2.

son, the *Grand Dauphin*, which was managed by the latter's governor, the duke of Montausier.

Strikingly, this private correspondence reveals a monarch acting like a common courtier, trying to introduce a controversial novelty by stealth. This is a far cry from the image of the authoritarian sovereign who supposedly moulded ceremony and etiquette at will. Louis gave secret instructions, while he was away from court, and hoped to efface his personal involvement. Concerned about possible reactions, he wanted to make the transition seem as 'natural' as possible. To ensure this, he even instructed his minister to resort to the avoidance tactic, keeping Vermandois away from 'overly marked' occasions. Only in the last resort was Colbert to assert the royal will in order to enforce equal treatment with the Contis.

For the king, the most obvious marks of Bourbon status were the chemise and the serviette. An ousting of the service by the Legitimated Prince, albeit at the dauphin's bedchamber only, would constitute too strong a signal at this early phase. Besides, the duke of Montausier might resent an augmentation of the ranks of those who superseded him—the senior officer—in handing the *honneurs* to the dauphin. If ousting were deferred, on the other hand, it would be easier to secure Montausier's cooperation in establishing equality between the Legitimated Prince and the Princes of the Blood in other respects. The king, therefore, instructed Colbert to ensure that Vermandois stayed away from the dauphin's *lever* and *coucher* when there were no legitimate Bourbons in the bedchamber.

As the process continued, the Legitimated Princes progressed from avoidance in the dauphin's bedchamber to an established honour in the royal one. The *État de la France* of 1677 already adds them to the ranks of those who oust the service of the king himself, as does a household regulation from 1681.[73] In 1679, we have seen, Sainctot justified the treatment of the Legitimated Princes and Princesses at the marriage of *Mademoiselle* with Charles II, 'since the king had accorded them the same honours enjoyed by the Princes of the Blood, such as that of handing him his chemise and presenting the serviette in preference to the Grand Officers'.[74] The definitive honour of everyday life thus paved the way for the extraordinary honours of high ceremony. Equality extended to inverted service too: in 1692, the duke of Maine received the nuptial chemise from James II of England, just as the duke of Chartres had a few weeks earlier.[75]

Honourable service figures again in the next phase of the dynastic drive: the promotion of the second generation. In his entry dated 16 March 1710, Dangeau announced the decision to award Maine's children the same rank enjoyed by their father. Two days later, he noted that the eldest child, the prince of Dombes, has 'already served the king in this status [*qualité*], giving him the serviette at his lunch and the chemise at his *lever*'.[76] The tactics called for to capitalize on an explicit decision were diametrically opposed to those required to introduce a precedent implicitly: publicity, clarity, and possession as opposed to secrecy, ambiguity, and

---

[73] *L'État de la France* (1677), p. 73; AN, O¹ 756, pp. 52–3.   [74] See p. 32.
[75] Dangeau, iv, 32, 49.   [76] Dangeau, xiii, 124, 126.

avoidance.[77] Honourable service thus aided the Legitimated Princes in 1710 for the same reasons that it threatened their agenda in 1675. As an everyday occurrence, moreover, it enabled them to take immediate *de facto* possession. This was particularly important at this juncture because of the dubious *de jure* ratification of the decision.[78] The Legitimated Princes, accordingly, orchestrated at least two oustings, involving both *honneurs*, within a day or two of the announcement. And the significance of these gestures was not lost on insider onlookers like Dangeau.[79]

By the end of the reign, the honours of bed and table seemed to be paving the way to the throne. As the position of the bastards was again becoming uncertain, however, honourable service resurfaced as a crucial stake. The edict that stripped the Legitimated Princes of the right of succession in July 1717 left much ambiguity surrounding their honours, in particular as regards the second generation. With ambiguity renewed, the bedchamber and the table of the infant Louis XV immediately turned into testing-grounds. Although Maine was in charge of the king's education, both arenas were managed by his rivals, from below and from above: by the First Gentlemen of the Bedchamber, members of the titled nobility, and by the duke of Bourbon, Grand Master of the Household and leader of the legitimate campaign against the Legitimated.[80]

On the day the edict was published, Louis XV supped in his chamber in the presence of Maine's son, the count of Eu, and of the duke of Mortemart, First Gentleman of the Bedchamber. When the moment of the serviette arrived, a subaltern officer passed the *honneur* to Maine's son—as has been customary since 1710—rather than to Mortemart as the First Gentleman. Mortemart reprimanded the officer, and ordered the Bedchamber staff to desist from handing the serviette or the chemise to the prince, based on the new edict.[81] Eu, as a member of the second generation, was an especially vulnerable target for challenges. He had to opt for avoidance during the *coucher*, while appeal was made to the regent.

The Legitimated based their continued claim to Bourbon honours on the patents of 1711, equally granted to both generations and untouched by the recent edict. The regent indeed ruled in Eu's favour, and the latter immediately took possession of the chemise. This, however, does not seem to have satisfied the duke of Bourbon, in charge of the table staff and of the king's service outside the chamber. Bourbon reportedly argued that the patents expired with Louis XIV, and forbade

[77] In the absence of recognition, Maine noted on a later occasion, 'mes enfants, au lieu de paroître, seroient obligés de s'aller cacher': SSB, xli, 394.

[78] See the Conclusion, p. 167.

[79] Since the Legitimated ranked at the bottom of the Royal House, they also had to ensure that other Bourbons would be absent from the lunch and the *lever* in question (or would agree to cede the honour on an extraordinary basis).

[80] What follows is based on Dangeau, xvii, 126–8; *Les correspondants de la marquise de Balleroy*, ed. Édouard de Barthélemy (2 vols, Paris, 1883), i, 181, 184, 186, 189; Marais, *Journal de Paris*, i, 71–2; Jean Buvat, *Journal de la Régence*, ed. Émile Campardon (2 vols, Paris, 1865), i, 291–2; *Lettres d'Élisabeth-Charlotte d'Orléans, duchesse de Lorraine, à la marquise d'Aulède*, ed. A. de Bonneval (Nancy, 1865), p. 62; SSB, xxxi, 262–6, 425; Saint-Simon, *Traités politiques et autres écrits*, ed. Yves Coirault (Paris, 1996), pp. 716–17.

[81] Though related by blood to the Legitimated through Madame de Montespan, Mortemart fought for his post and for his rank.

his own officers to pass the serviette to Eu. The king's supper was delayed while his governor, the marshal of Villeroy, searched for the regent in the streets of Paris. Once found, Orléans again ruled in favour of the Legitimated, and Eu retook possession of the serviette.[82]

A public challenge was a double-edged sword. Instead of denying the bastard progeny the honours of the Princes of the Blood, Mortemart and Bourbon ended up handing it memorable precedents and buttressing its weakest element, the second generation. Although the subsequent juridical blow of 1718 stripped Maine and his children of all Bourbon honours, the end of the regency signalled a return to the logic of custom and precedent. As was the case with mantled visits, so with honourable service: past examples would again become pertinent. In seeking to prove that Maine's children 'remained in full possession of the honours of the court' even after the edict of 1717, a memorandum submitted to Cardinal Dubois cited the regent's decision in Eu's favour when Mortemart 'made difficulties in letting him give the serviette to the king'.[83]

As the eighteenth century progressed, honourable service continued to figure prominently at key moments in the trajectory of the bastard progeny. The partial restoration of its status in the 1720s explicitly included the honours of the chamber and in particular the right 'to take the service after the Princes of the Blood'.[84] In the 1740s, when the Legitimated negotiated a permanent rank for their posterity, the right to 'oust the service of all the Grand Officers' was one of their first demands. In order to placate the opposition, however, they suggested a compromise in secondary service: 'that the chemise and the serviette would not be presented to [the posterity] by the same persons who present them to the Princes of the Blood'.[85] This did not satisfy their opponents, who argued that even the most discerning courtiers would be hard put to it to spot the differences, and that given the uneven levels of attendance by the king's officers on these occasions the two groups might end up being served by the same persons *de facto*. 'The real honour', they concluded, 'consists in the right to serve the person of the king'.[86]

Ever since the surreptitious manoeuvres of Louis XIV in the 1670s, honourable service to the monarch 'marked' the near-equality between legitimate and legitimated members of the Bourbon dynasty. The latter's inclusion in the line of

---

[82] According to Dangeau, Villeroy headed off from Louis XV's residence to the Palais Royal, only to discover that Orléans was supping at the Place de Vendôme. In noting the itinerary in such detail, the usually-concise writer may have sniggered at the expense of the wandering septuagenarian marshal. But this may also hint at the latter's resolve to uphold the rights of the bastards. Villeroy was allied to them politically and served as governor under Maine.

[83] AN, 300 AP I 91, 'Memoire concernant les rangs de M. le Duc du Maine, donné a M. le Cardinal du Bois'. See also SSB, xli, 394.

[84] AN, O¹ 67, pp. 255–6 (the patents of 1723). Initially, this applied to the first generation only, but a few years afterwards it was extended to the second.

[85] AN, O¹ 281, no. 103¹. This document also deals with other *honneurs* presented by the Legitimated, with nuptial train-bearing, and with the Legitimated as recipients e.g. of the holy bread.

[86] AN, O¹ 281, no. 100. The Princes of the Blood themselves, after all, were secondarily served by subaltern officers only (see the previous section).

succession at the end of the reign dramatically revealed the high stakes of near-equality. Later in the century, the rivals of the Legitimated did not want them to hold the same jumping-off point enjoyed by Louis XIV's bastards in the 1710s. For that, these rivals had to prevent future generations of Legitimated Princes from laying their hands on the royal chemise.

6

Epistolary Ceremonial: Manuscript Correspondence as Unmediated Status Interaction

In the spring of 1693, Nicolas Catinat, commander of the Italian theatre of operations in the Nine Years War, received the highest honour that a military career could offer: the marshal's baton. For Catinat, scion of a family of recent nobility, this entailed social as well as military promotion: he became a Grand Officer of the Crown, near-equal to dukes. A new rank, however, also entailed new challenges. Most immediately, the neophyte marshal had to respond to the mountain of congratulatory letters that accumulated on his field desk. Which formulae should he adopt in this new capacity? How should he address the Vendôme brothers, grandsons of a royal bastard, but also officers serving under his command? And how was his correspondence with the Secretary of State for War to be conducted henceforth? In a state of exasperation, Catinat turned to his brother Croisille, expounded his epistolary dilemmas, and urged his brother to help him. 'Ceremonial troubles me', he wrote on one occasion; 'I hope you will send me a reliable protocol in good form as soon as possible', on another. In the meantime, however, Catinat managed to make several blunders. On the one hand, some of his correspondents were offended by what seemed to them an unjustifiably imperious manner; on the other, some of his fellow marshals complained that his excessively deferential style failed to uphold the dignity of their rank.[1]

Modern scholars of status interaction cannot but empathize with Catinat's predicament. Indeed, three centuries removed, they cannot even rely on informants like Croisille. Nevertheless, epistolary ceremonial, embodied as it is in the written medium, offers them the rare opportunity to enjoy that other great benefit of contemporary ethnography: direct observation. In the codes discussed thus far, we generally had to make do with re-presentations of early modern status interaction. Even the most telling account by Gourville or by Maine could only mediate a past forever lost to us in its original form, be it objects, gestures, or situations. By contrast, when

---

[1] BN, FF 7888, fos. 42r, 48v, 53r, 56v–57r. This chapter is a shorter and slightly modified version of Sternberg, 'Epistolary Ceremonial'.

modern scholars inspect the many surviving letters from the seventeenth and eighteenth centuries, they can examine with their own eyes the signs that one early modern protagonist directed at another.[2]

This, of course, does not spare us the challenge of cracking the code. Even unmediated access to real-time material or behaviour is not sufficient in itself, as any archaeologist or anthropologist can testify. Reverse-engineering of cultural artefacts requires supporting evidence of insider perceptions. But such evidence, as noted in previous chapters, is hard to find, because for insiders everyday practices were normally too self-evident for comment. The explicit discussions generated during special moments of crisis—of which the Catinat case is a remarkable exemplar—are extremely useful; they are too sporadic, however, for anything approaching a systematic reconstruction.

Traditionally, the most popular source for this kind of scholarly endeavour has been 'how-to' literary works: in this case, epistolary manuals, which often dedicate a portion of their discussion to the ceremonial aspects of letter-writing. Comprehensive in scope and easily accessible and digestible for outsiders, manuals point out pertinent categories and variables in the potentially infinite sea of signs. Yet their value is limited for the study of the actual practice of any particular milieu: they are prescriptive rather than descriptive, and compound a motley of social strata: men of letters as authors, entrepreneurs as publishers, members of the elite as model protagonists, and the general public as intended audience.[3] Although they offer a useful context for discovery, for verification we must turn elsewhere.

Two types of manuscript sources prove particularly valuable for this purpose. First, there are epistolary 'protocols': formularies that letter-writers produced for their personal everyday use rather than for public edification. The protocol that Catinat desperately requested from his brother may not have survived (if it was ever delivered), but quite a few others did, now in various French archives.[4] The typical format of these protocols is a list of addressee groups, ordered more or less hierarchically; for each group, there appears a concise outline of the corresponding forms or options. Furthermore, protocols include occasional illuminating marginalia on

---

[2] This special case thus qualifies the general distinction between anthropologists and early modern historians in Burke, *The Historical Anthropology of Early Modern Italy*, p. 15, and alleviates the danger of extrapolating non-textual practices from texts highlighted in Buc, *The Dangers of Ritual*, p. 4.

[3] See Roger Chartier, 'Des "secrétaires" pour le peuple? Les modèles épistolaires de l'Ancien Régime entre littérature de cour et livre de colportage', in Roger Chartier et al. (eds), *La Correspondance: les usages de la lettre au XIXᵉ siècle* (Paris, 1991), pp. 159–207. The literature on epistolary manuals is extensive. For a good overview of the French context, see Marie-Claire Grassi, 'Lettre', in Alain Montandon (ed.), *Dictionnaire raisonné de la politesse et du savoir-vivre: du Moyen Âge à nos jours* (Paris, 1995), pp. 543–66. The most useful manual for our purposes is De Grimarest, *Traité sur la maniere d'écrire des lettres, et sur le ceremonial* (Paris, 1735[1709]).

[4] See later. A handful have been published: *Formulaires de lettres de François Iᵉʳ à Louis XIV et État de la France dressé en 1642*, ed. Eugène Griselle (Paris, 1919); [A. de Boislisle et al.], 'Le Président Rose et les lettres de la main', in SSB, viii, 407–20; Thierry Sarmant and Mathieu Stoll, 'Le style de Louvois: formulaire administratif et expression personnelle dans la correspondance du secrétaire d'État de la Guerre de Louis XIV', *Annuaire-Bulletin de la Société de l'Histoire de France* (1997), pp. 71–7. See also Jon D. Rudd, 'A Perception of Hierarchy in Eighteenth-Century France: An Epistolary Etiquette Manual for the Controller General of Finances', *French Historical Studies*, xvii (1992), 791–801.

practices, changes, and controversies. The other type of valuable manuscript source is minutes. Additions and corrections reveal the continuous presence, and significance, of status interaction throughout the process of letter-writing. At times, it seems to be the only reason for redrafts.[5]

Finally, of course, we have the letters themselves. Hypotheses arising from the other types of sources can thus be tested against unmediated evidence of practice— for those strata whose written production has been reasonably conserved. The question of conservation points to another advantage of epistolary ceremonial. Whereas the record of other status-related events and routines is uneven for all but the highest-ranking aristocrats, correspondence can consistently shed light on the practices of a broader cross-section of early modern society. This chapter, accordingly, casts a wider social net, including in its remit also members of army, church, judicature, and administration, and notably the illuminating case of ministers and their relations with the sword nobility.

What's in a letter, then, as far as epistolary ceremonial was concerned?[6] The means by which letter-writers signified and manipulated status relations can be divided into four main types. Forms of address ('Madam'; 'Your Majesty') made up the salutation that opened the letter and the superscription that covered it (*suscription*: the outside address on an envelope or equivalent), and could also appear elsewhere within the text. Subscriptions (*souscriptions*) were the formulae that ended the text ('Your most humble and most obedient servant'). The 'ceremonial of expression' consisted of other linguistic status signifiers, such as lexical and grammatical markers ('profound respect'). Finally, and probably least self-evident to most modern readers, non-verbal features such as letter material, spatial intervals, and graphic parameters were also laden with status. That all four types not only appeared in regular letters, but also crept into the familiar *billet* style—expressly designed to circumvent formality— highlights the pervasiveness of the hierarchical in early modern society.[7]

FORMS OF ADDRESS: *MONSEIGNEUR* OR *MONSIEUR?*

Among the arsenal of features at the writer's disposal, forms of address and subscription formulae were the primary means of reference to social position, always appearing in epistolary protocols and most common in disputes. It is useful to

---

[5] See also Sarmant and Stoll, 'Le style de Louvois', p. 62.   [6] See Figure 6.1.

[7] Other treatments include Ferdinand Brunot, *Histoire de la langue française des origines à nos jours*, new edn (13 vols, Paris, 1966–79), iv, pt 1, ch. 10; Kristen Neuschel, *Word of Honor: Interpreting Noble Culture in Sixteenth-Century France* (Ithaca, 1989), esp. ch. 4; Marie-Claire Grassi, *L'Art de la lettre au temps de La nouvelle Héloïse et du romantisme* (Geneva, 1994); Marie-Claire Grassi, 'Lettre'; Christophe Blanquie, 'Entre courtoisie et révolte: la correspondance de Condé (1648–1659)', *Histoire économie et société*, xiv (1995), 427–43; Sarmant and Stoll, 'Le style de Louvois'; Jean Duma, 'Les Formes de la civilité au XVIIIe siècle: la correspondance protocolaire du duc de Penthièvre', in Pierre Albert (ed.), *Correspondre jadis et naguère* (Paris, 1997), pp. 85–99. Outside France, see esp. James Daybell, *Women Letter-Writers in Tudor England* (Oxford, 2006); cf. the sociolinguistic approaches in *Letter Writing*, special issue of *Journal of Historical Pragmatics*, v, no. 2 (2004); Minna Nevala, *Address in Early English Correspondence: Its Forms and Socio-Pragmatic Functions* (Helsinki, 2004); Jonathan Culpeper and Dániel Z. Kádár (eds), *Historical (Im)politeness* (Bern, 2010).

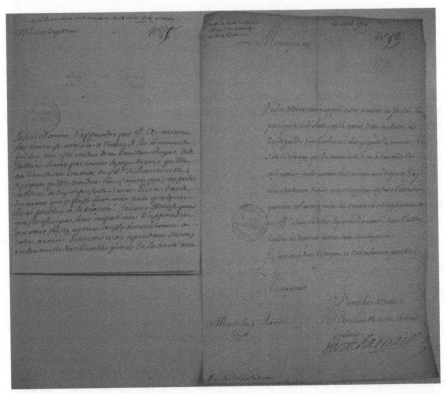

Fig. 6.1 Two letters from Jérôme de Pontchartrain to the duke of Vendôme, both dated 14 April 1706: SHD/DAT, A¹ 1958, nos. 156 and 159. The official one on the right, in scribal hand on *papier de ministre*, shows all aspects of deferential epistolary ceremonial: free address (*Monseigneur* in salutation and ending) and dignity address (*Vostre Altesse*); subscription (*tres humble et tres obeissant seruiteur*); ceremonial of expression (*respect* and *attachement* in the ending passage); and non-verbal space (esp. the vertical interval between salutation and body). Comparison with the letter on the left shows how Pontchartrain 'stretches' epistolary ceremonial in personal letters via the more flexible aspects: increased expressive and spatial deference as well as autograph writing. Reproduced by permission of the Service historique de la Défense.

divide forms of address into two main types, according to whether or not they were integrated into the sentence structure: free address (not integrated) and bound address (integrated).[8] The basic free-address forms in early modern French were the

---

[8] Free-address forms are indicated in modern punctuation by comma-separation from the rest of the text, either at the beginning, as salutation (*Madame,…*), or later in the body (*Veuillez agréer, Monsieur, l'expression de mes sentiments distingués*). Bound address consists of forms which are fully integrated into the sentence structure ('I received the letter which Your Highness did me the honour of writing to me'), and whose removal would thus result in ungrammatical utterances. See Friederike Braun, *Terms of Address: Problems of Patterns and Usage in Various Languages and Cultures* (Berlin, 1988), pp. 7–14; Hélène Merlin-Kajman, '"Une troisième espèce de simple dignité", ou la civilité entre l'honneur et la familiarité', in Cosandey (ed.), *Dire et vivre l'ordre social*, pp. 231–79.

male *Monseigneur* and *Monsieur* and the female *Madame* and *Mademoiselle*. Bound address included the second-person pronoun (*tu*, *vous*, and their derivatives) and what I refer to as 'dignity address': the combination of the possessive pronoun and an abstract 'dignity' noun ('Your Majesty').

Where exactly did these forms materialize? Formal-style letters began with a salutation of the addressee, which consisted of the appropriate (or inappropriate) free-address form. Both free address and bound address could subsequently appear throughout the text and in the ending. They also formed part of the superscription on the envelope, which was more detailed since it also served the prosaic purpose of pointing the letter to its destination. Its standard arrangement was twofold:[9] the first part consisted of the preposition 'to' (*à*) and the appropriate address term (*À Monsieur* or *À Son Altesse*); the second, of address term and name/title, sometimes adding noteworthy designations (*Monsieur le marquis de X, ministre et secrétaire d'état*). When rank difference was significant, superiors could save themselves the bipartite structure, writing *Monsieur*/*Madame* only once, or not at all.[10] Location details were often added at the end. Somewhat counter-intuitively, these particulars were to be minimized for higher-ranking addressees—the rationale being that the offices and whereabouts of such distinguished personages were supposed to be common knowledge. This 'inverted curtness' principle, postulating an inverse relation between elaboration and rank, is evident in the royal protocol's singling out of Louis XIV's most high-ranking cousin, the *Grande Mademoiselle*, by superscribing to her simply 'To my Cousin'.[11]

Superscriptions to the king show fine gradation by rank. Most addressers, following the inverted curtness principle, simply wrote 'To the King' (*Au Roi*). Addressers from the Royal House added a complement: Princes of the Blood appended *Mon souverain seigneur*; members of the Royal Family, *Monseigneur*; and the king's son and heir, *Monseigneur et père*. These seemingly minute distinctions were nonetheless closely regulated by the sovereign himself. When it was reported to him that the duke of Burgundy, then second in line to the throne, wanted to add 'et Grand père' to his superscription, Louis XIV—amidst the diplomatic crisis which was to lead to the War of the Spanish Succession—considered the matter important enough to scribble in the margin in his own hand: 'the dukes of Burgundy and Berry should only write on top of their letters *au Roi Mgr*, without adding anything else: tell them on my behalf'.[12]

The king's wish was his subjects' command. Epistolary exchanges among the latter, on the other hand, occasioned a great deal of strife. As usual, contention was at its highest when rank differences were small or when criteria for the evaluation of relative position were contradictory. Nowhere is this better illustrated than in the

---

[9] See Figure 6.2.

[10] See the superscription of the future regent in 1705, 'A Monsieur le Duc de Vendosme Mon Cousin': SHD/DAT, A¹ 1958, no. 72; cf. Arsenal, MS 5170, p. 9. For Princes of the Blood, the move to monopartite address was much lower down the addressee hierarchy: AN, K 577, no. 44.

[11] AAE, MD, France 1970, fo. 15r; BN, NAF 66, fo. Bv. Some writers adhered to the opposite, more intuitive principle, which indeed characterized other types of formal documents: Grimarest, *Traité*, pp. 153–7.

[12] *Le duc de Bourgogne et le duc de Beauvillier: lettres inédites, 1700–1708*, ed. le marquis de Vogüé (Paris, 1900), p. 404.

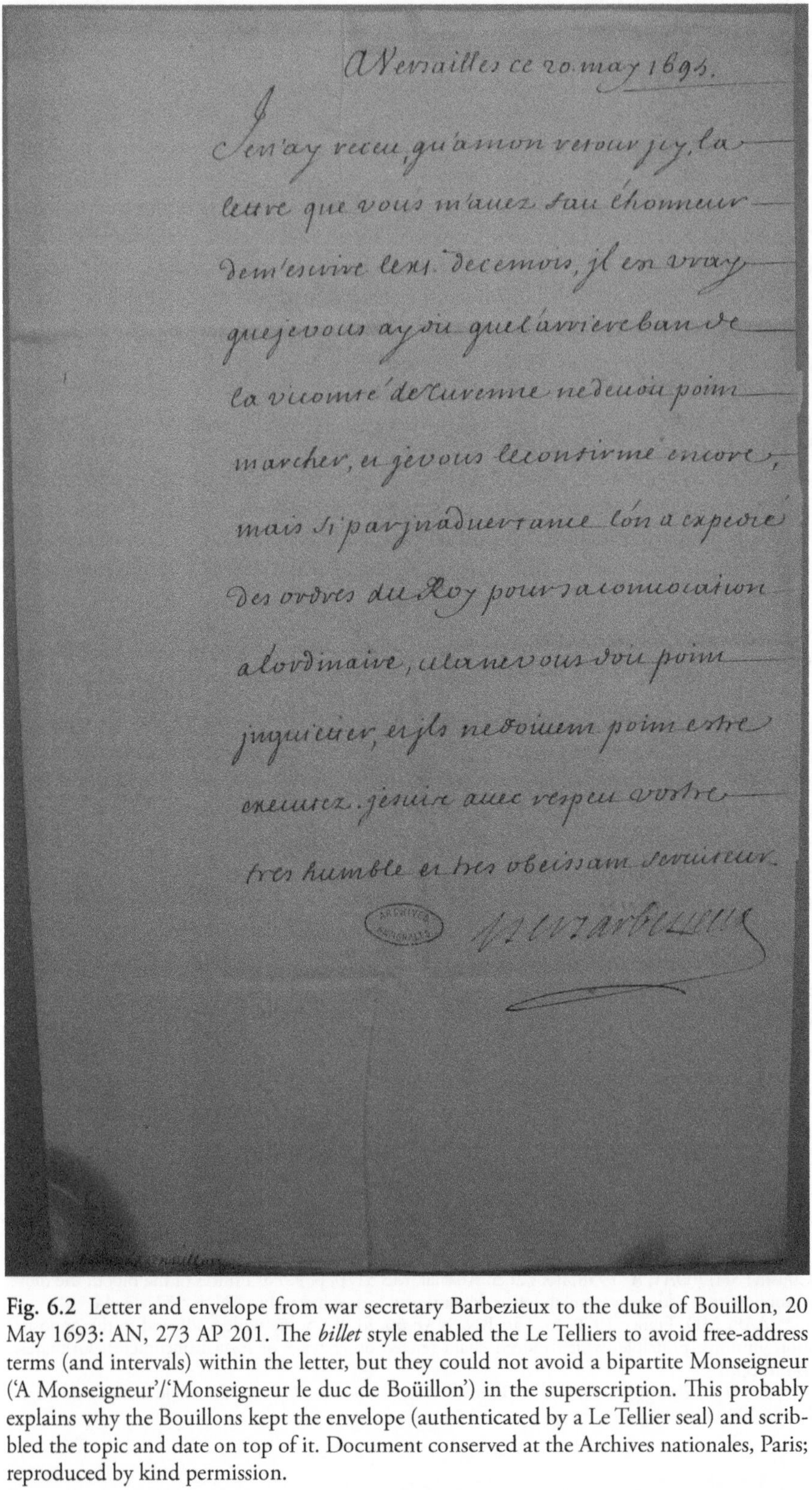

À Versailles ce 20 may 1693.

Je n'ay receu qu'à mon retour icy, la
lettre que vous m'aués fait l'honneur
de m'escrire le xj. de ce mois, il est vray,
que je vous ay dit que l'arriereban de
la vicomté de Turenne ne deuoit point
marcher, et je vous le confirme encore,
mais si par inaduertance l'on a expedié
des ordres du Roy pour sa convocation
a l'ordinaire, cela ne vous doit point
inquieter, et ils ne doiuent point estre
executez. je suis auec respect vostre
tres humble et tres obeissant seruiteur.

Fig. 6.2 Letter and envelope from war secretary Barbezieux to the duke of Bouillon, 20 May 1693: AN, 273 AP 201. The *billet* style enabled the Le Telliers to avoid free-address terms (and intervals) within the letter, but they could not avoid a bipartite Monseigneur ('À Monseigneur'/'Monseigneur le duc de Boüillon') in the superscription. This probably explains why the Bouillons kept the envelope (authenticated by a Le Tellier seal) and scribbled the topic and date on top of it. Document conserved at the Archives nationales, Paris; reproduced by kind permission.

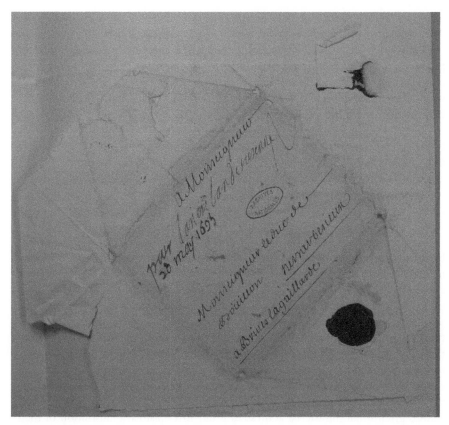

Fig. 6.2 Continued

usage of the term *Monseigneur*. Its appearance within a letter was the clearest sign of the addresser's recognition of his or her inferiority vis-à-vis the addressee. What mattered, with the *Monseigneur* as with other aspects of status interaction, was the relation between the two communicants, not the absolute rank of either. The same person would be addressed as *Monseigneur* by his subordinates, but as *Monsieur* by his peers.[13] This simple distinction was probably the thorniest issue of epistolary ceremonial, generating numerous conflicts throughout the social spectrum.

The army, a hierarchical institution even in more egalitarian societies, is a good case in point. There were two types of key positions at the top: the marshals, holders of the most exalted military rank, which conferred court status as well as field command; and the Secretary of State for War, head of the administrative hierarchy,

---

[13] A notable exception was in the ecclesiastical style, where prelates treated each other reciprocally: L'Abbé Sicard, *L'Ancien clergé de France*, 5th edn (2 vols, Paris, 1912), i, 46–53. This habit of *se monseigneuriser*, regarded as a ruse to make others use the term, was mocked by contemporaries (see e.g. AN, K 1712, no. 39). Ironically, this is almost the only surviving modern usage.

who drew his authority from representing the king. Marshals were entitled to the *Monseigneur* address from all sword nobles except princes, dukes, and Officers of the Crown. Nevertheless, contention periodically arose when addressers did not perceive distance to be significant enough for discursive subordination—in view of their ancestry, offices, or seniority. There were at least two cases where marshals who failed to secure the *Monseigneur* from provincial lieutenant-generals under their command brought their grievances before the king: Albret against Ambres in 1675 and Choiseul against Matignon and Beuvron in 1694.[14] In both cases, the king ruled in favour of the marshals. But royal arbitration was not necessarily the rule: less drastic means of conflict resolution included the agreement to disagree, or tacit avoidance of communication (either on the part of the subordinate, who would not initiate the exchange, or of the marshal, who would not reply).[15] Needless to say, this did not contribute towards the smooth running of the king's service.

The Secretary of State for War was also almost invariably addressed as *Monseigneur* by army officers. The minister's proximity to the king and his influence over governmental decisions, funds, and promotions seem to have overcome the repugnance of sword officers to bow before a parvenu. Unlike the case of marshal addressees, however, there are no known examples of open royal intervention, and ministerial rights seem to have been somewhat less all-encompassing, founded more on transient functional subordination than on inherent rank.[16] Ministers put up with *Monsieur* from the same recalcitrant officers who had refused the *Monseigneur* to marshals.[17] Top robe officials, such as intendants, addressed ministers as *Monsieur* as a matter of course. And the Le Tellier war secretaries may have been somewhat more demanding than their peers.[18] But the fact that the *Monseigneur* was the dominant form of address given to all ministerial addressees is our first epistolary illustration of their elevated status.

Another recurring *Monseigneur* dispute, this time with ministers as addressers, illuminates the problematic position of Foreign Princes in the French system. The latter considered the *Monseigneur* from Secretaries of State as one of their distinguishing honours. Ministerial protocol, however, denied the honour to houses whose claim to sovereign status was less established, and sometimes advised 'to abstain as much as possible from writing to cadets'.[19] When the prince of

---

[14] Sévigné, *Correspondance*, ed. Duchêne, ii, 85; Dangeau, v, 50.

[15] Blanquie, 'Entre courtoisie et révolte', p. 428.

[16] But cf. the post-facto report in AN, O¹ 281, no. 25. Saint-Simon posited Louvois as the main culprit behind ministerial pretensions, and claimed that he and his colleagues had used all the power invested in them to persecute recalcitrant officers and to wring the *Monseigneur* from all but the titled nobility: SSB, vi, 126–31; xiv, 226–9.

[17] e.g. SHD/DAT, A¹ 903, nos. 32, 72.

[18] Brunot, *Histoire de la langue française*, iv, pt 1, p. 360. But see Camille Rousset, *Histoire de Louvois et de son administration politique et militaire* (4 vols, Paris, 1862–3), iv, 557–8. Villars, who consistently *Monseigneur*-ed war secretaries until his elevation to the marshalate in 1702, treated foreign secretary Torcy with *Monsieur* in the late 1690s: *Mémoires du maréchal de Villars*, ed. le marquis de Vogüé (6 vols, Paris, 1884–1904), i, 459–60.

[19] BN, Clairambault 658, fo. 209. Princely rank and privileges were supposed to be enjoyed by all descendants in the male line.

Monaco demanded the *Monseigneur* address from the Secretary of State for Foreign Affairs in 1699, the latter expounded the reasons for the king's rejection of this pretension, citing precedents from the differential treatment of other houses and taking pains to address Monaco eleven times as *Monsieur* in the course of the letter.[20] In address as in other respects, Foreign Princes were far from homogeneous.

Developments in *Monseigneur* treatment show changes in ministerial as well as in princely status. In the seventeenth century, the house of Bouillon fared better than those of Rohan and of La Trémoille. Nevertheless, ministerial treatment was not invariable, and the Le Tellier dynasty, for example, exploited the *billet* style in order to write neither *Monseigneur* nor *Monsieur*. When François-Michel Le Tellier, marquis of Louvois, adopted this avoidance tactic in addressing the cardinal of Bouillon—a prince of the Church as well as a Foreign Prince—the latter exploded with indignation.[21] Louvois's father had already secured an exemption from awarding *Monseigneur* to princes of the Church upon achieving the ceremonially exalted post of chancellor in 1677.[22] Chamillart, less personally ambitious than his Le Tellier predecessors, put an end to this practice at the turn of the century and even extended the deferential address term to Bouillon cadets. Later in the eighteenth century, ministerial treatment mirrored the rise of the house of Rohan, as the latter joined Lorraine and Bouillon in lists of *Monseigneur* recipients.[23]

The female distinction between *Madame* and *Mademoiselle* was not simply a question of marital status. Women of lower rank were not supposed to be addressed as *Madame* even after their marriage, though by the second half of the seventeenth century all married noblewomen (and even those lower down the social hierarchy) assumed this honorific, an example of the process of linguistic inflation. Conversely, status considerations occasionally stipulated the *Madame* address for unmarried women, notably in the case of the king's daughters.[24] But there was no female equivalent of *Monseigneur* as a special distinction for superior addressees, and even the queen shared *Madame* with other married ladies. This may be part of the explanation why women seem to have been less involved in address disputes than men in this period.

In this language community, most addressers did not venture beyond these four basic free-address forms. The familiarity of names or kinship terms in formal discourse

---

[20] AAE, CP, Rome 392, fos. 123–124. See also SSB, vi, 125–6; Dangeau, vii, 53–4. Monaco's numerous status pretensions would hamper his mission as French ambassador to Rome.

[21] A seemingly final draft (14 July 1687) in reply by Bouillon to one of these *Monseigneur*-less letters from Louvois begins: 'Pour me conformer au style que vous me prescrivés par vostre exemple en bannissant toute ceremonie et supprimant tous les termes que La civilité ord.^re a jntroduits dans les lettres'; continues with a mimicking of the minister's curt and bureaucratic style—with no free-address term whatsoever; and ends with a haughty subscription formula (AN, 273 AP 188); cf. SHD/DAT, A¹ 770, fo. 466; BN, FF 7888, fos. 42–3.

[22] A contemporary, commenting on the meaning of this exemption with regard to the chancellor's status, thought that 'On veut mettre cette charge à un haut point': *Correspondance de Bussy*, ed. Lalanne, iii, 414; cf. AN, O¹ 279, no. 11.

[23] AN, O¹ 279, no. 3.

[24] [René Milleran], *Le Nouveau Secrétaire de la Cour* (Paris, 1723), pp. 12–13, 475ff.; Brunot, *Histoire de la langue française*, iv, pt 1, pp. 365–6.

was a show of superiority which only the Royal Family could afford.[25] The king never employed address terms alone. His relatives he addressed using kinship terms, such as 'My niece'. To the most illustrious of his other subjects—princes, dukes/peers, Grand Officers of the Crown, and a few select families—he granted the highly sought-after kinship term 'cousin' (*Mon Cousin/Ma Cousine*). What would be considered degrading familiarity from other quills was considered a special privilege from the king's.[26] His subjects further down the social hierarchy (including, interestingly, ministers) received a combination of address term and name/title (*Mons.ʳ Tel, Mad.ᵉ la comtesse Telle*). Other addressers from the Royal House adopted a scheme midway between the king and the rest of the aristocracy, finely balancing their position against that of the addressee.[27]

What about bound address? Pronominal address in French follows what sociolinguists call the 'T/V' distinction, notably including the deferential use of the plural form ('V-pronoun'; in French, *vous* and its derivatives) instead of the singular ('T-pronoun'; in French, *tu* and its derivatives) when addressing a single person.[28] By the mid-seventeenth century, the T-pronoun was virtually banished from aristocratic written discourse. Lower strata of society did however continue to make use of it, arousing the contempt of the authors of manuals.[29] Another indication of Catinat's mismatch with aristocratic society is the appearance of the T-pronoun in his personal correspondence with his brother. After the elevation, Croisille could no longer live with the anomaly of addressing a marshal in the singular form, and switched to the plural, despite Catinat's strong protests.[30]

But for the majority of correspondents, the V-pronoun was the norm—and hence no longer a special distinction. The devalued pronoun thus gave way to other means of conveying status difference. The device utilized was again cross-cultural: a combined second-person/third-person indirect address, using an abstract dignity noun with the possessive form of the V-pronoun ('Your Highness has'

[25] Brunot, *Histoire de la langue française*, iv, pt 1, pp. 363–4. A dispute over kinship terms threatened to cut off personal communication between the duke and duchess of Savoy and their daughter and son-in-law in France: Le Comte d'Haussonville, *La duchesse de Bourgogne et l'alliance savoyarde sous Louis XIV* (4 vols, Paris, 1898–1908), i, 484–6; AAE, CP, Sardaigne 99, fos. 204–205. See also Saint-Simon, 'Estat des changements', pp. 126–7; Braun, *Terms of Address*, p. 8.

[26] A duality of proximity versus subordination analogous to the duality of train-bearing or of service more generally (see Chapters Three and Five). The kinship status of royal bastards naturally formed an especially delicate question: AAE, MD, France 1970, fo. 15r. See the handling of petitions for *cousin* treatment in SHD/DAT, A¹ 3779, nos. 497–504. The (male) sovereign was also singled out as addressee, by the term *Sire*.

[27] Blanquie, 'Entre courtoisie et révolte', p. 433. See Appendix IV for a summary of free-address forms.

[28] First suggested in Roger Brown and Albert Gilman, 'The Pronouns of Power and Solidarity', in Thomas A. Sebeok (ed.), *Style in Language* (Cambridge, Mass., 1960), pp. 253–76, and attested from Africa to Sri Lanka: Penelope Brown and Stephen C. Levinson, *Politeness: Some Universals in Language Usage* (Cambridge, 1987), pp. 198–204.

[29] Grimarest, *Traité*, p. 140. In a sample of minor-nobility correspondence from 1700 to 1770, only 5 per cent employ the T-pronoun: Grassi, *L'Art de la lettre*, pp. 199ff. It seems reasonable to assume that figures for the aristocracy at the time of Louis XIV are even lower. In an earlier period, the T-pronoun was in use among Henri III's entourage: Le Roux, *La faveur du Roi*, pp. 278–88.

[30] BN, FF 7888, fos. 28, 32, 34v, 43, 50.

instead of 'you have').[31] The dignity variants were differentiated according to rank: the king received 'Majesty' (*Majesté*); princes, 'Highness' (*Altesse*); and cardinals, 'Eminence' (*Éminence*).

The evolution of the 'Highness' address provides a classic example of a status arms race. Intertwined with the international ceremonial of the Society of Princes, it underwent continual devaluation in the course of the seventeenth century, forcing the more highly placed to take on new variants as the older ones were being adopted (or usurped—depending on perspective) by their inferiors.[32] Earlier in the century, 'Highness' was limited to children of royalty. But in 1622 the prince of Condé secured it from the Roman Curia, and this paved the way for its adoption by other Princes of the Blood and Legitimated Princes. A decade later, Louis XIII's brother Gaston had the adjective 'Royal' (*Royale*) added to his 'Highness', first in the Spanish Low Countries and then in France. His daughter, the *Grande Mademoiselle*, added it in turn, as did other Grandchildren of France. This inflationary process led Louis XIV to forbid the use of 'Royal Highness' with regard to the dauphin, who—somewhat paradoxically—was treated with a mere *vous* in order to distinguish him from other princes. Some Children of France followed suit.[33]

Unable to equate themselves with the Grandchildren on this count, the Princes of the Blood had to settle for another adjective, gradually exacted from their inferiors.[34] The 'Most Serene Highness' (*Altesse Sérénissime*) was first adopted by the *Grand Condé* as he returned from his 1650s exile, in order to distinguish himself from the rest of the princely pack. But it was soon coveted by others too. These princes established their claim precedent by precedent, with the circle of accommodating addressers gradually increasing quantitatively and qualitatively. By 1704, even some of their most exalted inferiors had to acquiesce, when Louis XIV had thrown his weight behind the claim. Minister Chamillart thus wrote to his son-in-law, the duke of La Feuillade, that

> it is established presently that when writing to the Princes of the Blood and even to the Legitimated one must treat them with Most Serene Highness, the Duke of Rohan received an express order [to do so] with regard to the count of Toulouse[;] it is a capital crime to doubt it.[35]

As was to be the case with mantled visits a few years later, the Princes of the Blood, supported by their near-equated legitimated colleagues, succeeded in convincing the king to force the hand of the titled nobility.[36]

[31] See Irma Taavitsainen and Andreas H. Jucker (eds), *Diachronic Perspectives on Address Term Systems* (Amsterdam, 2003).
[32] Bély, *La société des princes*, pp. 180–1; Le Roy Ladurie with Fitou, *Saint-Simon*, pp. 86–8; cf. Descimon, 'Un langage de la dignité', p. 102; Croq, 'Des titulatures', p. 151; Hennings, 'The Semiotics of Diplomatic Dialogue', pp. 525–6.
[33] AAE, MD, France 1848, fos. 15–18; BN, NAF 9757, fo. 359r. See also Saint-Simon, 'Matériaux pour servir a un mémoire sur l'occurrence présente', p. 252.
[34] See AC, MS 1131, fo. 18.
[35] SHD/DAT, A¹ 1765, no. 132. See also Saint-Simon, *Hiérarchie et mutations*, ed. Coirault, p. 104.
[36] The question seems to have remained contentious, though: Arsenal, MS 5170, pp. 143–4.

Ironically but inevitably, these developments lowered the value of 'Most Serene' in the symbolic market.[37] While Bourbons were establishing their claim for the adjective, lesser princes struggled to receive simple 'Highness' from French aristocrats. The crucial issue with interactional status symbols, whether sartorial or linguistic, was the rank of those who awarded them; obsequiousness from the lowly offered little comfort. The duke of Vendôme trailed behind Louis XIV's bastards in this as in other respects.[38] The cardinal of Bouillon had himself titled 'Your Most Eminent Highness' (*Votre Altesse Éminentissime*) by subordinates and well-wishers, but did not secure it from independent aristocrats. From ministerial pens, the simple *vous* served here too as an avoidance compromise: Bouillon was treated in a different manner from other cardinals (who were addressed as 'Your Eminence'), but without receiving princely 'Highness'.[39] Below princely level, aristocrats did not manage to secure dignity address from respectable inferiors. French grandees did not have an equivalent for 'Excellency'; nouns like *Grandeur* were granted only by humble servants.[40]

SUBSCRIPTION FORMULAE: ON SERVANTS AND FRIENDS

At the end of the letter came the subscription: the most explicit positioning of addresser vis-à-vis addressee. It was composed of a noun which described the relationship between the two, most commonly 'servant' (*serviteur* for male addressers and *servante* for female ones), plus adjectives and adverbs serving as deference building-blocks. Building-blocks followed an internal hierarchy: for adjectives, 'humble' (*humble*) and 'obedient' (*obéissant*) were more deferential than 'affectionate' (*affectionné*) and 'good' (*bon*); for adverbs, 'most' (*très*) was followed by 'more' (*plus*) and 'very' (*bien*).[41] The words had long lost their literal sense: their meaning derived from their relative position in the graded sequence they formed together. The number of items correlated with deference: normally one to three adjectives, each possibly further upgraded by an adverb.[42] Among lexical groups, nouns were more important than adjectives, and adjectives more than adverbs. Combined together, these variables generated multiple distinctions. By the end of Louis XIV's

---

[37] It was reportedly discarded by a new incumbent of the very position for which it had originally been created: when the Orléans branch took over as First Princes of the Blood, the duke of Chartres made do with simple *vous* address: AN, O¹ 279, no. 3.

[38] 'Point d'altesse' from ministers: BN, NAF 9757, fo. 359v. The Pontchartrains did grant it, though: see Figure 6.1.

[39] See Sarmant and Stoll, 'Le style de Louvois', p. 72, and the subscription of a letter of 26 February 1690 from Torcy (AN, 273 AP 190, dossier 7), where the minister apparently began writing 'De V.E.', and then amended it, writing 'Votre tres humble, et tres obeïssant seruiteur' instead.

[40] Callières, *Des mots à la mode*, pp. 168ff., 250–1; Saint-Simon, 'Matériaux pour servir a un mémoire sur l'occurrence présente', p. 252.

[41] In rendering subscriptions into English, I preferred 'most' to 'very' for translating *très* (following, inter alia, early modern translations).

[42] See Chartier, 'Des "secrétaires" pour le peuple?', p. 188. Sometimes as many as four adjectives were used: BN, NAF 66, fos. 70r, 74v–75r.

reign, the standard formula towards superiors or near-equals was 'Your most humble and most obedient servant' (*votre très humble et très obéissant serviteur*). Adding a further adjective expressed extra deference, resulting from marked inferiority/subordination or from a desire to ingratiate oneself with the addressee.[43] A sole adjective was usually a show of superiority.

In subscribing to their sovereign, subjects were expressing political allegiance as well as social deference. Subscriptions to the king consisted of a triple-superlative, double-noun structure: 'Sire, Your Majesty's most humble, most obedient, and most faithful subject and servant' (*Sire, De Votre Majesté, Le très humble, très obéissant, et très fidèle sujet et serviteur*). In this special case, literal meaning was not entirely lost, the rule being most salient in its breach: the cardinal of Bouillon's renunciation of his subjection to the French crown in 1710 culminated in the striking omission of 'most faithful subject' from his subscription, the form of the letter thus reinforcing its content.[44] Conversely, the *Grand Condé's* ultimate loyalty was subtly conveyed by the fact that even at the height of his 1650s rebellion, as he was fighting alongside the Spaniards against his own countrymen, he remained only the most humble and most obedient servant of the king of Spain, reserving the fidelity and subjection of the full royal subscription for letters addressed to Louis XIV.[45]

The delicate line between 'most humble and most affectionate' and 'most humble and most obedient' illustrates the tensions between near-equals and the evolutionary processes of epistolary ceremonial. Earlier in the seventeenth century, the former was standard usage between status-equals: in ducal protocols from that period, this is the variant exchanged among peers.[46] In the course of the reign, following a process of inflation, 'obedient' began to be awarded to near-equals as well as to superiors. By the end of the seventeenth century it became the norm, 'affectionate' now normally reserved for inferior addressees.[47] It is, however, the transition period that is most revealing. Writers were hesitant about upgrading their subscription style, since they feared that addressees might not reciprocate.

Take, for example, the manoeuvres between ministers and the top echelon of the (non-princely) sword nobility. A protocol prepared for Colbert after he was appointed Secretary of State notes in the entry 'Officers of the Crown, Dukes, Pairs, and Marshals' that 'affectionate' should be used, 'unless they treat equally, by writing also the most obedient'.[48] A later version gives 'obedient' as the default option, but remarks that if the sword correspondents wrote in a different manner, they would be offered a taste of their own medicine.[49] The minutes of the war

---

[43] 'suiuant les dependances et les obligations': BN, NAF 66, fos. 74v–75r. The *commissaires des guerres*, for example, added 'très obligé' when subscribing to their superior, the war secretary.

[44] A. de Boislisle, 'La désertion du cardinal de Bouillon en 1710', pts 2–3, *Revue des questions historiques*, 2nd ser., xli (1909), here pt 2, pp. 61ff.

[45] Blanquie, 'Entre courtoisie et révolte', p. 432.

[46] Arsenal, MS 4109, fo. 421r; cf. the epistolary instructions of a provincial *parlementaire* to his son in 1658: 'Le Président Bouhier', *Le Cabinet historique*, vii (1861), 92–3.

[47] See also Callières, *Du bon, et du mauvais Usage*, pp. 222–32; Brunot, *Histoire de la langue française*, iv, pt 1, pp. 374–5.

[48] BN, Clairambault 658, fos. 212–213.   [49] Sarmant and Stoll, 'Le style de Louvois', p. 73.

ministry from the late 1680s, which usually omit the ending formula, have the word 'obedient' scribbled in the margin of letters addressed to certain dukes: no doubt an indication to the scribe that in these cases the deferential variant was required.[50] This illustrates both the change in the norm and the anxiety of correspondents about possible implications to their status. Variants in themselves are meaningless—it is their relative application that counts. The crux of the matter as far as the ministers were concerned was to ensure equal treatment.[51]

In a climate of inflation, the conservative stance of keeping the old style, in whole or in part, created in effect a novel distinction. The same ministers who, as addressees, expected the 'obedient' even from dukes and Grand Officers of the Crown, insisted, as addressers, on retaining the 'affectionate' when writing to sword nobles below that level. Bussy-Rabutin noted bitterly that in the past, when 'birth and arms still retained their rank', the Secretarial 'your most humble and most affectionate' was met by the (degrading) 'your most affectionate to do you service' (*votre très affectionné à vous faire service*). But

> since the Secretaries of State have felt their power and recognised their credit, they have continued the old style despite the politeness of our times; and the holders of *grandes charges*, knowing that the Secretaries of State could make or break them, have been their most humble and most obedient servants.

As Blanquie remarks, the *formule de politesse* was not impolite in itself, but only because its counterpart had evolved.[52]

Saint-Simon accused the Princes of the Blood of similar 'haughty conservatism' in their persistent use of 'most affectionate servant' with regard to dukes. By the end of the seventeenth century, this single-adjective subscription was employed towards marked inferiors only.[53] One could argue that this is a case of incongruity rather than of haughtiness, since the 'most affectionate' (sometimes even coupled with kinship terms instead of 'servant') was regularly exchanged within the Society of Princes between correspondents who saw themselves as near-equals. However, as in the case of mantled visits, the ultimate key lies in the question of reciprocity. Whereas with regard to princely correspondents the protocolar rule of the Princes of the Blood was that received upgrades should be matched, the 'most humble and most obedient' awarded by lower-ranking aristocrats did not meet with similar treatment.[54]

---

[50] e.g. SHD/DAT, A¹ 814, fo. 311.

[51] BN, FF 5764, fo. 3v; cf. Saint-Simon, 'Estat des changements', pp. 118ff.

[52] *Correspondance de Bussy*, ed. Lalanne, ii, 347–8; Blanquie, 'Entre courtoisie et révolte', pp. 428–9. See also SSB, xiv, 229. It might have come as a small comfort to Bussy to know that Chateauneuf (the Secretary whose letter to the exiled nobleman sparked this comment) insisted on keeping the old style with regard to dukes and to marshals too: Saint-Simon, 'Estat des changements', p. 119; *Mémoires de Nicolas-Joseph Foucault*, ed. F. Baudry (Paris, 1862), p. 320.

[53] See Saint-Simon, 'Matériaux pour servir a un mémoire sur l'occurrence présente', p. 252. For an example, see BN, FF 22797, fo. 164. Lesser princes maintained the intermediate formula of *très humble serviteur*: Vendôme to La Feuillade, SHD/DAT, A⁴ 6, dossier '1704–1706'; SHD/DAT, A¹ 904, no. 134.

[54] AN, K 1712, no. 6/2; AN, K 577, no. 44, fos. 1v–2r. On mantled visits, see Chapter Four.

Writers could manifest an even greater sense of superiority by substituting 'friend' (*ami/amie*) for 'servant' as subscription noun.[55] Those at the very top of the hierarchy might drop the relational formula altogether. Louis XIV did not subscribe as his subjects' servant or even friend. Instead, he ended his formal-style letters 'without subscription', only commending the addressee to God's protection. To those entitled to 'cousin' address he awarded 'I pray God to keep you, my cousin, in His holy and worthy protection' (*Je prie Dieu qu'il vous ait, mon cousin, en sa sainte et digne garde*). Lower-positioned individuals were deemed worthy of no more than holy protection (without 'et digne'). Only hereditary sovereigns and their children were eligible to the monarch's subscription—within the realm, this meant queens and Children of France.[56] The *Grande Mademoiselle*'s special treatment during the previous reign and the regency included a subscription, but when he came into his own, Louis XIV refused to award this honour to his turbulent cousin.[57]

The subscription code did allow for significant exceptions. Men granted women more than was their due according to other criteria, and sometimes received less in return. In his manual, René Milleran allowed exceptions 'in favour of the sex to which all must defer', but complained about women's tendency to deny two-adjective subscriptions even to unfamiliar male equals.[58] The protocol of the Princes of the Blood, so conservative and niggardly as far as subscriptions to men were concerned, awarded 'most humble and most obedient servant' to ladies who did not even belong to the top echelon.[59] Surviving ducal protocols are also more deferential towards women.[60] On the other hand, the protocols of the Royal Family or of ministers appear less occupied with such courtesies. Exceptions, in any case, were not limited to gender. When writing to prelates, ministers converted the customary 'affectionate' into 'obedient' in the case of those 'for whom one can have consideration'.[61] The crucial criterion for such special treatment of God's servants seems to have been links to ministerial clan networks rather than piety.[62]

At the very end of the letter, signatures indicated rank as well as personal identity. In another example of the inverted curtness principle, the king, queen, and Children of France signed their Christian name only. Other members of the Royal House had to add a surname, usually the *apanage* of the founder of their branch. The rest of the aristocracy normally used a surname, sometimes coupled with title

---

[55] An intermediate variant was *affectionné à vous faire service* (or, even haughtier, *servir*).

[56] Even then, a kinship term was used rather than 'servant': AAE, MD, France 1970, fos. 14ff.

[57] BN, NAF 2038, p. 44; cf. AAE, MD, France 1970, fo. 15r. Another Grandchild of France, the future regent, was also denied subscriptions but received the distinction of two superlatives in the commendation—'tres sainte et tres digne': 'Correspondance de Louis XIV et du duc d'Orléans', ed. Pallu de Lessert.

[58] [Milleran], *Le Nouveau Secretaire de la Cour*, pp. 19–20. See also Grimarest, *Traité*, pp. 127–9.

[59] In a special section dedicated to female addressees: BN, NAF 9757, fos. 276ff. See also *La marquise d'Huxelles et ses amis*, ed. Édouard de Barthélemy (Paris, 1881), pp. 22–3.

[60] Arsenal, MS 4109, fos. 419–426; BN, Clairambault 718, fos. 91–95.

[61] BN, Clairambault 658, fos. 211–212.

[62] e.g. the archbishop of Lyon, allied to the Le Telliers: Sarmant and Stoll, 'Le style de Louvois', p. 73; SHD/DAT, A¹ 770, fo. 443; AAE, MD, France 1206, fo. 77.

or office, but without their Christian name. Here again the Legitimated and the Foreign Princes offer interestingly intermediate cases.[63]

THE CEREMONIAL OF EXPRESSION: GIVING RESPECT AND TAKING LIBERTIES

Address terms and subscriptions were formulaic: mandatory and—as a rule— invariable for any specific 'dyad' (pair of communicants) at a given moment. Other forms of linguistic status interaction were fuzzier, ranging from quasi-formulaic constructions to nuances of vocabulary and grammar. Grimarest calls these forms the 'ceremonial of expression' (*cérémonial de l'expression*). As he observes, an exhaustive description of such stylistic variation is impractical.[64] What I attempt here is an outline of some of the more frequent and more clear-cut lexical and grammatical markers of status.

The first subtle marker came at the very beginning. Letters often began with a phrase that acknowledged reception of previous correspondence from the addressee. Sarmant and Stoll have noted that ministerial reception phrases were divided hierarchically into three main variants (in ascending order of deference): 'I received your letter'; 'I received the letter which you took pains [*pris la peine*] to write to me'; 'I received the letter which you did me the honour to write to me' (*que vous m'avez fait l'honneur de m'écrire*).[65] The third, most deferential variant is normally awarded to near-equals and to superiors (including government colleagues and the top echelon of the sword nobility); the 'pains' variant, to respectable inferiors; and the simplest one to the rest. Usage, however, is not unwavering, and it remains to be ascertained in each case whether exceptions are due to indifference, negligence, or perhaps strategic variation, where reversible upgrades and downgrades reflect transient interests rather than fixed social distances.[66] In the less bureaucratized language of sword nobles, the second variant seems less common. The king used only the simplest one, even when addressing his most highly ranked subjects.

At the other end of the letter, diverse quasi-formulaic constructions appeared in the passage leading into the subscription. The shortest was the simple predication of the subscription (*Je suis votre...*), but it was usually 'wrapped' with further linguistic items, the degree of ornamentation roughly correlating with deference. These wrappers included adverbs, adverbial phrases, and other constructions (such as *J'ay l'honneur d'estre*, or *Je vous prie de me croire*).[67] A common adverbial phrase

<hr />

[63] For the Legitimated, see BM, MS 2741, fo. 80v. For the Foreign Princes; cf. BN, FF 22797, fos. 161, 181; SHD/DAT, A¹ 2135, no. 241; Spangler, *The Society of Princes*, p. 121; AN, K 1718, no. 2ᵈ.

[64] Grimarest, *Traité*, pp. 174ff.

[65] Sarmant and Stoll, 'Le style de Louvois', p. 61; cf. Grimarest, *Traité*, pp. 178–9.

[66] Draft revisions not infrequently modify these phrases: e.g. SHD/DAT, A¹ 814, fo. 311. Later in the eighteenth century, reception phrases are noted in epistolary protocols—evidence of increased standardization of the ceremonial of expression: AN, O¹ 279, no. 5.

[67] See the last-minute addition of 'très parfaitement' in letters from ministers to dukes from the last decade of the reign: BN, Châtre de Cangé, Réserve, F 228, fo. 233; BN, FF 22797, fo. 67.

was the preposition 'with' (*avec*) complemented by one noun or more and possibly by other deference building-blocks (adjectives and adverbs). For some dyads of correspondents, these passages remain constant over long stretches of letter exchange. They may have been increasingly formalized during the first half of the eighteenth century. In some protocols from the middle of this century, they are inseparable from the core of the subscription. The core's devaluation processes, outlined in the previous section, may explain the need for new formulaic distinctions.[68]

The most clear-cut lexical mark of deference in these constructions was *respect* and its derivatives (*respectueux, respectueusement*)—generally reserved for superior addressees. In a ministerial protocol compiled around the 1720s, 'with most profound respect' (*avec un très profond respect*) is awarded to the First Prince of the Blood, 'profound respect' to the others, and 'respect' to lesser princes.[69] Even when they denied the *Monseigneur*, war ministers often gave respect to the house of Bouillon—sometimes in the course of draft revisions.[70] They also gave it to women below that rank.[71] As with most features of the ceremonial of expression, practice was not always consistent, and here too we must determine for each case whether variance was meaningful. Sometimes it can simply be a question of hand, given that aristocrats did not write all their letters themselves, and that some of them had several scribes. Among near-equals, there was some reluctance over the use of *respect*. Chamillart wrote to Villars in 1703: 'I cannot help telling you that your letters include expressions which cause me pain, I pray you to suppress the terms of *respect*, to agree to remain with those of *amitié*'.[72] That a marshal would contemplate such *respect*ful treatment of a minister (let alone stick to it) is revealing in itself; from the quill of lower-ranked sword nobles it was common practice.

Other lexical markers ranged from milder deference to outright superiority. 'Attachment' (*attachement*) and its derivatives belonged to the mild deference section. Expressing 'esteem' (*estime*) or 'friendship' (*amitié*), on the other hand, could mark non-inferiority of the writer. It was a common idiom in the closing passages of superior addressers—another demonstration of the potential condescension implied by familiarity.[73] When writing to non-inferiors, a polite corrective to the offer of *amitié* was often deemed necessary.[74] An alternative formulation reversed

---

[68] AN, O¹ 279, no. 5; BN, Châtre de Cangé, Réserve, F 228, fos. 199ff.

[69] AN, O¹ 279, no. 3; cf. Arsenal, MS 5170, p. 25.

[70] See the minutes addressed to the counts of Auvergne and of Evreux in SHD/DAT, A¹ 3779. In an autograph letter of 22 January 1707 to the duke of Bouillon, Chamillart superimposes the 'r' of 'respect' on the trace of a 'p'—presumably deleting the beginning of an over-deferential *profond*: AN, 273 AP 201. In a minute of 1686 to the duke, 'respect' is deleted rather than added: SHD/DAT, A¹ 771, fos. 108, 130.

[71] SHD/DAT, A¹ 2136, no. 350; cf. Callières, *Des mots à la mode*, p. 94.

[72] SHD/DAT, A¹ 3779, no. 566. See also BN, FF 22797, fo. 173; Grimarest, *Traité*, pp. 180–1.

[73] Arsenal, MS 5170, pp. 183ff.

[74] 'Je vous prie d'en estre bien persuadé ainsi que du respect et de la veritable amitié, *si vous voulés bien me le permettre*, auec laquelle je suis monsieur vostre tres humble et tres obeissant serviteur': duke of Noailles to Vendôme, SHD/DAT, A¹ 1958, no. 44, my emphasis. My discussion here concerns conventional epistolary usage of the term 'amitié' rather than the complicated concept of 'friendship'

directions, demanding the honour of the addressee's friendship rather than offering one's own. Finally, the term 'consideration' (*considération*) was reserved for inferior addressees.[75] The hierarchical nuances of these terms were not limited to ending passages. They appear, for example, throughout a letter of 1713 from the princess of Conti to Villars: the marshal had 'attachment' towards her late husband; the prince held Villars in 'esteem' and 'friendship'; and she herself ends her letter by professing 'esteem' and 'consideration'.[76]

Seventeenth-century correspondence bears out the sociolinguistic universal that utterances which concern the communicants are potentially offensive and therefore require linguistic buttressing, and that the intensity of this protective layer depends (inter alia) on the respective social positions of addresser and addressee. Grimarest calls the linguistic devices that perform this function *correctifs*.[77] A common corrective which we have already seen in action is the term 'honour'. 'To do the honour' (*faire l'honneur*) was used not only with regard to letter reception, but also to other actions performed by the addressee. 'Giving oneself the honour' (*se donner l'honneur*) was used to wrap utterances in the opposite direction (performed by the addresser). It is by now probably not surprising that *honneur* was regularly added and erased in the drafting process. Philippe de Vendôme began writing the 'your' of 'your esteem and your friendship', but then erased it, preposing 'the honour of'. The addressee Catinat may have been inferior by birth, but he was superior in command.[78]

The classic case for *correctifs* is the language of requests and demands. Louis XIV's secretary observed that 'The king as king writing in his own hand within his realm does not pray [*prie*] anyone but queens and without the realm he does not pray or supplicate [*suplie*] anyone but the pope; he delicately avoids these terms with all other foreign princes'.[79] An early eighteenth-century protocol noted that ministers 'give each other *honneur* reciprocally and *je vous supplie*'.[80] In a minute to the bishop of Metz from 1692, Secretary of State Barbezieux had originally put

in early modern society. Term and concept cannot of course be neatly separated, but the distinction would seem to be fruitful analytically: see Sharon Kettering, 'Patronage in Early Modern France', *French Historical Studies*, xvii (1992), 839–62, for a discussion of terminological confusions. Subscribing as the addressee's *ami* implied great superiority, not friendship: AN, K 577, no. 44, fos. 6v–8r. The ultimate test, here and throughout, would be quantitative: whether usage was differentially distributed according to rank. See Grassi, *L'Art de la lettre*, pp. 202ff. On friendship in this context, see Dewald, *Aristocratic Experience*, pp. 104ff.; Christian Kühner, '"Quand je retournai, je trouvai toutes les cabales de la cour changées": Friendship under the Conditions of Seventeenth-Century Court Society', in Bernadette Descharmes et al. (eds), *Varieties of Friendship: Interdisciplinary Perspectives on Social Relationships* (Göttingen, 2011), pp. 59–75.

[75] Grassi, 'Lettre', p. 553; Callières, *Des mots à la mode*, pp. 94–7.

[76] *Mémoires du maréchal de Villars*, ed. Vogüé, iii, 345. See also Callières, *Du bon, et du mauvais Usage*, pp. 192ff.

[77] Grimarest, *Traité*, pp. 134ff., 181ff. This is a forerunner of Brown and Levinson's 'FTA[Face Threatening Act]-redress': see their *Politeness*, pp. 68ff.

[78] B. Le Bouyer de Saint Gervais, *Mémoires et correspondance du maréchal de Catinat* (3 vols, Paris, 1819), iii, 147–8.

[79] [Boislisle et al.], 'Le Président Rose et les lettres de la main', p. 412. See also AAE, MD, France 1970, fo. 14r.

[80] BN, NAF 9757, fo. 362r.

down 'I pray you' in a demand phrase; then had 'pray' erased and 'supplicate' written down instead; and finally instructed the scribe that the same letter was to be dispatched to two other addressees, but with 'pray' instead of 'supplicate'. An intendant, after all, was not worthy of the same lexical deference as a bishop.[81] Higher up the deference scale we find wrappers such as 'take the liberty' (*prendre la liberté*) and 'dare' (*oser*). Grammatical devices included the future, conditional, and subjunctive at the expense of the imperative, interrogative, and negative.[82] And these devices were often used in conjunction, occasionally producing rather spectacular exemplars such as 'Shall I dare, Madam, take the liberty of supplicating Your Majesty to…'[83]

The papers of a prominent *parlementaire* from the end of the reign offer a textbook example of the ceremonial of expression. A draft of a request letter concerning the family's holdings in Beaumont is marked by several corrections, none of which has anything to do with 'content'. 'Pray' in 'I dare pray you' is changed to 'supplicate'. 'Friendship' is considered too familiar, and is thus erased from 'the marks which I have always received of your goodness and of your friendship'. The wrapper 'to have the pleasure' (*avoir le bonheur*) is added to the next phrase. Finally, 'with all possible respect and attachment' is appended to the ending passage. By orchestrating the expressive features discussed in this section, the writer significantly upgraded deference without, however, resorting to the *Monseigneur*.[84]

The crucial point for our purposes is not the intricacy of linguistic devices per se, but rather their differential application according to relative social position. 'A superior rarely inserts correctives to verbs of command […] When he refuses, he does not search for detours', whereas inferiors must studiously apply themselves to employ the 'terms of respect'.[85] These remarks by Grimarest largely reflect the practice of his contemporaries. On the other hand, he also noted that 'the *grand Seigneur* does not scrimp his courtesies when his interests are at stake'.[86] The greater flexibility of the *cérémonial de l'expression* allowed other factors besides the official hierarchy to play their part. Even princes sometimes deigned to award lexical and grammatical deference to the socially inferior yet highly influential ministers.[87]

---

[81] SHD/DAT, A¹ 3779, no. 554. See also SHD/DAT, A¹ 1033, fo. 223r.

[82] Brunot, *Histoire de la langue française*, iv, pt 1, pp. 369–70; Grimarest, *Traité*, pp. 134–5, 181–2; cf. Brown and Levinson, *Politeness*, pp. 130–44.

[83] 'Oserai-je, Madame, prendre la liberté de supplier V.M. de…': *Madame Palatine: Lettres françaises*, ed. Van der Cruysse, p. 742. Quadruple indirection—three wrappers (*oser, prendre la liberté* and *supplier*) and one grammatical marker (future interrogative instead of imperative)—as well as two adjacent address forms (*Madame* and *V.M.*); cf. Catherine Kerbrat-Orecchioni, 'From Good Manners to Facework: Politeness Variations and Constants in France, from the Classic Age to Today', *Journal of Historical Pragmatics*, xii (2011), 141.

[84] BN, FF 22816, fo. 282.   [85] Grimarest, *Traité*, pp. 176, 177, 181.

[86] Grimarest, *Traité*, p. 103. More generally, superiors had more freedom in choosing ceremonial strategy: p. 118.

[87] See e.g. the dossiers of finance ministers Chamillart and Desmaretz in the duke of Bouillon's correspondence: AN, 273 AP 201.

NON-VERBAL ASPECTS: THE HIERARCHY
OF MATERIAL, SPACE, AND GRAPHICS

Letters were not simply transparent vehicles of language in the abstract. They were also objects, pieces of paper upon which words were arranged and inscribed in the most physical sense. The non-verbal aspects of correspondence—material, spatial, and graphic—made an impact on recipients even before they started reading the letter and taking in its content. Like the ceremonial of expression, degree of formalization and codification varied for different aspects or writers, but there was hardly a feature of epistolary exchange which was not utilized in one way or another for status interaction.[88]

Letter material—substance, size, colour, folding, seals, and so forth—is discussed at length in royal formularies.[89] By the reign of Louis XIV, letters were generally written on paper (parchment reserved only for a handful of foreign addressees). The seal was usually either applied on the folded rear page, or on an envelope. According to the manuals, the latter expedient was more deferential.[90] Folded letters could be wrapped with silk thread: the king's formulary stipulated white silk for the pope, blue silk for princes, and red silk for the rest. For seals too, material, colour, design, and perhaps also number, could be differentiated according to addressee.[91] Finally, size mattered, especially in the two extremes: inferiors were expected to use larger paper, while superiors got away with jotting on tiny scraps. But size was also a question of function: those who handled large quantities of paperwork used folio for official letters, and smaller sheets for personal ones. Thus the smaller (but not tiny) format could be more prestigious or deferential than the large.[92]

Page layout, or the spatial organization of the text, was the most codified of non-verbal features. Certain margins (space between the edges of the paper and the text) and intervals (space between text components) were supposed to be proportionate to deference, physical distance thus mirroring social distance.[93] The opening interval—the position of the salutation vis-à-vis the body of the text—was most significant. When writing to inferiors, one would begin the body on the same line as the opening free-address form, horizontal distance often being measured in

---

[88] cf. the references and discussion in Daybell, *Women Letter-Writers in Tudor England*, esp. pp. 47–52, 183–4.

[89] The king's correspondence was divided into two types: official letters, handled and countersigned by the four *Secrétaires d'État*; and personal letters, handled by the *Secrétaires du Cabinet*. For the first, see the beautifully crafted formulary prepared for Colbert upon his nomination as Secretary in 1669: BM, MS 2653. For the second, see [Boislisle et al.], 'Le Président Rose et les lettres de la main'.

[90] Grimarest, *Traité*, pp. 147–9. But cf. AAE, MD, France 310, fo. 162v.

[91] BN, Clairambault 718, fos. 91–95; Grimarest, *Traité*, pp. 163–4.

[92] See Figure 6.1. See also, on single versus double pages, [Boislisle et al.], 'Le Président Rose et les lettres de la main', p. 410; *Madame Palatine: Lettres françaises*, ed. Van der Cruysse, p. 551; Duma, 'Les formes de la civilité', p. 90. And see Grimarest, *Traité*, pp. 106, 114–15, 149–50; [Antoine de Courtin], *Nouveau Traité de la Civilité qui se pratique en France parmi les honnêtes-gens* (Paris, 1728), pp. 235–6, 239–40. Were all writers aware of all these fine distinctions? One assumes that considerations of paper availability also played a part.

[93] Grassi, 'Lettre', p. 552; Chartier, 'Des "secrétaires" pour le peuple?', p. 175.

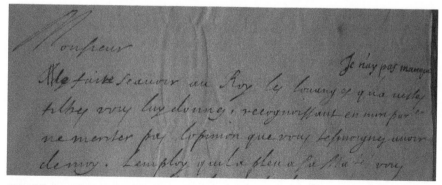

Fig. 6.3 First lines of a letter from Cardinal Richelieu to the prince of Condé, 21 May 1629 (AC, M ii, fo. 273). Initially, the cardinal 'gave the line' to the prince, with 'J'ay fait' beginning the text on a new line below the *Monsieur* salutation. He then decided to downgrade deference to 'words on the line', by adding 'Je n'ay pas manque' at the end of the salutation line, and turning 'J'ay fait' into 'de faire'. Photo kindly provided by the Bibliothèque et archives du château de Chantilly.

words (either the number of 'blank' words constituting the interval between the salutation and the body, or the number of actual words written at the right end of the salutation line). Members of the Royal Family left no interval at all to most addressees, starting the body of the text immediately after the salutation.[94] When addressees were near-equals, one would 'give the line' (*la ligne*): begin the body on a new line immediately below the salutation. Finally, deference to superiors required vertical blank space between salutation and body, measured in either lines or fingers. In extreme cases, such spatial deference resulted in the first page including only a few text lines, and in a significant upper margin on subsequent pages.[95]

Intra- and inter-protocol comparisons are already instructive. A mid-seventeenth-century formulary of a duke finely differentiates the vertical space between salutation and body according to addressee rank: seven to eight lines for the king, five to six for the king's brother, and three for the First Prince of the Blood.[96] The closing of the status gap between Princes of the Blood and Legitimated Princes during the final years of Louis XIV's reign is evident in the elimination of differences in the intervals awarded in ministerial protocols.[97] Practice also shows painstaking attention to spatial distinctions. They appear at early stages of the drafting process, occasionally corrected there.[98] In the final product, a conspicuous

---

[94] Again, a noticeable difference in everyday routines compared with the Princes of the Blood. Protocols can be so punctilious as to differentiate between no interval and an interval that is only a fraction of a word: BN, NAF 9757, fos. 269–270. Length of words and number of syllables were also taken into consideration: BN, Clairambault 658, fo. 226.

[95] e.g. AN, K 120A/2, fo. 2; Grimarest, *Traité*, pp. 105–7.

[96] Arsenal, MS 4109, fos. 419ff.

[97] Compare Sarmant and Stoll, 'Le style de Louvois', p. 72 (end of the seventeenth century) and AN, O¹ 279, no. 3 (early eighteenth).

[98] See e.g. BN, Châtre de Cangé, Réserve, F 228, fo. 193.

modification could serve as a political message. Until 21 May 1629, Cardinal Richelieu always gave the line to the prince of Condé. On that date, he visibly corrected a letter to the prince, adding a few words at the end of the salutation line.[99] And this deference downgrade was continued henceforth.[100]

Writers were fairly consistent as far as the basic tripartite division (words on the line, *la ligne* and vertical space) was concerned. Beyond that, comparisons are tricky: fingers or lines (on unlined paper) are far from precise measures, and the visual effect of distancing varies with page size and handwriting. But fuzziness was in fact a potential strategic advantage. It gave writers more room for manoeuvre than did codes with clearly distinct alternatives like address and subscription.[101] In a group of letters sent by Secretary Pontchartrain to Vendôme in 1705–6, there is a contrast between official dispatches in folio and autographs written on smaller paper. Address and subscription are invariable in both, but the opening intervals or upper margins of the autographs (which sometimes contain personal requests) are more extensive: Pontchartrain appears to stretch ceremonial 'outside the office'.[102] In other cases, the more ambiguous non-verbal code seems to compensate in part for the verbal. The formulaic defiance of the sword nobles who denied the *Monseigneur* was tempered by their spatial deference to war secretaries. Intendants similarly followed the initial *Monsieur* with a half-page interval.[103]

Different sub-code, similar logic: in non-verbal opening space one re-encounters the phenomena of inflation, anxious reciprocity, haughty conservatism, and gender courtesy. A mid-seventeenth-century ministerial protocol is less generous with space than later prescription and practice. In this earlier period, respectable inferiors were normally not given the line; this seems to have fulfilled the function of distinguishing non-inferiors as the 'obedient' would later in the century. Aware that 'courtesy and submission rather augment than diminish as they go on', the protocol redactor notes that initial intervals were even stingier in the past: ministers only gave the line then to Princes of the Blood. As for dukes and marshals, one gave them the line mainly in return for the same honour.[104] The general devaluation of space later in the reign, when 'words on the line' were normally relegated to markedly inferior addressees only, skipped the conservative protocols of the chancellor and of the Royal House. In the early eighteenth century, Princes of the Blood still wrote several words on the line even to dukes, but gave the line to many noblewomen.[105]

---

[99] See Figure 6.3.
[100] Le Duc d'Aumale, *Histoire des princes de Condé pendant les XVIᵉ et XVIIᵉ siècles* (8 vols, Paris, 1885–96), iii, 525 n. 1. On the epistolary rise of cardinals, see Saint-Simon, 'Estat des changements', pp. 92–6; BN, NAF 9757, fos. 104–105; NAF 66, fos. 70–75. On Richelieu and signs of respect, see Ranum, 'Courtesy, Absolutism, and the Rise of the French State', pp. 431ff.
[101] cf. the difference between discrete type and continuous size in chairs (Chapter Two, p. 50).
[102] See Figure 6.1. The difference is unambiguous, since greater space is left in the smaller, denser format (I thank Sara Chapman for kindly helping me verify Pontchartrain's handwriting). But cf. Jonathan Gibson, 'Significant Space in Manuscript Letters', *Seventeenth Century*, xii (1997), p. 4.
[103] SHD/DAT, A¹ 903, nos. 32, 72 (officers); nos. 1, 14 (intendants).
[104] SHD/DAT, A¹ 154, fo. 28r.
[105] AN, O¹ 279, no. 11; BN, FF 22797, fo. 164; NAF 9757, fos. 276ff.

Page layout injunctions concerned other areas besides the opening sequence. Some manuals and protocols specified intervals and arrangement of the final components leading to the subscription and the signature. Most writers placed the latter two at the bottom-right corner of the final written page. Extra deference might be shown by placing the passage leading into the subscription on a new page, thereby allowing spacious intervals on a page dedicated to courtesy.[106] High-ranking addressers, on the other hand, could subscribe 'without distance' even if the body of the text ended higher up on the page.[107] According to the manuals, spacing in the external superscription also denoted deference.[108]

Compositional considerations involved not only spatial organization, but also the number and location of address forms. Contemporaries counted *Monsieur*s and *Altesse*s, and to maintain dignity address instead of the V-pronoun throughout marked special deference.[109] As for location, it involved a hierarchization of letter components. The subscription was the most consequential of loci: Secretary of State Chateauneuf reportedly gave 'Eminence' in the body of the text, but not in the subscription.[110] The external superscription, on the other hand, seems to have been least prestigious. The royal formulary offers a possible explanation: 'In 1667 the king ordered that the *Monsieur* in the superscription [to the chancellor] be written in full, because it is in the hand of the secretary and not of His Majesty as [is] the inside of the letter'.[111] Outside address was unavoidable if the letter was to reach its destination. The Le Telliers thus had to award *Monseigneur* to the Bouillons on the envelope even when managing to avoid it within the text, and the latter clung to such precious evidence of ministerial deference.[112] More ingenious solutions to this dilemma included the ambiguous abbreviation *M.*, or the resort to foreign languages: envelopes to cardinals were sometimes written in Italian for this reason.[113]

The hierarchy of layout was complemented by the hierarchy of graphics. Its most elaborate feature was abbreviation. The general rule followed the 'effort

---

[106] [Courtin], *Nouveau Traité de la Civilité*, pp. 238–40; SHD/DAT, A¹ 3779, no. 370. See also Arsenal, MS 5170, p. 5.

[107] AAE, MD, France 1206, fo. 23v. In a minute of chancellor Pontchartrain (AAE, MD, France 1093, fo. 158r), the subscription was first corrected *in situ* ('faire service' is changed to 'servir') and then erased and copied above, so that it would follow the text without intervals.

[108] [Jean Puget de la Serre], *Le Secretaire de la Cour: ou, La Maniere d'ecrire selon le Tems* (Lyon, 1713), p. 5; Grimarest, *Traité*, pp. 150–5.

[109] Grimarest, *Traité*, pp. 137–8; BN, NAF 9757, fo. 296v; Arsenal, MS 5170, p. 52; AAE, CP, Espagne 177, fo. 64v ('V.A.R.' instead of an erased 'vous'). See also the rise and fall of the *Excellence* in Condé's correspondence as an indicator of his political position: Blanquie, 'Entre courtoisie et révolte', pp. 441–3.

[110] BN, FF 5764, fo. 2v.

[111] AAE, MD, France 1970, fo. 15v.

[112] See Figure 6.2. For other *Monseigneur*-ed envelopes of *Monseigneur*-less letters kept by the Bouillons, see AN, 273 AP 188, Louvois to the cardinal; cf. AN, O¹ 279, no. 3; AN, K 578, no. 68; BN, FF 7888, fo. 42v.

[113] AN, O¹ 279, no. 11; Saint-Simon, 'Estat des changements', p. 95; BN, NAF 9757, fos. 102, 105. *M.* usually stood for *Monsieur*, but was apparently ambiguous enough. See also the dispute between France and Savoy (n. 25 earlier in this chapter); *Madame Palatine: Lettres françaises*, ed. Van der Cruysse, p. 501; Nevala, *Address in Early English Correspondence*.

principle': fewer abbreviations, more deference. Particularly with terms of address and reference, diminution of the signifier might be construed as diminution of the signified. Short versions of the four main terms thus usually appear only in the less exacting third-person reference.[114] In free address, *Mons.ʳ* or *Mad.ᵉ* marked a significant status gap between correspondents. The sovereign never offered the full-length *Monsieur* to his subjects: the higher-ranking among them received kinship terms anyway, and the others were given the abbreviated form coupled with name/title (except in superscriptions to the chancellor—see earlier). In 1665, Louis ordered to abbreviate the full-length *Messieurs* that had been awarded to the General Assembly of the Clergy during the preceding regency.[115] Other addressers from the Royal Family drew the distinction line lower down the hierarchy of addressees. Abbreviations for dignity address, on the other hand, were more common practice, though deference occasionally obliged the first appearance at least to be unabbreviated.[116]

Another important graphic parameter was handwriting. Autograph writing signified respect or esteem, especially in personal letters. Addressers often apologized when they did not take the trouble to write in their own hand, common justifications being malady and illegible handwriting.[117] In the special case of the king, the senior personal secretary (known as *la plume*) was allowed to imitate the royal hand. This created a tripartite distinction: some letters were simply written in the secretary's hand; others carried the honour of the king's hand, albeit imitated; and some specimens were actually inscribed by Louis himself.[118] There were also cases of partial autograph, especially in the final passage. The Condés kept up this usage despite its decline in the second half of the seventeenth century: a case of polite conservatism.[119] The signature, in any case, was normally autograph. The effort principle was also invoked in the expectation that one rewrote one's letter on a clean sheet if the original draft accumulated too many additions, deletions, or postscripts.[120] Finally, the physical size of the graphic signifier sometimes denoted the social stature of the person signified: some inferiors emphasized the addressee's superiority by writing address forms in larger script than the rest of the text. 'Your Grandeur' was thus taken literally.[121]

---

[114] For details, see Grimarest, *Traité*, pp. 144–6.   [115] AAE, MD, France 1970, fo. 19r.

[116] In BN, Châtre de Cangé, Réserve, F 228, fo. 227, an abbreviated first appearance of 'Votre Majesté' is crossed out and written in full; cf. 'altesse auec un V. et un A. seulement': BN, NAF 9757, fo. 282v.

[117] See BN, NAF 9757, fo. 296v; BN, FF 7888, fos. 52–53; Grimarest, *Traité*, pp. 146–7; Boislisle, 'La désertion du cardinal de Bouillon', pt 3, p. 472.

[118] [Boislisle et al.], 'Le Président Rose et les lettres de la main', pp. 412, 417. See also AAE, MD, France 311, fo. 65v; Duma, 'Les formes de la civilité', p. 96.

[119] BN, FF 7888, fos. 21, 134, 158. Blanquie notes that this non-verbal feature was more flexible than the formulae it embodied: see his 'Entre courtoisie et révolte', pp. 432–5, 438–9; cf. the evolution of ministerial hand in BN, FF 8564.

[120] Or at least apologized for untidiness: *Madame Palatine: Lettres françaises*, ed. Van der Cruysse, pp. 556, 581; SHD/DAT, Aˡ 1779, no. 17.

[121] cf. Chartier, 'Des "secrétaires" pour le peuple?', p. 194; Grimarest, *Traité*, p. 109. For the printed equivalent, see Fogel, *Les cérémonies de l'information*, esp. pp. 371–5.

BILLET STYLE: AVOIDING THE UNAVOIDABLE

Even within a milieu that perceived social divides and their explicit signification as natural, the constant attention to minute ceremonial detail often proved cumbersome for regular exchanges and undesirable for intimate ones. Furthermore, when rank differences or epistolary distinctions were uncertain or contested, communication might break down altogether. These problems help to explain the success of the *billet*, a style which seemed to offer a bypass, or avoidance, of formalities.[122]

Écrire en billet was in fact an umbrella-term, covering a variety of practices, with a lesser or greater relaxation of the various injunctions of epistolary ceremonial. The fundamental criterion that distinguished *billets* from regular letters in this period was formality (not length). The minimal characteristics involved layout: the salutation as a separate component at the beginning was abolished, and interior intervals were eliminated. The next step down the formality scale was to eliminate the subscription formula. Alternatives for leave-taking in this case included various expressions of sentiment, some of which became conventional. A common template was 'I am X yours' (*je suis X à vous*), where 'X' represents an adverb (such as *tout, parfaitement, entièrement* or *absolument*). Writers sometimes ornamented these templates with adverbial phrases: 'with all my heart', 'more than anyone in the world', and so forth.

Like straw-upholstered chairs or like the dispensation from mantled visits, the *billet* style provided an alternative that could save the face of social inferiors and reduce rank contestations by eliminating most manifestations of status.[123] Inequality of layout and subscriptions could be suspended, and since free address was no longer structurally inevitable, this provided a possible way out of the *Monseigneur/Monsieur* dilemma. Ministers were happy to use this style for their correspondence with respectable nobles who did not, however, belong to the highest echelon. An early eighteenth-century protocol noted with regard to Knights of the Order of the Holy Spirit: 'One does not give them the obedient, but should avoid giving them the affectionate, by writing to them *en billet* and putting entirely yours'.[124] In similar circumstances, Catinat was grateful to the war secretary for 'the courtesy of ending his letters with I am all yours'.[125]

But in fact this expedient functioned well only in cases where there was goodwill on both sides. Manifestation of status differences did not entirely disappear, as a result of two main phenomena: irreciprocity and formalization. Relaxation of ceremonial

---

[122] See Geneviève Haroche-Bouzinac, '"Billets font conversation". De la théorie à la pratique: l'exemple de Voltaire', in Bernard Bray and Christoph Strosetzki (eds), *Art de la lettre, art de la conversation à l'époque classique en France* (Paris, 1995), pp. 341–54; Bernard Bray, 'Recherchez la brièveté, évitez l'extrême concision: théorie et pratique du billet à l'époque classique', *Révue de l'AIRE*, xxv–xxvi (2000), 52–64; Christophe Blanquie, 'Saint-Simon épistolier?', *Cahiers Saint-Simon*, xxix (2001), 75–84.

[123] See pp. 52–3 and 100–1 on chairs and mantled visits, respectively.

[124] BN, NAF 9757, fo. 360v. This did not, of course, apply to Knights whose rank entitled them to *obéissant* anyway (such as princes); cf. AAE, CP, Sardaigne 95, fos. 128ff.

[125] BN, FF 7888, fo. 53r. Some perceived ceremonial concessions within a *billet* as less consequential: *Correspondance de Bussy*, ed. Lalanne, iv, 364, 374.

injunctions was not always reciprocal: the inferior correspondent would sometimes continue to offer subscription formulae or even full-formal style well after s/he stopped receiving them.[126] Thus, within a dyad, symbolic subordination was softened—by the elimination of haughty subscriptions and by the fact that the two ending styles were in a sense incommensurable—but not abolished. Catinat himself was accused of *billet* haughtiness following his promotion to the marshalate. Many people complained 'that I could and should end with most humble and most obedient servant, and not make use of the liberty of the *billet*, having little familiarity with them'.[127] Once again, what might have been considered a privilege from recognized superiors is resented from addressers who are perceived as near-equals.

Resentment against Catinat may have stemmed not only from the implied evasion of deferential subscription formulae, but also from a subtler facet of irreciprocity. Even when both sides eventually switched to the informal register, the superior was expected to make the first move. This is evident in the correspondence between Vendôme and La Feuillade on the Italian front. The prince and senior general—who gave no more than 'most humble servant' to dukes—is the one who initiated suspension of formalities: 'and in order to banish from now on any kind of ceremony, I finish this letter, *Monsieur*, completely informally [*sans aucune façon*], and I pray you to do the same on your side'.[128] Ceremony may have been banished, but the expression of superiority only changed level from the text to the meta-text.[129] Among near-equals, the move to informality normally presupposed familiarity, and even then this epistolary rite of passage was often accompanied by polite compensation for the liberty taken.[130]

What is more, formality was pulled back in (if it was ever out). Hierarchical differences were expressed in other ways rather than completely eliminated. This is evident in all aspects of epistolary ceremonial. First, abolition of the salutation spot did not do away with address injunctions. Free forms were still expected in the first sentence, preferably in the first line. While it is hard to prove Grimarest's assertion that even the position within this line mattered, writers did perceive the difference between 'beginning' and 'middle' of the text as meaningful.[131] Further appearances,

---

[126] See the Toulouse-Aumont exchange in BN, FF 22797, fos. 86, 90, 159, 201; and Bray, 'Recherchez la brièveté', p. 59 n. 76. An indicator for irrecirocity is the comparative paucity of *billets* with *Monseigneur* address.

[127] BN, FF 7888, fo. 57r; cf. Grimarest, *Traité*, pp. 129–30.

[128] SHD/DAT, A⁴ 6, dossier '1704–1706', 8 February 1704. Vendôme repeated the suggestion a few weeks later, and many subsequent letters from La Feuillade are indeed in *billet* form.

[129] As with the dispensation from mantled visits, another code where reciprocity was crucial. For superior permission, see also AC, T ii, fo. 6; Blanquie, 'Entre courtoisie et révolte', p. 431; *Madame Palatine: Lettres françaises*, ed. Van der Cruysse, pp. 116, 186. Even then, inferiors (like Croisille) sometimes remained hesitant.

[130] Haroche-Bouzinac, '"Billets font conversation"', pp. 343–4; Grassi, *L'Art de la lettre*, p. 183. Saint-Simon apparently had this delicacy in mind when he suggested that in cases of ceremonial incertitude with regard to near-equals, the dukes 'finiront en billet, s'ils écrivent les premiers, *mais très-poliment*': see his *Traités politiques et autres écrits*, p. 443 (my emphasis).

[131] Grimarest, *Traité*, p. 116; BN, NAF 9757, fos. 295–296; Arsenal, MS 5170, p. 184. The *Monsieur* is occasionally squeezed in at the end of the first line rather than demoted to the second: SHD/DAT, A¹ 2108, no. 41. See also Henri-Jules's autograph addition of several *Monsieur*s to a draft to Conti: AC, T i, fos. 348ff.; this also illustrates that formal address was customary even among close relatives.

especially in the ending passage, were also common. This underscores the singularity of the total omission of free address from Le Tellier *billets*, which so piqued the Bouillons.[132] Second, the *à vous* ending constructions, which were supposed to signify sentiment rather than rank, were integrated into protocols by the early eighteenth century. Marshal Villars as war minister employed 'Very perfectly yours' with regard to colonels and 'Entirely yours' to lieutenant-colonels.[133] Third, the ceremonial of expression did not disappear, and was even accentuated according to Grimarest: superiors were more attentive to style in *billets*, 'in order to mark their *bonté*, their *estime*, their *amitié* with haughtiness'.[134] Finally, writers continued to offer generous spatial margins at the top of the page.[135]

* * *

In *billets* as in letters, epistolary ceremonial touched on the many sensitive spots in the social-political fabric of early modern France: the rise of cardinals, ministers, and Legitimated Princes; the contested and graded status of Foreign Princes; tensions between sword and robe, and other divisions in provincial as well as Parisian circles. Letters, of course, were not only about form or hierarchy, nor were all letter-writers as querulous and obsessed about their status as were Saint-Simon or the cardinal of Bouillon. But the accumulation of contestations and dilemmas presented here (which are only a sample of known documented cases) points to its wide-ranging significance in early modern society. Formal correspondence had to go on, and even people of a non-ceremonious constitution like Catinat had to learn its intricacies if they were to take part in the *commerce du monde*. Or correspondence might in fact not go on when its formal aspects were in dispute, disrupting not just social exchanges, but also diplomatic communications and even military chains of command.

Epistolary ceremonial enriches and nuances our understanding of status interaction.[136] The more consistent documentary basis of the inquiry, grounded on the abundance of surviving original correspondence, allows a finer-grained analysis of the code and of its evolution. Letters, moreover, enable us to observe status interactions between diverse strata of society, juxtaposing parties who might not have been forced to articulate their rank relations in other settings. Epistolary ceremonial, finally, was less susceptible to public scrutiny and to monarchical control than were high ceremonies, dress codes, or court routines. Whether or not it was to be exposed to the eye of the public or of the sovereign was at the correspondents' discretion. This allowed greater autonomy and flexibility, and may explain why epistolary distinctions seem to have been more immediately indicative of power relations and constraints. In the potentially private

---

[132] See earlier and Figure 6.2.

[133] SHD/DAT, A¹ 2541. This generated a spectacular incident: Giora Sternberg, 'Are *formules de politesse* Always Polite? The Bauffremont-Villars Incident, Discursive Struggles and Social Tensions under the *Ancien Régime*', *Zeitsprünge*, xiii (2009), 219–34. *Tout à vous*, the most common variant, was largely relegated to social inferiors by the end of the seventeenth century. Ending a *billet* abruptly, with no final *civilité*, was reserved for cases of great superiority of the addresser (or great familiarity): see Grassi, *L'Art de la lettre*, pp. 178ff.

[134] Grimarest, *Traité*, pp. 124–5.   [135] AAE, CP, Espagne 177, fo. 97.

[136] While, from a methodological perspective, it brings to light a neglected dimension of one of the most widely-used historical sources: Sternberg, 'Epistolary Ceremonial', esp. pp. 35–6, 82–5.

context of correspondence, interactants could cede more ground than they would in the public arena of the court.

The most vivid example is the case of ministers. These newcomers were normally relegated to a secondary position, if any, during the ceremonial routines of the court. At most, they could assume (or usurp) the status symbols of the rank-and-file 'people of quality'.[137] Ministerial attempts to equate themselves with the pinnacle of the sword nobility were thwarted by a monarch still keen to uphold the pre-eminence of birth and arms.[138] Against such a background, it is all the more remarkable that ministers could demand, and obtain, complete ceremonial equality in their bilateral epistolary exchanges with the highest echelon of the non-princely aristocracy, and clear superiority in their dealings with the rest—including lieutenant-generals and members of prominent old families. Among the latter, even those who insisted on equal *Monsieur* treatment did not object to a ministerial edge in subscriptions, expression, and space.

Another corollary of the dyadic and potentially private nature of correspondence was greater inconsistency. Unlike processions, letter exchanges only confronted two individuals at a time and hence could not offer anything approaching a comprehensive image of the social order. The question of dukes versus ministers is again instructive. While direct bilateral exchanges were roughly equal, correspondence with third parties in some cases gave the edge to the dukes, in others to the ministers. The latter often received more deference from inferiors, while the Royal House maintained the advantage of the older aristocracy.[139] Epistolary ceremonial was sometimes inconsistent even between members of the same two status-groups. Its structural complexity, moreover, makes evaluations and comparisons far from straightforward, since different features (verbal, non-verbal) may lead to different conclusions, especially in borderline cases.

Yet comparisons, within dyads and between them, remained the fundamental key for the meaning of epistolary ceremonial.[140] Here too, the crucial measure was relative, not absolute. Epistolary signs made sense only in relation to each other and to dyadic histories (the question of reciprocity). Degree of deference was not inherent in the form. Seemingly obsequious constructions like 'Your Highness' or 'Your most humble servant' were in fact disrespectful when 'Most Serene Highness' or 'most humble and most obedient servant' were expected. Honour was not simply incremental, and aristocrats relinquished deference forms that they had to share with their inferiors. In opposing the manner in which dukes were expected to treat Princes of the Blood, Saint-Simon does not argue so much against the *Monseigneur* and *Altesse Sérénissime* per se as he does

---

[137] As we have seen e.g. in the case of mourning mantles in Chapter Four, esp. p. 100 n. 16.

[138] See SSB, xv, 241–51; BM, MS 2746, fos. 100–102.

[139] As in 'cousin' treatment. Interestingly, the chancellor protocol also maintained the edge of the sword nobility, even though chancellors were generally of robe, and sometimes of ministerial, origin: AN, O¹ 279, no. 11. On deference from inferiors, see Saint-Simon, 'Estat des changements', pp. 142–5.

[140] See BN, NAF 9471, fos. 124–129, and Le Vaillant to cardinal of Bouillon, 17 April 1690 (AN, 273 AP 190, dossier 10).

against their implications in relation to other cases: that such treatment was shared with the lowliest addressers; that Foreign Princes escaped it; and that dukes received no dignity address in return.[141]

The special communication setting of correspondence also made the logic of precedent-making trickier than that operative in other status interactions. Letters as ceremonial events involved at least two separate and potentially private occasions—writing and reading—each normally controlled by one of the parties. A new precedent, therefore, could not be unilaterally usurped: its successful introduction required the collaboration of its intended victim. This is obvious in the case of 'indirect' challenges (the pretender demands to be treated more deferentially, as in other codes), but is also true for 'direct' ones (the pretender treats less deferentially). For addressees could block irreverent letters simply by refusing to accept or to reply. The penalty for such avoidance, if any, was lower than that paid in more public ceremonial battlefields. Alternatively, addressees could escalate the situation by retaliating in kind.[142] In the absence of resolution, the parties could cease communications entirely, agree on a temporary bypass, or solicit royal adjudication.

To return to the question of structural complexity, the interplay between the different components of the code involved a division of labour and occasional trade-offs, especially between formulaic and flexible aspects. In most cases, forms of address served to distinguish superior addressees: *Monseigneur* and dignity address as opposed to the 'unmarked' *Monsieur* and *vous*. Subscription formulae, for their part, exposed inferiors: 'friend', 'affectionate', and single-adjective constructions as opposed to the unmarked 'most humble and most obedient servant'. The ceremonial of expression and non-verbal aspects were fuzzier and hence more applicable for strategic variation, as in the obsequious terminology that writers employed in times of need; or for trade-offs, as in the generous spatial intervals that apparently compensated for the lack of the *Monseigneur*. Finally, the 'familiar' *billet* style established a series of variants of the formal style rather than its absolute negation.

How did such a complex code evolve, in the course of the reign and beyond? In relating signifiers (letter form) to signified (status relations), it is important to distinguish between at least two types of change. The first is change on the level of the signifier that is related to 'external' developments on the level of the signified: an upgrade or downgrade of epistolary ceremonial that correlates with an increase or a decrease in status difference. For example, the growing influence of ministers over the sword nobility in the seventeenth century can explain changes in their respective epistolary ceremonial. As in other codes, the logic of the precedent provides a mechanism for such change: beginning with isolated novelties, continuing with insinuations and challenges, and ending with the establishment of a new norm. The new cultural norm, in turn, reinforces or advances social transformations. This positive

---

[141] Saint-Simon, 'Matériaux pour servir a un mémoire sur l'occurrence présente', pp. 251–2.
[142] See also BN, NAF 9757, fo. 270v; Callières, *Des mots à la mode*, pp. 164–5.

correlation can be methodologically fruitful from both perspectives: status interaction can indicate or explain social and political changes, and vice versa.

The dynamics of signifiers does not, however, always go hand in hand with the dynamics of the signified. Discursive arms races, a climate of politeness, or simple linguistic drift can all lead to a total 'internal' translation of epistolary signifiers without a correlating external change in the signified social relations. This is arguably the case with the shift in subscription formulae that occurred in the seventeenth century. The fact that 'obedient' replaced 'affectionate' as the adjective for non-inferior addressees does not necessarily indicate change in the relations between specific seventeenth-century subscribers and 'subscribees'. When the crucial measure is relative, inflation across the board may amount to nothing in the final count.[143] This calls for caution in comparative diachronic studies: superficial differences may obscure underlying similarities. In other respects, though, the motors behind internal change may signal important external phenomena. Discursive arms races, for example, are proof of the continuing vitality of the quest for distinction.

Finally, a diachronic analysis, like a synchronic one, must also take into account the structural complexity of epistolary ceremonial and the interplay among its diverse aspects. For instance, the distinction between inferior and equal addressees may have been realized by different components in different periods, not least as a result of the levelling effect of inflationary processes. In the early seventeenth century, spatial layout may have been critical for this distinction. In the course of the reign of Louis XIV, addressers increasingly gave the line to inferiors as well as to equals and superiors, and the subscription seems to have become the determining factor. In the eighteenth century, as 'obedient' filtered down, lexical variation of the preceding ending passage became more important, formally incorporating constructions that originated in the 'familiar' *billet* style. If this hypothesis is substantiated, then what seems like increased courtesy or egalitarianism (or the opposite) when components are considered in isolation, may well turn out to be no more than an internal shift, when the system is considered as a whole.

---

[143] Except for those who lag behind in discursive arms races or continue to receive the old form from 'haughty conservatives' despite a polite *Zeitgeist*, like the untitled sword nobility in the case of the 'obedient'/'affectionate' transition, or the sub-Bourbon aristocracy and its difficulties in assuming dignity address or receiving respectable subscriptions from the Princes of the Blood.

Conclusion

This book has showcased early modern status interaction by studying ceremony, dress, gesture, and writing during the reign of Louis XIV. Each of the angles was focused enough to allow in-depth, systematic analysis and the recovery of insider perspectives 'on the ground'; together, they create a comparative framework that ranges across the broad spectrum of symbolic interaction. The marriage of 1679 has illustrated the complex interplay among status codes on one key ceremonial occasion, while the *affaire des sièges* has opened an extraordinary window into the micro-politics of crisis and negotiation. The case of mantles, in high ceremonies and on social occasions, has illuminated the interactional dimension of dress and the diachronic development of status codes. The analysis of court routines has underscored the advantages of extending our gaze beyond the sovereign's, even when considering his own domestic service. Finally, epistolary ceremonial has offered the rare opportunity to observe early modern status interaction in its original form, in relative abundance, and among diverse social groups.

This conclusion draws together key themes that have recurred in the chapters and points out inter-connections and wider implications. The first section draws on preceding discussions to analyse the logic and workings of some of the general, cross-code principles, including the questions of relativity and avoidance. Next, I examine the dynamics of codification. What were the relations between status symbols and status, between status *de facto* and status *de jure*, and between customary and positive law? What light can they shed on the fluidity of social position, on the power of the written medium, and on the limitations of royal control? The following section illuminates the macro-political impact of these questions via a longitudinal analysis of the Legitimated Princes. I end by highlighting the significance of the phenomenon in this and in other social, geographical, and temporal contexts and hence the importance of developing a comparative framework of status interaction in the early modern world.

THE MECHANICS OF STATUS INTERACTION

Let us begin by analysing some of the cross-code regularities, or the general principles of status interaction that recurred in the preceding chapters. The first is the question of arbitrariness. Although it is sometimes possible to think of plausible rationales, much was arbitrary in status symbols, as in symbols in general: domains, parameters, mappings, and orderings. Anything could serve as a sign for distinction, from the most precious object to the most daily routine. Within the same domain, certain distinguishing parameters were meaningful (or more meaningful) while others were not: for example, seat-type as opposed to seat-size. Conversely, the same parameter functioned differently across domains: seat-size as opposed to mantle-size (train-length). Mappings—the assignment of specific values—did not follow an obvious logic either: why leave three lines rather than four (or two) to the First Prince of the Blood? Even orderings were not always consistent: while the common-sense notion of 'the more the better' explains many instances (ells in mantles, links in chains of service, adjectives in subscriptions), the inverted curtness principle contradicts it. And how should we order three-dimensional space? The ultimate demonstration of arbitrariness lies in the variability between different contexts: the insignificance of seat-size did not hold in Italy. This principle—or rather, anti-principle—poses a serious methodological challenge, since it entails that we cannot assume status codes a priori, and must identify the meaningful in each code and in each context anew.

Once a particular status symbol became meaningful in a given context, the competition over mappings that made up status interaction generally followed the relativity principle.[1] What mattered, with ells or with adjectives, were not the absolute measures per se, but the differences vis-à-vis one's rivals. From a historical or cultural distance, it is often tempting to marvel at seemingly prodigious lengths or obsequious formulations, but these should always be evaluated in the context of their specific code and relative to the available alternatives. In a system guided by precedent, the alternatives included not only the measures of co-present parties, but also relevant past cases. In 1685, for example, the six ells of Henri-Jules's daughter-in-law referred back to those of the Granddaughters of France in 1679 and in 1684. In view of the variation and evolution of status codes in time, however, co-presence offered the most definitive comparison. Thus, the ultimate confirmation of the equality of trains occurred only in the 1710s, when the Orléans and the Condés appeared mantled together for the first time in decades.

In cases of direct interaction, the relative standing of parties was signified not only by comparisons between their respective, co-present status symbols, but also by the structure of the situation. Visits and letters provide good examples. Any visit triggered, by definition, a set of interactional parameters. Where did the host meet the visitor? Who preceded whom? Did the visitor wear garments specific to the interaction, such as mourning mantles? Similarly with letters: Did the addresser use *Monseigneur* or *Monsieur* (in the case of a male addressee)? Which ending formula did s/he use? What was the spatial distance between salutation and body of text? The answers to these questions—whether they went one way or the other—constituted statements about relative status. In the special case of service, the very performance of the interaction decided the matter by definition, signifying the subordination of server to served.

---

[1] On this fundamental principle, cf. Faudemay, *La distinction à l'âge classique*; and Merlin-Kajman, ' "Une troisième espèce de simple dignité" '.

Situations of direct interaction could, of course, also involve comparisons between co-present status symbols, as in the question of seat-types in visits. Furthermore, each direct statement also entailed multiple indirect comparisons, in time or in space. The treatment of an addressee, for example, would compare with past or future treatments of other addressees by the same letter-writer, or of the same addressee by other letter-writers. The notion of reciprocity, or role-reversal between parties, introduces a particular type of comparison (did both correspondents employ the same subscription formula to one another?). Sometimes only such a comparison among a series of interactions would supply a definite statement about status relations.[2] Service was exceptional in this respect because it was irreciprocal by definition.[3] To comparisons within codes or sub-codes one must, of course, add the complex interplay among them. A single ceremonial occasion could involve multiple status interactions. In some cases, they acted in unison; in others, they expressed compromises or trade-offs (titles offsetting *plume* in 1679; secondary service offsetting primary service; epistolary space offsetting form of address).

Status symbols, moreover, were not simply incremental. The negative corollary of the relativity principle was that parties would prefer to diminish their absolute honours or to relinquish them altogether rather than share them with their inferiors or receive less than their near-equals. Distinctions had to distinguish. The dauphin received a simple 'vous' address instead of the devalued 'Royal Highness', and the regent waived train-bearers in 1715 to make a comparative point. Another aspect of this principle was that protagonists did not simply accumulate as many advantages as they could. Indeed, they cared more to obtain small advantages vis-à-vis their near-equals than greater ones offered by marked inferiors. As Maine put it, 'the more below us in status [*etats*], the less one has to observe the forms'.[4] These advantages, besides, did not just determine relative precedence. Those who denied mantled visits or the *Monseigneur* did not necessarily question the superiority of hosts or of addressees; they contested its degree and the extent of subordination that it entailed.[5]

Parties who could not openly challenge the advantages sought by rivals, or who failed to secure their own claims, would frequently resort to the avoidance tactic, by staying away from the event altogether or by circumventing the specific act under dispute. This tactic worked better in direct interactions that depended on presence or active cooperation (like the handing of the chemise), than in comparisons, where rivals could still take possession of their own status symbols (as in 1665, when Condé avoidance could not prevent *Monsieur* from wearing seven ells for the first

---

[2] This was the case in the question of spatial precedence in visits. Since hosts were expected to cede precedence (*donner la main*) to near-equals as well as to superiors, the choreography of a single visit might not determine status relations. For some near-equals, only the order of precedence on neutral ground (*en lieu tiers*) would decide the matter.

[3] Extraordinary inversions being the exception that proves the rule. Of course, there was nothing inherently irreciprocal about service (the arbitrariness principle); it evolved that way in this particular context; cf. the discussion of 'symmetrical' versus 'asymmetrical' rules of conduct in Goffman, *Interaction Ritual*, pp. 47–95.

[4] AN, K 577, no. 72, fo. 1v; cf. Duindam, *Myths of Power*, pp. 144–8.

[5] Conversely, symbolic equality does not always indicate status equality.

time). Relatedly, avoidance was more salient on high ceremonies than on everyday routines. A subtle variant served to introduce a new claim surreptitiously: usurpers would initially avoid marked occasions, building their claim gradually in ambiguous or intermediate situations (mantled visits). Parties with a strong case, in contrast, would adopt the opposite tactic, trying to force avoiders into clear-cut interactions. (Compare the cases of the chemise in 1675 and in 1717; or of Le Tellier *billets* to the Bouillons versus the eleven *Monsieur*s to Monaco.)

Avoidance was not only an adversarial tactic, though. In many cases, conflicting parties who could not agree on the substance nevertheless mutually found some expedient, like the *billet* style, that allowed them to bypass unresolved problems. In others, the monarch forced avoidance on the parties. For an indecisive ruler like Louis XIV, to conduct affairs 'without ceremony' or 'without consequence', or even to prohibit those in dispute from attending a larger event, was an easy way out of a ruling dilemma. In the international arena, avoidance was built into diplomatic ceremonial in the form of the *incognito*, which allowed visiting dignitaries to suspend formalities by conventional denial of their identity, and hence of their status claims.[6] These various expedients, however, failed to eliminate status interaction altogether. Differences, for example, might remain on the 'meta' level (one-sided dispensation from mantled visits, initiation of the *billet* style), or implied in the situation (armchair behind a standing host).

These general principles are of course abstractions and approximations only, never fully articulated as such in the mind of any single contemporary. The latter differed in perspective and in competence; even a connoisseur like Saint-Simon overlooked and misconstrued (and not just out of bias). All the same, this general model, like the more specific ones detailed in the preceding chapters, underscores the complexity of status interaction, and the degree of alertness, perseverance, and sophistication required of its protagonists.

THE DYNAMICS OF CODIFICATION: *DE FACTO, DE JURE, DE REGISTRO*

Any status interaction might have far-reaching consequences because, contrary to the traditional image of the Society of Orders and of the Sun King's court in particular, neither ceremonial nor rank was ever definitively codified there. Status symbols did not mirror a rigid, pre-determined hierarchy, but rather operated as a powerful tool for shaping an unstable and constantly evolving system. In high ceremonies as in everyday routines, these symbols created, as well as reflected, status and rank. Participants had to remain vigilant at all times, identifying opportunities to further their own claims while keeping guard against those of their rivals. In these circumstances, just to preserve the status quo demanded considerable effort.[7]

---

[6] Bély, *La société des princes*, chs. xxii–xxv.
[7] The methodological corollary of the last point is that 'bottom line' change is not a sufficient measure for the rigidity or stability of the system.

In dynastic contexts, demographic fluctuation and uncertainty introduced a structural instability that gave greater scope to status interaction.[8] Just as the contraction of the nuclear royal family in the late sixteenth century had facilitated the elevation of the Princes of the Blood as a distinct rank, so its expansion in the course of the seventeenth century provided the setting for the invention of the Grandchildren of France. What began as a miscellany of symbolic pretensions by individuals in a genealogical position unheard of since the fifteenth century ended up in the consolidation of a new level in the court hierarchy. By 1679, this new rank was becoming established *pace* the Princes of the Blood, and the birth of a male incumbent (the duke of Chartres) opened the possibility—or danger—of a further step down the genealogy. A generation later, hypothetical debate turned into overt dispute between Orléans and Condés.

It was only then, towards the end of the reign, that Louis XIV made a first attempt to codify rank and precedence in the Royal House. The formal regulation of 1710 confirmed the arrangement secretly offered to Gourville thirty years earlier, of recognizing the rank of Grandchildren of France while turning down the aspirations of the great-Grandchildren.[9] In retrospect, the former rank may seem a natural part of ancien-régime hierarchy, but it had been as insecure to begin with as its abortive descendant. In both campaigns, the Orléans relied on status interaction to build their case, seeking distinctions *de facto* before demanding the recognition of a novel rank *de jure*. The persistent struggle of the Condés against the pretensions of the third generation—in seats, trains, and other respects—ultimately bore fruit in the fourth.

The last years of the reign saw a couple of other cases of official codification: the edict on the peerage and the decisions on the status of the Legitimated Princes (see the next section). These exceptions, however, prove the rule. They came about as a result of sustained pressure from interested parties and never cohered into anything resembling a unified table of ranks. The edict on the peerage, for example, did not specify the relations among the different types of dukes, let alone settle the perennial rivalry between them and the even worse defined Foreign Princes. What codification there was, moreover, never spelt out status interaction in any comprehensive way. In the same years, for example, the monarch refused to make an unequivocal decision on mantled visits. Legislation on the Legitimated Princes gave them the 'same honours' as others—whose honours had never been codified in the first place. Statute thus ultimately referred back to custom. The patents of 1723 followed this logic to its extreme, setting the honours of Maine and Toulouse 'as has been practiced in their regard before 1710'.[10]

Did the monarch fear that detailed codification might limit his room for manoeuvre as arbiter? Was he 'paralysed by indecision' at court as he sometimes appears to have been in the war cabinet? Or was the Sun King a traditionalist who

---

[8] In other contexts, the processes of creation and reproduction that destabilised the social order were administrative as well as biological, as in the appearance and transformation of office-holders in both centre and periphery; cf. Descimon and Haddad, *Épreuves de noblesse*.

[9] AN, O¹ 54, fos. 38v–40r. See also SSB, xix, 61–78, 497–516.

[10] AN, O¹ 67, p. 256.

adhered to the priority of custom over statute?[11] Whatever the cause, effect is clear: the ceremonial court was far less well-ordered and codified than its myth would have us believe. Rule by precedent remained fundamental, and this, in turn, placed a premium on mechanisms of ceremonial memory. In the seventeenth century, these mechanisms were becoming increasingly reliant on the written medium. The Masters of Ceremonies and other officials regularly kept record of proceedings under their charge, and the crown would call on their registers to refresh its ceremonial memory in cases of uncertainty or contestation. A pertinent precedent, duly recorded, could thus make a difference.

The striking consequence of the growing importance of written records in status-related decision-making was that they became a contested stake in themselves. Knowledge was power, and protagonists worked hard to amass it. Saint-Simon was not alone in creating a knowledge-base of status interaction. The Condés collected evidence and maintained their own ceremonial registers and epistolary protocols. The duke of Maine produced remarkably detailed memoranda on high ceremonies and everyday routines. His nephew, the duke of Penthièvre, would carry on these documentary efforts in the eighteenth century. And the Bouillons preserved *Monseigneur*-ed envelopes that proved the epistolary deference of the Le Telliers. Such independent repositories of past precedents aided their owners in future contestations. Based on memoranda written in the last decade of the reign, Maine could successfully challenge the official version in 1723.

To an extent, the written record became more important than the event it purported to reflect. Information warfare was the continuation of status interaction by other means. A precedent had to reach a reputable repository in order to sustain authority over time. In 1690, Henri-Jules was willing to sacrifice the immediate gratification of public glory for the assurance of lasting official documentation. Conversely, one might cover up a defeat by keeping it off the record, as the *Grand Condé* tried to do in 1679. In other cases, the official version was altered after it had already been noted down. Interested parties thus succeeded in infiltrating the organs of the monarchy and manipulating ceremonial memory to suit their partisan agenda. This calls into question both the effectiveness of central control and the reliability of the sources it produced.[12]

STATUS LEGITIMATING POWER

The extraordinary rise of the Legitimated Princes provides us with a strong case for the link among status symbols, rank, and power, or between micro-politics and macro-politics. From bastards of dubious legal standing in the early years of the

---

[11] We have encountered on more than one occasion the assumption that secure possession was superior to royal directive, and that the latter could accordingly be counter-productive: see e.g. pp. 104, 119, 124–5. On royal paralysis, see Guy Rowlands, *The Dynastic State and the Army under Louis XIV: Royal Service and Private Interest, 1661 to 1701* (Cambridge, 2002), p. 293; cf. Cosandey, 'L'insoutenable légèreté du rang'.

[12] For a detailed analysis, see Sternberg, 'Manipulating Information'.

reign, the Legitimated became full-fledged Princes of the Blood at its close. Hindsight tells us that this constitutional revolution ultimately failed, and that the bastard progeny, removed from the line of succession a few years after the death of its progenitor, never acceded to the French throne. But in 1715 these were far from foregone conclusions. Contemporaries had seen the number of legitimate successors shrink by almost half in the princely 'hecatomb' of the preceding few years.[13] The inclusion of the bastards in the line of succession had passed without resistance in 1714. Some even suspected that the next step would reorder successors and place the Legitimated immediately after Louis XV. After all, if they were full princes of royal blood, why not go by degree of consanguinity?

Looking forward, 'the affair of the princes' would become a major controversy in the years that followed the death of Louis XIV and would continue to influence legal and constitutional debates and the evolution of a political public sphere in the course of the eighteenth century.[14] As I have argued throughout, however, the legal and political crisis of the 1710s cannot be understood without the socio-cultural micro-interactions of earlier decades, and the public debates of the regency—without the clandestine manoeuvres of the previous reign. The spate of demographic accidents in the final years was, of course, a necessary condition for the constitutional revolution of 1714. But so was the gradual and premeditated advancement of the royal bastards since the 1660s. By the time they became Princes of the Blood by right, they had long become like Princes of the Blood in fact. It is unlikely that Louis XIV would have dared to change the 'fundamental law' of royal succession without this long accumulation of precedents. Let us, then, reconsider the trajectory of the Legitimated Princes from obscurity to integration, and in particular the interplay between *de facto* possessions and *de jure* promotions.[15]

Louis legitimated the children of Madame de La Vallière and of Madame de Montespan at an early age, giving them special titles and privileges. He named them after royal lands, made the count of Vermandois Admiral of France at the age of two, and the duke of Maine Colonel-General of the Swiss and Grison forces at the age of four. The king's secret instructions to Colbert show that the decision to treat them at court like Princes of the Blood can be dated as early as 1675.[16] On the other hand, they also show the monarch's reluctance to declare his will in the matter and his appreciation of the power of *de facto* possessions, introduced gradually and 'naturally'. He instructed, in the first instance, to avoid marked honours like the chemise or the serviette and, for decades, would not turn verbal order into formal legislation.

---

[13] Colin Jones, *The Great Nation: France from Louis XV to Napoleon* (London, 2003), p. 29. In 1709, there were twelve legitimate French successors; in 1714, only seven, two of them infants.

[14] Ellis, *Boulainvilliers and the French Monarchy*, ch. 6; Claire Saguez-Lovisi, *Les lois fondamentales au XVIIIᵉ siècle: recherches sur la loi de dévolution de la couronne* (Paris, 1984); and, most recently, Matthew Gerber, *Bastards: Politics, Family, and Law in Early Modern France* (Oxford-New York, 2012), ch. 3.

[15] cf. SSB, xxiv, 341–58; Brocher, *À la cour de Louis XIV*, ch. 5; Leferme-Falguières, 'Le monde des courtisans', pp. 612–31.

[16] See pp. 124–5. See also *Lettres, mémoires et instructions de Colbert*, ed. Clément, vi, 272–3.

The marriage of 1679 formed the next landmark in the status of the bastards: their first appearance in a major high ceremony. Literally elevated together with the legitimate Bourbons above all other participants, the Legitimated Princes and Princesses shared other honours exclusive to the Royal House, including train-bearing and the appellation of *très hautle et puissantle* in the marriage contract. They were also named 'Bourbon' there, anticipating the *de jure* conferral of this right a few months later.[17] 'To authorise these novelties better', Louis extended them to the duke of Verneuil, surviving son of Henri IV.[18] In the following decade, he showered military and court offices on his male bastards, and married the female ones into the legitimate line.[19] Each bridegroom raised the stakes further: first, a junior Prince of the Blood in 1680; then, a future head of the Condé branch in 1685; and finally, the king's nephew, a Grandson of France, in 1692. That year, Maine married the daughter of the prince of Condé.[20]

De jure, the first significant recognition came in 1694, in the creation of an intermediate rank for Maine, Toulouse, and their future children: after the Princes of the Blood and before the rest of the aristocracy, 'in all places, acts, ceremonies and assemblies, public and private', notably including the *parlement*.[21] The king was building on the precedent of Henri IV, who had tried to create a similar rank for his own legitimated son, the duke of Vendôme. In addition, Louis personally met with the leaders of the *parlement* to arrange intermediate honours for his sons in the ceremonial of the assembly.[22] He thus officially confirmed decades of *de facto* precedence at court, and gave the Legitimated Princes a rank in formal state occasions.

In fact, at court intermediate rank shaded into equality with the Princes of the Blood. In the spatial choreography of weddings, the Legitimated shared the exclusive right to place their cushions on the Persian rug, though they formed a class of their own behind the Princes of the Blood. In everyday life, one would be hard pressed to spot differences between the two groups: they shared, *inter alia*, the quintessential Bourbon honour of ousting the service, and the right to receive 'Most Serene Highness' from dukes. Indeed, for a while at least, legitimate and legitimated seem to have joined forces in order to extract novel honours from other groups, as in the case of mantled visits from the titled nobility. Many courtiers put it simply: the Legitimated enjoyed the 'rang' of Princes of the Blood.[23]

---

[17] See Chapter One and Isambert et al. (eds), *Recueil général des anciennes lois françaises* (29 vols, Paris, 1821–33), xix, 230–1. In the same period, the king ordered the mayor of Paris to extend the traditional New Year visits to the Legitimated Princes, and to give them the same presents as to the Princes of the Blood: BM, MS 2741, fo. 76.

[18] Sourches, i, 14.

[19] Rowlands, *The Dynastic State*, esp. pp. iv–v, 307–8, 343–5.

[20] Since women had to adopt the rank of their husband, female hypogamy was more marked than its male counterpart. See Le Roy Ladurie with Fitou, *Saint-Simon*, ch. 5.

[21] AN, O¹ 38, fos. 125v–126v.

[22] e.g. one *huissier* would accompany them on their way out, as opposed to two in the case of the legitimate Bourbons. For a recent discussion of the precedent of Henri IV, see Fanny Cosandey, 'Ordonner à la cour: Entre promotion du sang et célébration de la personne royale', in Michel De Waele (ed.), *Lendemains de guerre civile: réconciliations et restaurations en France sous Henri IV* (Québec, 2011), pp. 221–44.

[23] Sourches, i, 14; Dangeau, vi, 240; Arsenal, MS 3863, p. 385.

Unlike the intermediate rank, though, this customary near-equality of honours was yet to receive *de jure* confirmation. As the reign of Louis XIV was drawing to its close, Maine realized that he needed more durable recognition of his status. There was no guarantee that his honours would survive his aging progenitor. What is more, Maine had to provide for his descendants, whose rank at court was yet to be defined. And finally, near-equality was not quite equal to the real thing.

The dynastic hecatomb of the last years of the reign accelerated developments. In the obsequies of Henri-Jules in 1709, the Legitimated Princes tightened their *de facto* possessions. To paraphrase the famous 'duck test', if they represented the mourning like Princes of the Blood and received and exchanged mantled visits like Princes of the Blood, it would be easier for them to become Princes of the Blood. Maine researched the ceremonial past and would henceforth meticulously record the ceremonial present.[24] When the duke of Bourbon died in 1710, Maine pushed forward the question of his children. Louis agreed to give them the same honours enjoyed by their father, but the manner of ratification hints at his uneasiness about the decision: he ordered a cryptic note on the register rather than a dedicated document, and exhorted the *Grand Dauphin* and the duke of Burgundy to uphold it when they acceded to the throne.[25] In the absence of substantial *de jure* confirmation, *de facto* public possession became crucial, and the prince of Dombes, accordingly, hastened to hand the chemise and the serviette.

In May 1711, shortly after the death of the *Grand Dauphin*, the king issued two pieces of legislation. The first and more famous one was the public edict on the peerage; among other things, it expanded the intermediate rank of 1694, specifying new state honours and extending them to the legitimated posterity—not just to the second generation. In parallel, Maine conducted secret negotiations with the king's ministers concerning private patents that would reflect the more elevated *de facto* status of near-equality. In order to allay Louis's reluctance, the bastard argued that these documents would merely confirm existing possessions and may therefore never need to come to light. The monarch finally agreed to confirm Maine, his children, and Toulouse, in the enjoyment of the 'same honours that are and could in the future be rendered to the Princes of the Blood', albeit on a personal basis and with the exception of the (intermediate) state honours specified in the edict.[26] Reservations notwithstanding, for the first time the monarch recognised, formally and explicitly, the near-equality between legitimated and legitimate.

What is more, contrary to Maine's (deliberately misleading?) assurances, the transition from *de facto* to *de jure* did more than confirm existing possessions. Until 1711, the Legitimated were constrained by past precedents and had to present a case for each honour anew. The patents, on the other hand, enabled them to

---

[24] For details see Sternberg, 'Manipulating Information', pp. 255–61.

[25] AN, O¹ 54, fo. 40v; BM, MS 2745, fo. 194. The note awarded the children the treatment of their father without specifying what that treatment was. In his own register, Maine added: 'or, les honneurs dont je jouis à la cour sont tous les mêmes que ceux des princes du sang': SSB, xix, 517. See also SSB, xix, 91–108. The unusual act of royal request implied that the thing requested was not self-evident even after the decision.

[26] AN, O¹ 55, fos. 52–53. On the secret negotiations, see SSB, xxi, 462–3; AN, 257 AP 2.

demand equality a priori, arguably even where it had been denied them in the past. Maine did precisely that in 1713, invoking the patents in order to force the Princes of the Blood to accept the Legitimated cushions in the same row with their own on the Persian rug, contrary to the precedents of 1679 and of other occasions.[27] The *de jure* title thus fed back into the *de facto* possessions that had substantiated it in the first place. The bastards became Princes of the Blood for nearly all practical purposes.

The ultimate promotion followed the death of the duke of Berry in 1714. The sovereign issued the famous public edict that gave his bastards and their legitimate posterity the full rank of Princes of the Blood, including, most importantly, the right to inherit the throne after the legitimate Bourbons. The Legitimated Princes were now a few heartbeats away from the fountain of power. The next year, the king made them Princes of the Blood in title as well.[28] The trigger, and official explanation, for this breach of the 'fundamental laws' of the kingdom was the state of dynastic emergency. In the space of three years, Louis XIV had lost a son, two grandsons, and a great-grandson. Three of his Condé cousins had died in the preceding two years. His only surviving descendant eligible to inherit the throne was the future Louis XV, a four-year-old child who had nearly died with his parents and older brother in 1712.

This sudden demographic crisis in the Royal House was, of course, a necessary condition for the constitutional revolution. But, I argue, the decision to award the Legitimated Princes the ultimate dynastic right would have been equally unthinkable if they had not gradually obtained nearly all other Bourbon rights in the course of the previous half century. The monarch who agonized on almost every step along the way would hardly have taken the plunge in one jump. The chemise-handing of the 1670s, the spatial elevation and trains since 1679, the dignity address of the turn of the century, and the mantled visits and tentative *de jure* honours of the early 1710s all finally converged in the decision of 1714.

Even when the revolution was undone after the death of Louis XIV, accumulated possessions were hard to disregard. In 1717, the annulment of the decisions of 1714–15 still left Maine and Toulouse in personal possession of their honours. Maine's children retained their court honours, not least in the bedchamber and at the table of Louis XV—for all the protests of Mortemart and of Bourbon. Toulouse's honours remained intact even after the *lit de justice* of 1718. Although it would not revive the *de jure* promotions of the last years of Louis XIV's reign, post-regency legislation confirmed earlier *de facto* possessions in rehabilitating Maine and his children. The patents of 1723 explicitly invoked the logic of the precedent: 'as has been practiced in their regard before the year 1710'.[29] Once

---

[27] This occasion (the double Condé-Conti marriage in July 1713) also demonstrates Maine's growing control over the official repository of possessions, the registers of the Masters of Ceremonies: Sternberg, 'Manipulating Information', pp. 259–60.

[28] Both decisions received the highest *de jure* stamp: registration at the *parlement* (unlike e.g. the elevation of the house of Longueville). Isambert, *Recueil*, xx, 619–23, 641–2.

[29] AN, O¹ 67, p. 256.

again each distinction counted towards equality, and Maine could draw on his past meticulousness in status interaction and documentation.

From the 1720s onwards, legislation on the Legitimated maintained the pre-1711 possessions but limited the scope for new precedents by explicitly specifying differences, rather than similarities, between legitimate and legitimated. These specifications concerned precisely the few aspects that had remained distinct until 1711 or 1714, such as the spatial position of cushions in marriages or the number of escorting *huissiers* in the *parlement*.[30] This explicit delimitation eliminated the margin of ambiguity that had characterized earlier legislation and had facilitated the transition from near-equality to equality in the twilight of Louis XIV's reign. After 1714, both sides recognized the far-reaching potentialities of status interaction.

Years later, when Maine was already dead, a secret memorandum prepared for the younger generation of Legitimated Princes advised them to keep up the fight, pointing out the crucial link between status symbols and continued aspirations to the throne:

> Although this rank and these honours could never in themselves give to those who possess them the slightest right to succeed to the Crown, they nonetheless serve to maintain this claim. They accustom the populace, that does not know enough about them to [be able to] distinguish between appearance and reality, to regard the Legitimated Princes as Princes of the Blood. And [they accustom] the grandees of the state to a deference [to the Legitimated], which, by the sentiment of jealousy that is only too natural to human nature, would make [the grandees] rather place [the Legitimated] on the throne than submit to the power and to the dictates of one of their own, in the case of the extinction of all the Princes of the Blood.[31]

AN EARLY MODERN MODE OF BEHAVIOUR AND INTERACTION

Status interaction suffused French aristocratic society. It was not limited to celebrated aficionados like Saint-Simon, *Monsieur*, or the cardinal of Bouillon, or to groups whose rank was particularly unstable like the Legitimated Princes. The duke of Beauvillier, a member of the small circle of confidants in the king's High Council, still worried about his spatial position in carrying the dauphin's mantle in 1711. Victory at Rocroi in 1643 did not satisfy the *Grand Condé*, who went on to fight the battles of the mantles a year later, and remained committed to the cause in the *affaire des sièges* of 1679. Though untypical as a courtier and, like Condé, a man of broad learning and interests in the arts and sciences, Philippe II of Orléans too demanded train distinctions at his son-in-law's obsequies in 1714. Status symbols were honours, and contemporaries had to take them seriously even when they joked about it.

---

[30] AN, O¹ 67, p. 264; O¹ 71, pp. 123–5.
[31] AN, 300 AP I 91, 'Mémoire sur les Jntérests les plus Essentiels, et les plus délicats des Princes Légitimez'.

If anything, our sources under-represent the pervasiveness of status. They probably report the high points of open dispute more than the everyday tensions and frustrations. One suspects, for example, that for every unruly lieutenant-general there were many others who regularly flinched when they had to sign their name below another *Monseigneur*. Much status negotiation happened face-to-face or behind the scenes, without leaving an extensive paper trail. In some cases, parties made a conscious effort to hush it up. Were it not for the special communicational circumstances and fortuitous survival of the Condé-Gourville correspondence, one would never have suspected the scope of the *affaire des sièges*. Subsequent generations of archivists and editors, who no longer shared the values of the ancien régime, added to these lacunae of documentation by 'rationalizing' archival holdings and trimming source editions.[32] They thus perpetuated their anachronistic opinions about the insignificance of status interaction.

Even from a traditional historiographical perspective, however, the phenomenon is far from inconsequential. For one, the case of the Legitimated Princes has clearly demonstrated the macro-political ramifications of status interaction. For another, the pervasiveness of status meant that policy-makers too either had direct personal stakes or had to consider its implications in their dealings with others. The *Grand Condé* during the Fronde and the correspondents of ministers at all times offered epistolary concessions to their addressees because they knew that they might obtain 'hard' political currency in return. The instrumental approach to ceremony and etiquette similarly assumes that these played a key role in the monarchy's power politics. And one need not accept it wholesale to appreciate the amount of time and energy that a busy ruler like Louis XIV spent on dealing with status disputes among his family, court, and kingdom at large.

Not least, the monarch had to intervene because status contestations continued to disrupt the smooth running of the state throughout his reign. Nowhere is this more striking than in the army, where the *Monseigneur* and other status symbols jeopardized the communication between field commanders at times of war or rebellion.[33] The same can be said for the other quintessential realm of high politics: foreign affairs. Those familiar with the unedited archives of foreign ministries will know the prevalence of status and ceremony in early modern international relations. Here too the historiography has been lagging behind, but is now gradually catching up.[34] Any diplomatic interaction, whether face-to-face or in writing, carried immediate implications for the status of its protagonists: from the question

---

[32] Henri-Jules's intelligence operation of 1701 (see Chapter Three) offers a case in point: it left no trace in the standard sources, and the secret folders, though escaping total destruction during the Revolution, were mutilated almost beyond recognition.

[33] I am completing an article on this matter. On the tensions between social prestige and military command, see David Parrott, 'Richelieu, the *Grands*, and the French Army', in Joseph Bergin and Laurence Brockliss (eds), *Richelieu and his Age* (Oxford, 1992), pp. 135–73, and Rowlands, *The Dynastic State*, esp. pt III.

[34] Roosen, 'Early Modern Diplomatic Ceremonial'; Hennings, 'The Semiotics of Diplomatic Dialogue'.

of spatial positioning to the recognition of sovereignty in forms of address. For communication to take place at all, these implications had to be resolved one way or another. Time and again, however, disagreement over protocol seriously hindered the relations between states.[35]

Status interaction thus poses new problems for older questions; to unlock its mechanisms is to provide novel tools for the analysis of moves in both the domestic and the international arenas. But macro-politics was not all. Status interaction should not just be evaluated on the basis of its impact—negative or positive—on 'modern' preoccupations. Over the last decades, historians have increasingly been interrogating early modern action via the perspectives, expectations, and priorities of contemporaries themselves. For these men and women, the micro-politics of personal relations and private interest mattered no less, if not more, than the macro-politics of grand strategy. Status interaction needed no external justification then; it deserves to be studied on its own terms now.[36] Like other modes of social behaviour and interaction, such as patronage, faction, or friendship, it promises not only to inform older questions, but also to provide an analytic framework of its own for understanding early modern action and agency.

Though developed here mainly in the context of courtly, aristocratic society, this framework is clearly applicable to other social arenas. The Culture of Orders operated throughout the Society of Orders: one did not have to belong to the in crowd of Versailles to partake in this fundamental mode of early modern interaction and competition. 'Status disputes were a pervasive feature of Old Regime society [...] While it is tempting for the modern-day reader to dismiss such status disputes as petty affairs, it would be a mistake to do so'. These phrases are taken from a recent study of merchants, not courtiers.[37] In town processions as in diplomatic encounters, in village churches as in aristocratic assemblies, contemporaries regularly expressed, negotiated, and contested social positions through 'dress, address, and demeanour'.[38] Provincial archives abound with examples of status interaction and contestation, among protagonists such as legal magistrates, administrative officials, municipal authorities, and members of religious

---

[35] Status interaction also disrupted the official purpose of court ceremonial, as quarrels and absences detracted from the grandeur and solemnity of occasions and hence from its intended effects both domestically and internationally.

[36] A recent illuminating study of interaction codes still contrasted a gestural contest with 'more serious matters' behind it: Walter, 'Gesturing at Authority', p. 110. I am by no means questioning the possible interrelatedness, only the implied hierarchy: in some cases, other matters lay behind status interaction; in others, it was the reverse. On early modern priorities, see Campbell, *Power and Politics*; Carroll, *Blood and Violence*, esp. p. 330; Horowski, '"Such a Great Advantage for My Son"'.

[37] Amalia D. Kessler, *A Revolution in Commerce: The Parisian Merchant Court and the Rise of Commercial Society in Eighteenth-Century France* (New Haven-London, 2007), pp. 247, 248. Despite the title, the disputes considered (pp. 247–55) range well beyond the capital, involving merchants in Angers, Toulouse, Bordeaux, and elsewhere.

[38] Besides the studies cited at the beginning of the Introduction, see Sylvie Mouysset, 'Au premier rang, à main dextre, de rouge et noir vêtus: les signes du pouvoir municipal dans le Sud-Ouest de la France à l'époque moderne', *Revue de l'Agenais*, cxxxi (2004), 131–48. The tripartite division is taken from Anna Bryson, *From Courtesy to Civility: Changing Codes of Conduct in Early Modern England* (Oxford, 1998).

corporations.[39] Localized studies have frequently noted and occasionally analysed these examples, but they remain isolated and underdeveloped in the absence of a comparative analytic framework. The rich case of aristocratic society can provide thematic and methodological insights that would contribute towards a wider framework, suggesting differences as well as similarities and shedding light on the reciprocal relations between centre and periphery.

The same applies to other early modern geographical and political contexts. As emphasized throughout—whether in the discussion of chairs, mantles, or honourable service—one can trace analogous codes in other settings, across and beyond Europe. It is hard to think of early modern polities more different from one another than Bourbon France and the Holy Roman Empire. Yet in both contexts protagonists highly valued and passionately contested the minutest expression of social and political position. Other arenas, such as colonial America, are also beginning to receive attention.[40] There is much scope for further study, then, leading to a comparative history of status interaction in the early modern world. Such a framework, moreover, is crucial for a proper understanding of how the system functioned on the international level, where protagonists themselves operated comparatively and supranationally. As we have seen, a crisis within the French ruling house could hinge on the treatment of Roman cardinals in Madrid.

Finally, what happened after 1715? Just as the rising of the Sun King did not initiate status interaction, so his setting did not signal its downfall. On the contrary, latent tensions erupted during the regency that followed Louis XIV's death, as various parties took advantage of the transition period to push forward their agendas. The affair of the princes involved not only the rival camps within the Royal House, but also the Dukes and Peers, who sided with the legitimate Bourbons against the legitimated; the untitled nobility, who voiced its resentment of titled privileges and supported the other side; and the public who followed the outpour of pamphlets from all directions. The peers faced the nobility of the robe too, here and in the celebrated *affaire du bonnet*, which revolved around their respective spatial and gestural interactions at the chief law court of the realm.[41] Epistolary ceremonial, for its part, continued to disrupt military chains of command. In 1718, a colonel of untitled but ancient nobility was thrown in the Bastille following an altercation with the war minister, Marshal Villars, over ending formulae.[42]

[39] These are the local bodies that have usually left the most abundant traces. Like their courtly analogues, they documented status in registers of deliberations, in folders assembled at times of dispute, and in dedicated ceremonial records. I am currently drawing on the materials emanating from the southern towns of Languedoc and Provence (especially Montpellier) for a project on the power of writing in the ancien régime.

[40] For details, see the studies cited at the beginning of the Introduction.

[41] Ellis, *Boulainvilliers and the French Monarchy*, chs. 5 and 6; Jean-Dominique Lassaigne, *Les assemblées de la Noblesse de France aux XVIIᵉ et XVIIIᵉ siècles* (Paris, 1965), pt 4. See also Franklin L. Ford, *Robe and Sword: The Regrouping of the French Aristocracy after Louis XIV* (Cambridge, Mass., 1953), ch. 9.

[42] Sternberg, 'Are *formules de politesse* Always Polite?'. The colonel had already been incarcerated during the affair of the princes. See also the altercation over the ceremonial of expression of the Colonel-General of the cavalry: 'Querelle de mots', *Le cabinet historique*, xiii (1867), pt 1, 168–74; and an analogous case from 1737 involving a Spanish naval officer in Quito: Herzog, *Upholding Justice*, pp. 221–5.

The death of Orléans in 1723 occasioned a crisis over co-presence and train-bearing between the Bourbons and the dukes, and the matter remained contested in subsequent years.[43] Louis XV may have appreciated ceremony less than his great-grandfather did; his subjects, though, did not cease to clash over status. If anything, the codes reflected in the memoirs of the duke of Luynes seem more intricate than those depicted in Dangeau or in Saint-Simon.[44] The Foreign Princes nearly came to blows with the dukes in holy water ceremonies during the 1740s and 1750s. In the affair of the minuet in 1770, the parties threatened to boycott the marriage of the future Louis XVI with Marie-Antoinette if their status claims were not met. Around the same period, they engaged public opinion in a war of treatises concerning 'the ranks and the honours of the court'. These publications boasted a high standard of scientific inquiry, based on wide-ranging research in ceremonial archives. Evidently, new media could also serve old agendas.[45]

Status symbols were still much to the fore in the final years of the ancien régime. The obsequies of Louis XV gave rise to familiar contestations across the kingdom, from the order of salutes at the funeral in Saint-Denis to a dispute between municipality and seneschalsy at a memorial service in Marseille.[46] The coronation of Louis XVI may have seemed archaic or absurd to some; others jealously watched over their privileges during the event.[47] When Joseph II, a European monarch celebrated for his disdain of ceremonial, visited Versailles incognito in 1777, he and the French royal couple nevertheless sat throughout their dinner on uncomfortable stools rather than on armchairs because of the imperial claim to superiority in seat type.[48] In 1787, the Assembly of Notables continued to argue over status, in the substance of the reforms discussed as well as in the procedure of discussions. Here, moreover, precedence determined presidency, the right to chair the committees and hence to influence the agenda.[49]

Throughout the spring of 1789, the syndics of the small town of Pont-de-Vaux in Bresse negotiated the hierarchical gradations of official dress with the local sub-delegate of the intendant of Burgundy. Many municipalities in the region had upgraded their sartorial appearance to violet robes over the previous couple of decades. In addition to these recent examples, the syndics cited a fifteenth-century

---

[43] Sternberg, 'The Culture of Orders', pp. 79–80.

[44] Duindam, *Vienna and Versailles*, p. 216. See e.g. the intricacies of service and co-presence in *Mémoires du duc de Luynes*, xii, 104–5, 122–4; and the analysis of the year 1751 in Bernard Hours, *Louis XV et sa cour: le roi, l'étiquette et le courtisan* (Paris, 2002), pp. 89–98.

[45] Sternberg, 'Manipulating Information', pp. 269–71, 274–5, 279; Thomas E. Kaiser, 'Ambiguous Identities: Marie-Antoinette and the House of Lorraine from the Affair of the Minuet to Lambesc's Charge', in Dena Goodman (ed.), *Marie-Antoinette: Writings on the Body of a Queen* (New York, 2003), pp. 171–98. The two main treatises are: [Joseph-Balthasar Gibert], *Mémoire sur les rangs et les honneurs de la cour* ([Paris, 1771]); L'Abbé Georgel, *Réponse a un écrit anonyme, intitulé: Mémoire sur les rangs et les honneurs de la cour* (Paris, 1771).

[46] AN, K 624, nos. 9² and 9⁴; AM, Marseille, BB 209, fos. 88–89.

[47] Jones, *The Great Nation*, pp. 300–1; AN, K 624, no. 9¹.

[48] Duc de Croÿ, *Journal inédit*, ed. Vicomte de Grouchy and Paul Cottin (4 vols, Paris, 1906–7), iv, 7–8, 255.

[49] John Hardman, *Overture to Revolution: The 1787 Assembly of Notables and the Crisis of France's Old Regime* (Oxford, 2010), pp. 81, 131–3; 168–9, 185–6, 197.

precedent from their archives, and argued that external distinctions were necessary for securing the respect of the populace. The subdelegate approved the introduction of municipal robes in Pont-de-Vaux, finely balancing their colour and fabric in order to differentiate them from the populace on the one hand and from the capital of the bailliage on the other. The accessories of the new robes, in turn, established an internal hierarchy among the syndics.[50]

The municipal officials did not enjoy their new status symbol for long. Viewed from the retrospect of the French Revolution, this provincial sartorial arms race may seem like an irrelevant residue of an ancient regime. From the opposite temporal perspective, however, one can trace the continuing relevance and vitality of the phenomenon from the fifteenth-century precedent down to the new robes of 1789.[51] Indeed, the Revolution itself began with ceremonial conflict at the convening of the Estates General. Members of the Third Estate 'were quick to seek symbolic representations of the equality which they sought to promote', because the alternative and its symbols were still very much in presence, in Versailles as in the provinces.[52] Deputies felt slighted at being reduced to sombre black dress and relegated to a secondary position during the inaugural ceremonies; such distinctions, noted one of their prominent members, carried great 'political consequences'.[53] The minutest aspects of status interaction—material, spatial, gestural, and linguistic—continued to impact the relations between the national assembly and the crown; in 1792 still, the number of doors opened before a delegation to Louis XVI could cause uproar among the ranks of the Legislative Assembly.[54]

Status interaction, then, remained highly significant to the end of the ancien régime. But what did and what did not change between the seventeenth and eighteenth centuries, and between the seventeenth century and earlier periods? For proper answers, we would need systematic reconstructions of these contexts that would compare with the framework presented here. The analysis of status interaction during the long reign of Louis XIV already suggests a few lessons for the study of its longer *durée*. For one, the perspective, agenda, or inclination of rulers does not offer reliable shorthand to the system as a whole. For another, caution is called

---

[50] Turrel, 'L'identité par la distinction', pp. 481–7.

[51] For the sixteenth-century antecedents, see the Introduction, esp. pp. 12–14.

[52] The quote is from Timothy Tackett, *Becoming a Revolutionary: The Deputies of the French National Assembly and the Emergence of a Revolutionary Culture (1789–1790)* (Princeton, 1996), p. 121.

[53] Edna Hindie Lemay, *La vie quotidienne des députés aux États Généraux 1789* ([Paris], 1987), pp. 17–30, here p. 27. See also *Mémoires de Bailly*, ed. Berville and Barrière (3 vols, Paris, 1821–2), i, 136–7, 206–7; Jones, *The Great Nation*, pp. 411–12; Richard Wrigley, *The Politics of Appearances: Representations of Dress in Revolutionary France* (Oxford, 2002), pp. 61–2; Ambrogio A. Caiani, *Louis XVI and the French Revolution, 1789–1792* (Cambridge, 2012), pp. 42–3, 152–3.

[54] Caiani, *Louis XVI and the French Revolution*, pp. 110–13. Other bones of contention included head cover, seating, kneeling, and forms of address: Caiani, *Louis XVI and the French Revolution*, pp. 30, 46; Lemay, *La vie quotidienne*, pp. 79–89; Antoine de Baecque, 'From Royal Dignity to Republican Austerity: The Ritual for the Reception of Louis XVI in the French National Assembly (1789–1792)', *The Journal of Modern History*, lxvi (1994), 671–96; *Mémoires de Bailly*, ed. Berville and Barrière, i, 34–5, 104–5, 135–6, 204–5, 210–11, 291; ii, 168–9. See also *Mémoires de Bailly*, ed. Berville and Barrière, ii, 251–2.

for in making diachronic comparisons: the dynamics of status symbols does not always go hand in hand with the dynamics of status; superficial differences may mask underlying similarities—and vice versa; absolute figures or isolated components can be misleading.[55] Much ground remains to be covered, but the endeavour is worth the while: for to uncover status interaction in all its historical complexity is to recover an indispensable facet of early modern life.

---

[55] See also Sternberg, 'Epistolary Ceremonial', pp. 86–8.

The Royal House of Bourbon, 1643–1715[1]

A. MEMBERS BY RANK[2]

King and queen

- Anne of Austria (1601–1666)—Queen Mother and sometime regent
- Louis XIV (1638–1715)
- Maria Theresa of Austria (1638–1683)—married Louis XIV in 1660

Dauphin and dauphine

- Louis (1661–1711)—known as the *Grand Dauphin* or *Monseigneur*
- Maria-Anna-Christina-Victoria of Bavaria (1660–1690)—married the *Grand Dauphin* in 1680

Children of France

- Gaston (1608–1660)—brother of Louis XIII, duke of Orléans, known as *Monsieur*
- Marguerite of Lorraine (1614?–1672)—duchess of Orléans, second wife of Gaston
- Philippe (1640–1701)—brother of Louis XIV, duke of Anjou and then of Orléans, known as *Monsieur*
- Henrietta-Anne of England (1644–1670)—first wife of Philippe and duchess of Orléans from 1661, known as *Madame*
- Elisabeth-Charlotte (1652–1722)—second wife of Philippe and duchess of Orléans from 1671, known as *Madame*
- Louis (1682–1712)—son of the *Grand Dauphin*, duke of Burgundy, dauphin from 1711
- Marie-Adélaïde of Savoy (1685–1712)—wife of Louis and duchess of Burgundy from 1697, dauphine from 1711
- Philippe (1683–1746)—son of the *Grand Dauphin*, duke of Anjou, king of Spain from 1700
- Charles (1686–1714)—son of the *Grand Dauphin*, duke of Berry
- Louis XV (1710–1774)—son of the duke of Burgundy, duke of Anjou, dauphin from 1712[3]

---

[1] Based especially on P. Anselme et al., *Histoire généalogique et chronologique de la maison royale de France*, 3rd edn (9 vols, Paris, 1726–33). This appendix should not be taken as an exhaustive prosopographic or genealogical guide; it is intended to help readers navigate the data necessary for following the arguments in the text.

[2] Members appear under the first rank they held during the reign; in some cases, it changed in the course of their lives: on marriage (for women) or on the death of a previous incumbent (king or dauphin). Naming is pragmatic. French names generally follow standard French orthography, with the particle 'de' translated unless preceded by a form of address.

[3] Children of France who died in their infancy include five children of Louis XIV and two sons of the duke of Burgundy.

Grandchildren of France

- Anne-Marie-Louise of Orléans (1627–1693)—daughter of Gaston, known as the *Grande Mademoiselle* or Mademoiselle d'Orléans
- Marguerite-Louise of Orléans (1645–1721)—daughter of Gaston, married the grand-duke of Tuscany in 1661, returned to France in 1675
- Elisabeth of Orléans (1646–1696)—daughter of Gaston, Mademoiselle d'Alençon, married the duke of Guise in 1667
- Françoise-Madeleine of Orléans (1648–1664)—daughter of Gaston, Mademoiselle de Valois, married the duke of Savoy in 1663
- Marie-Louise of Orléans (1662–1689)—daughter of Philippe, known as *Mademoiselle*, married the king of Spain in 1679
- Anne-Marie of Orléans (1669–1728)—daughter of Philippe, Mademoiselle de Valois, married the duke of Savoy in 1684
- Philippe II of Orléans (1674–1723)—son of Philippe, duke of Chartres and, from 1701, of Orléans, regent from 1715
- Elisabeth-Charlotte of Orléans (1676–1744)—daughter of Philippe, Mademoiselle de Chartres, married the duke of Lorraine in 1698[4]

Princes and Princesses of the Blood[5]

- Henri II of Bourbon (1588–1646)—prince of Condé, heir to the throne until 1601, known as *Monsieur le Prince*
- Marie of Bourbon (1606–1692)—of the Soissons line, granddaughter of the first prince of Condé, married the prince of Carignan in 1625
- Louis II of Bourbon (1621–1686)—son of Henri II, duke of Enghien and, from 1646, prince of Condé, known as the *Grand Condé* or *Monsieur le Prince*
- Henri-Jules of Bourbon (1643–1709)—son of Louis II, duke of Enghien and, from 1686, prince of Condé, known as *Monsieur le Prince*
- Anna of Bavaria (1648–1723)—married Henri-Jules in 1663, known as *Madame la Princesse*
- Louis-Armand of Bourbon (1661–1685)—prince of Conti from 1666, proxy to the king of Spain in the marriage of 1679
- François-Louis of Bourbon (1664–1709)—prince of La Roche-sur-Yon and, from 1685, of Conti
- Louis III of Bourbon (1668–1710)—son of Henri-Jules, duke of Bourbon and, from 1709, prince of Condé, known as *Monsieur le Duc*
- Louis-Henri of Bourbon (1692–1740)—son of Louis III, duke of Enghien and, from 1710, duke of Bourbon and prince of Condé, known as *Monsieur le Duc*, First Minister (1723–1726)
- Marie-Louise-Elisabeth of Orléans (1695–1719)—daughter of Philippe II, known as *Mademoiselle*, became a Daughter of France upon marrying the duke of Berry in 1710
- Louis of Orléans (1703–1752)—son of Philippe II, duke of Chartres and, from 1723, of Orléans

---

[4] Grandchildren of France who died in their infancy include two children of Gaston, three of Philippe, and three of the duke of Berry.
[5] For the following two ranks I mention only persons discussed in the text.

Appendix I

Legitimated Princes and Princesses

- César, duke of Vendôme (1594–1595[6]–1665)—son of Henri IV[7]
- Henri, duke of Verneuil (1601–1603–1682)—son of Henri IV
- Charlotte Séguier (1622–1704)—married the duke of Verneuil in 1668
- Marie-Anne of Bourbon (1666–1667–1739)—daughter of Louis XIV and Madame de La Vallière, Mademoiselle de Blois, became a Princess of the Blood upon marrying the prince of Conti in 1680
- Louis of Bourbon (1667–1669–1683)—son of Louis XIV and Madame de La Vallière, count of Vermandois
- Louis-Auguste of Bourbon (1670–1673–1736)—son of Louis XIV and Madame de Montespan, duke of Maine
- Louise-Françoise of Bourbon (1673–1673–1743)—daughter of Louis XIV and Madame de Montespan, Mademoiselle de Nantes, became a Princess of the Blood upon marrying the duke of Bourbon in 1685
- Françoise-Marie of Bourbon (1677–1681–1749)—daughter of Louis XIV and Madame de Montespan, Mademoiselle de Blois, became a Granddaughter of France upon marrying the duke of Chartres in 1692
- Louis-Alexandre of Bourbon (1678–1681–1737)—son of Louis XIV and Madame de Montespan, count of Toulouse
- Louis-Auguste of Bourbon (1700–1710–1755)—legitimate son of the duke of Maine, prince of Dombes
- Louis-Charles of Bourbon (1701–1710–1775)—legitimate son of the duke of Maine, count of Eu

---

[6] The middle number indicates year of legitimation, except for the last two, where it indicates year of promotion to the rank of their father.

[7] César's legitimate descendants, including his grandsons, the duke and chevalier of Vendôme, always ranked below first-generation bastards. See section E for more details.

B. THE MAIN LINE[8]

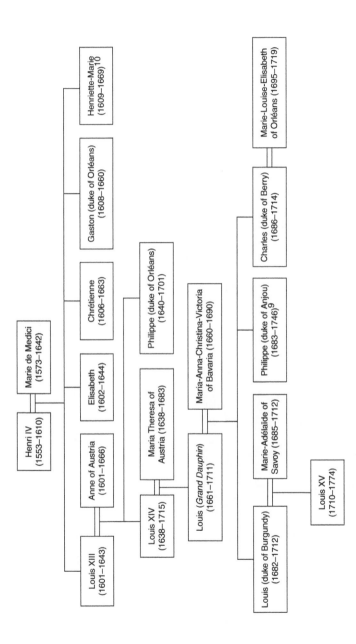

[8] As in section A, sections B–E generally omit those who died in infancy. On occasion, familiar appellations are added in brackets after the name to facilitate identification; for further details, see section A. In the main line depicted here, those who are not kings or queens are dauphins, dauphines, or Children of France. For illegitimate progeny, see section E.

[9] Philippe founded the Bourbon line in Spain in 1700.

[10] Elisabeth, Chrétienne, and Henriette-Marie were married outside the dynasty, to Philip IV of Spain, Victor Amadeus of Savoy, and Charles I of England, respectively. For Gaston's and Philippe's marriage and descendants, see the next section.

C. THE HOUSE OF ORLÉANS[11]

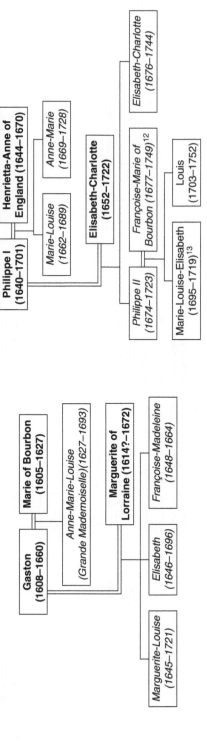

[11] Children of France are marked in bold and Grandchildren of France in italics (here women are marked according to the rank they held while members of the house of Orléans).

[12] Besides the children noted here, who are discussed in the text, Philippe II and Françoise-Marie had five more daughters who reached adulthood.

[13] Marie-Louise-Elisabeth became a Daughter of France upon marrying the duke of Berry. The other native female Orléans here married outside the dynasty. See section A for details.

D. THE HOUSE OF BOURBON-CONDÉ[14]

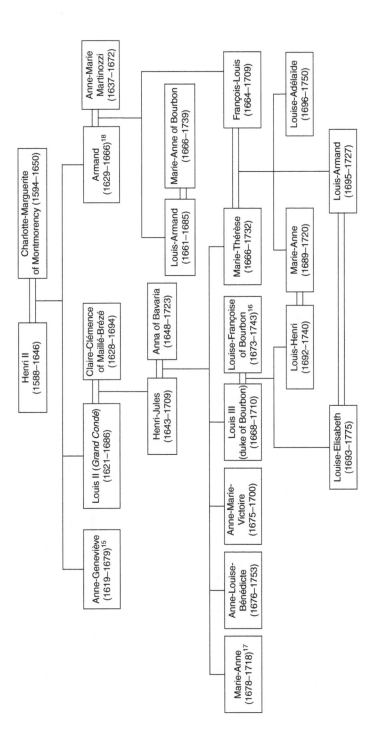

[14] All members are Princes or Princesses of the Blood. Of the Soissons cadet line (descended from the first prince of Condé), Marie of Bourbon, princess of Carignan, survived into the reign of Louis XIV (as did her mother for a year).

[15] Anne-Geneviève married the duke of Longueville, of an early Valois bastard line.

[16] Besides the children noted here, Louis III and Louise-Françoise had two more sons and five more daughters who reached adulthood.

[17] Anne-Louise-Bénédicte and Marie-Anne married illegitimate members of the dynasty: the duke of Maine and the duke of Vendôme (see next section).

[18] Armand refounded the cadet line of Conti.

E. LEGITIMATED DESCENDANTS

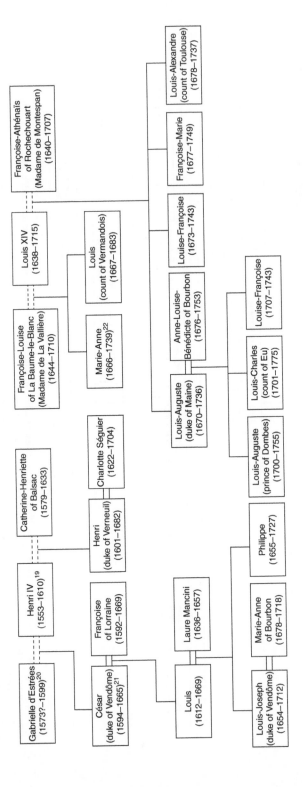

[19] Dotted lines mark illegitimate liaisons. Another child of Henri IV, by Charlotte des Essarts, survived into the reign as abbess of Fontevrault.

[20] Another surviving child of d'Estrées married the duke of Elbeuf of the house of Lorraine.

[21] César's descendants did not enjoy the same rank that Maine's would. Besides Louis, he also had a daughter and a son (the duke of Beaufort) who both died early in the reign.

[22] Louis XIV's legitimated daughters married legitimate Bourbons: see the previous sections.

APPENDIX II

The Condé-Gourville Correspondence

The folder described as 'Correspondance entre le Grand Condé et Gourville, 1679', in AN, K 1712, contains twenty-four items, numbered 33 to 56. They include eight letters from Gourville to his masters (probably copies or final drafts);[1] eleven original letters from the *Grand Condé* to Gourville (all but one autograph); and three autographs from Henri-Jules to Gourville.[2] Nearly all of these sixty-odd pages concern status interaction. Most were written in the space of three days, between 30 August and 2 September 1679.

Many of these items are undated, and the archival numbering is unhelpful. The following two tables thus form an attempt to reconstruct the chronological sequence.

GOURVILLE TO CONDÉ

No.	Date	No. of pages
45	29 August, evening	2
33	30 August, [afternoon/evening]	3
44	30 August, 9 p.m.	4
54, 55[3]	31 August, 11 [a.m.]	5
56	31 August, 3 p.m.	4
39	31 August, 11 p.m.	16
41	1 September, 11 p.m.	2
40	2 September, 1 p.m.	4

[1] The *Grand Condé* is the primary addressee of these letters, but the readership of Henri-Jules is assumed. Nos. 44 and 56 are signed.

[2] Of these three, no. 49 concerns complimentary letters; no. 53 (four pages) was probably written towards the end of the *affaire des sièges*; and no. 52 is a one-page (fragment?) follow-up.

[3] No. 55 is the last page of the letter begun in no. 54.

Appendix II

CONDÉ TO GOURVILLE

No.	Date	No. of pages[4]
36	15 [August], noon	2
34	[30 August], noon	1
48	[30 August], evening[5]	1
35[6]	31 August, morning	1
43	[31 August, afternoon/evening]	1
46	[31 August, afternoon/evening]	2
38	[31 August, evening]	1
42, 47[7]	1 September, 10 [a.m.]	7
50	[1 September, 10 a.m.]	1
51	[1 or 2 September]	2
37	[2 September, afternoon/evening?]	1

[4] Not including the address page.

[5] At the end of this letter, the *Grand Condé* began writing 'ce mar', then erased the second word (presumably the beginning of 'mardi'), wrote 'mercredi' (?) instead, and added 'au soir'. '29' is next added in a different ink, possibly on top of another date, and followed by 'aoust 1679' in another hand. The body of the letter seems to respond to Gourville's no. 33, from 30 August. I have therefore dated no. 48 to Wednesday, 30 August, rather than Tuesday, 29 August.

[6] This is the only non-autograph letter by the *Grand Condé* (it contains a few additions in his hand, though).

[7] No. 47 continues no. 42.

Train-Length and Train-Bearing in Bourbon Funerary Services at Saint-Denis and at Notre Dame, 1643–1715[1]

Year	Service	Representatives	Train-length (ells)	Train-bearers (number)
1643	Louis XIII (SD)	**Duke of Orléans**	5	?
		Prince of Condé	5	?
		Prince of Conti	5	?
1643	Louis XIII (ND)	Queen Mother†	9	3[2]
		Duchess of Orléans	7	2
		Mademoiselle	*7*	*1*
		Princess of Condé	7	1
		Countess of Soissons	7	1
1644	Queen of Spain (ND)	*Mademoiselle*	*5*	*1*
		Duchess of Enghien	5	1
		Duchess of Longueville*	5	1
1647	Prince of Condé (ND)	Prince of Condé	5	1
		Prince of Conti	5	1
1661[3]	Duke of Orléans (ND)	Prince of Condé	5	1
		Duke of Enghien	5	1
1664	Duchess of Savoy (ND)	*Mademoiselle d'Alençon*	*5*	*1*
		Princess of Condé	5	1
		Duchess of Enghien	5	1
1665	King of Spain (ND)	**Duke of Orléans**	7	2

[1] Adult members of the Royal Family normally received a solemn funeral service for their burial in Saint-Denis. In Notre Dame, a memorial service was celebrated for kings, queens, dauphins, dauphines, First Princes of the Blood, and members of foreign houses allied to the Bourbons (notably female members of the Royal Family who married foreign sovereigns). 'SD' = Saint-Denis; 'ND' = Notre Dame. Among the representatives of deep mourning, Children of France are marked in bold, Grandchildren of France in italics, Princes and Princesses of the Blood in regular type. In a few other, exceptional cases, '†' marks senior members (queen or dauphin) and '‡' Legitimated Princes. '*' indicates married women who represented according to their (higher) birth rank. Finally, square brackets indicate assumed but unstated figures. See Chapter Three, esp. pp. 86–96, for details and references.

[2] These three bearers were Bourbon princesses themselves. Strictly speaking, only Anne of Austria represented the mourning on this unusual occasion, but the duchess of Orléans and the three bearers enjoyed long-trained mantles and bearers of their own.

[3] Gaston's service took place a year after his death and burial.

Year	Service	Representatives	Train-length (ells)	Train-bearers (number)
1666	Queen Mother (SD)	**Duchess of Orléans**	7	3
		Mademoiselle d'Orléans	5	2
		Mademoiselle d'Alençon	5	2
1666	Queen Mother (ND)	(same as SD)		
1669	Queen of England (SD)[4]	**Duchess of Orléans**	7	3
		Mademoiselle	5	2
		*Duchess of Guise**	5	2
1669	Queen of England (ND)	(same as SD)		
1670	Duchess of Orléans (SD)	Princess of Condé	5	2
		Duchess of Longueville*	5	2
		Princess of Carignan*	5	2
1672	Dowager Duchess of Orléans (SD)	*Mademoiselle*	5	2
		Mademoiselle d'Orléans	5	2
		*Duchess of Guise**	5	2
1683	Queen (SD)	**Duchess of Orléans**	7	3
		Mademoiselle	5	2
		Mademoiselle d'Orléans	5	2
1683	Queen (ND)	(same as SD)		
1687	Prince of Condé (ND)	Prince of Condé	5	2
		Duke of Bourbon	5	2
		Prince of Conti	5	2
1689	Queen of Spain (ND)	*Mademoiselle*	6	2
		*Grand-duchess of Tuscany**	6	2
		*Duchess of Guise**	6	2
1690	Dauphine (SD)	**Duchess of Orléans**	7	3
		Mademoiselle	6	2
		*Grand-duchess of Tuscany**	6	2
1690	Dauphine (ND)	Princess of Condé	5/6?	2
		Dowager Princess of Conti	5/6?	2
		Princess of Conti	5/6?	2
1693	Grande Mademoiselle (SD)	*Duchess of Chartres*	5	2
		Mademoiselle	5	2
		*Duchess of Guise**	5	2
1701	Duke of Orléans (SD)	**Duke of Burgundy**	7	2
		Duke of Berry	7	2
		Duke of Orléans	5	2
1709	Prince of Condé (ND)	Prince of Condé	[5]	2
		Duke of Enghien	[5]	2
		Prince of Conti	[5]	2
		Duke of Maine‡	[5]	2

[4] Henriette-Marie, daughter of Henri IV and wife of Charles I of England, spent her last years in her native country and was buried in Saint-Denis.

Year	Service	Representatives	Train-length (ells)	Train-bearers (number)
1711	Grand Dauphin (SD)	Dauphin (duke of Burgundy)†	8	3
		Duke of Berry	7	2
		Duke of Orléans	5	2
1711	Grand Dauphin (ND)	(same as SD)		
1712	Dauphin (SD)	**Duke of Berry**	7	3
		Duke of Orléans	5	2
		Count of Charolais	5	2
1712	Dauphine (SD)	**Duchess of Berry**	7	3
		Princess of Condé	5	2
		Mademoiselle de Bourbon	5	2
1712	Dauphin (ND)	(same as SD, train-length unstated)		
1712	Dauphine (ND)	**Duchess of Berry**	[7]	3
		Mademoiselle de Bourbon	[5]	2
		Mademoiselle de Charolais	[5]	2
1714	Duke of Berry (SD)	Prince of Condé	[5]	2
		Prince of Conti	[5]	2
		Prince of Dombes‡	[5]	2
1714	Queen of Spain (ND)	Princess of Conti	5	2
		Mademoiselle de Charolais	5	2
		Mademoiselle de Clermont	5	2
1715	Louis XIV (SD)	*Duke of Orléans*	5	*0/1*
		Prince of Condé	5	0/1
		Count of Charolais	5	0/1
1715	Louis XIV (ND)	(same as SD)		

APPENDIX IV

A Schematized Hierarchy of Free-Address Forms[1]

Royal address term	*Sire*
Deferential address term	*Monseigneur* [*Madame, Mademoiselle*]
Address term	*Monsieur, Madame, Mademoiselle*
Address term + kinship term	*Madame Ma Sœur*
Kinship term	*Mon Cousin*
Address term + name/title	*Mons.ʳ le Comte Tel*

[1] In order of decreasing deference.

Bibliography

MANUSCRIPT AND ARCHIVAL SOURCES

Archives du ministère des Affaires étrangères, La Courneuve
Correspondance Politique, Espagne 63; 64; 177
Correspondance Politique, Rome 392
Correspondance Politique, Sardaigne 95; 99
Mémoires et Documents, Espagne 69; 73
Mémoires et Documents, France 304; 310; 311; 948; 1093; 1206; 1848; 1851; 1970; 2192
Traités, Espagne 16790010

Archives nationales, Paris
257 AP 2
273 AP 188; 190; 201
Série K 118; 119; 120A/2; 121; 542; 577; 578; 1712; 1717; 1718
Série KK 600; 601; 1424; 1430; 1448
Série O¹ 34; 38; 54; 55; 67; 279; 281; 391; 756; 821; 822; 1042; 1043; 1044; 3262

Bibliothèque de l'Arsenal, Paris
MSS 3863; 4109; 5170

Bibliothèque et archives du château de Chantilly
MSS 1131; 1174; 1176; 1182; 1194; 1201; 1217; 1218
Série M ii
Série P lxxv
Série R ix
Série T i; ii

Bibliothèque Mazarine, Paris
MSS 2285; 2346; 2653; 2737; 2738; 2739; 2740; 2741; 2742; 2743; 2744; 2745; 2746; 2747; 2748; 2750

Bibliothèque nationale de France, Paris
Cinq cents de Colbert 141; 142
Châtre de Cangé, Réserve, F 228
Clairambault 515; 658; 718; 814
Fonds français 6679; 7888; 8564; 14117; 14119; 14120; 16633; 18536; 18538; 18540; 22797; 22816; 23315; 23939
Nouvelles acquisitions françaises 66; 2038; 9471; 9757; 9770

Service historique de la Défense, Département de l'armée de terre, Vincennes
Série A¹ 154; 770; 771; 814; 903; 904; 1033; 1765; 1779; 1958; 2108; 2135; 2136; 2541; 3779
Série A⁴ 6

PRINTED PRIMARY SOURCES

Archives de la Bastille: documents inédits, ed. François Ravaisson (19 vols, Paris, 1866–1904).

Aubineau, Léon, ed., *Notices littéraires sur le dix-septième siècle* (Paris, 1859).

Barbier, Edmond-Jean-François, *Chronique de la régence et du règne de Louis XV* (8 vols, Paris, 1857–66).

Bonnardot, François, et al., eds, *Registres des délibérations du bureau de la ville de Paris* (15 vols, Paris, 1883–1921).

Breteuil, baron de, *Mémoires*, ed. Evelyne Lever (Paris, 1992).

Briefe der Herzogin Elisabeth Charlotte von Orléans, ed. Dr Wilhelm Ludwig Holland (6 vols, Stuttgart-Tübingen, 1867–1881).

Buvat, Jean, *Journal de la Régence*, ed. Émile Campardon (2 vols, Paris, 1865).

Callières, François de, *Des mots à la mode, et des nouvelles façons de parler*, 3rd edn (Paris, 1693).

Callières, François de, *Du bon, et du mauvais Usage* (Paris, 1693).

Coniez, Hugo, ed., *Le Cérémonial de la Cour d'Espagne au XVIIᵉ siècle* (Paris, 2009).

'Correspondance de Louis XIV et du duc d'Orléans (1707)', ed. C. Pallu de Lessert, *Mélanges publiés par la société des bibliophiles françois*, pt 1 (1903).

Correspondance de Roger de Rabutin, comte de Bussy, ed. Ludovic Lalanne (6 vols, Paris, 1858–9).

Les correspondants de la marquise de Balleroy, ed. Édouard de Barthélemy (2 vols, Paris, 1883).

[Courtin, Antoine de], *Nouveau Traité de la Civilité qui se pratique en France parmi les honnêtes-gens* (Paris, 1728).

Croy, duc de, *Journal inédit*, ed. Vicomte de Grouchy and Paul Cottin (4 vols, Paris, 1906–7).

Dictionnaire de l'Académie Françoise (Paris, 1694).

Le duc de Bourgogne et le duc de Beauvillier: lettres inédites, 1700–1708, ed. le marquis de Vogüé (Paris, 1900).

Écrits inédits de Saint-Simon, ed. P. Faugère (8 vols, Paris, 1880–93).

'Entrée en Espagne de Marie-Louise d'Orléans, femme du Roi Charles II', ed. Godefroy Ménilglaise, *Annuaire-bulletin de la société de l'histoire de France* (1868), pp. 148–56.

L'Etat de la France.

An Exact Relation of the Grand Ceremony of the Marriage of Charles the II. The Most Catholick King, with the Most Illustrious Princess Mademoiselle Marie Louise D'Orleans (London, 1679).

Formulaires de lettres de François Iᵉʳ à Louis XIV et État de la France dressé en 1642, ed. Eugène Griselle (Paris, 1919).

Gazette.

Georgel, L'Abbé, *Réponse a un écrit anonyme, intitulé: Mémoire sur les rangs et les honneurs de la cour* (Paris, 1771).

[Gibert, Joseph-Balthasar], *Mémoire sur les rangs et les honneurs de la cour* ([Paris, 1771]).

Godefroy, Theodore, *Le Ceremonial de France* (Paris, 1619).

Godefroy, Theodore, and Godefroy, Denys, *Le Ceremonial François* (2 vols, Paris, 1649).

Le Grand Condé et le duc d'Enghien: Lettres inédites à Marie-Louise de Gonzague, reine de Pologne, ed. Émile Magne (Paris, 1920).

De Grimarest, *Traité sur la maniere d'écrire des lettres, et sur le ceremonial* (Paris, 1735[1709]).

Grimoires de Saint-Simon, ed. Yves Coirault (Paris, 1975).

Hanovre, Sophie de, *Mémoires et lettres de voyage*, ed. Dirk Van der Cruysse (Paris, 1990).

Isambert et al., eds, *Recueil général des anciennes lois françaises* (29 vols, Paris, 1821–33).

Journal d'Olivier Lefèvre d'Ormesson, ed. Chéruel (2 vols, Paris, 1860–1).

Journal du marquis de Dangeau, ed. Soulié et al. (19 vols, Paris, 1854–60).

Le Bouyer de Saint Gervais, B., *Mémoires et correspondance du maréchal de Catinat* (3 vols, Paris, 1819).

Lettres d'Élisabeth-Charlotte d'Orléans, duchesse de Lorraine, à la marquise d'Aulède, ed. A. de Bonneval (Nancy, 1865).

Lettres du maréchal de Tessé au prince Antoine Ier de Monaco, ed. André Le Glay (Monaco-Paris, 1917).

Lettres, mémoires et instructions de Colbert, ed. P. Clément (7 vols, Paris, 1861–73).

Madame Palatine: Lettres françaises, ed. Dirk Van der Cruysse ([Paris], 1989).

Maintenon, Madame de, *'Comment la sagesse vient aux filles': propos d'éducation*, ed. Pierre E. Leroy and Marcel Loyau ([Etrepilly], 1998).

Marais, Mathieu, *Journal de Paris*, ed. Henri Duranton and Robert Granderoute (2 vols, Saint Etienne, 2004).

La marquise d'Huxelles et ses amis, ed. Édouard de Barthélemy (Paris, 1881).

Masson, Papirius, *Entier discovrs des choses qvi se sont passees en la reception de la Royne, & mariage du Roy* (Paris, 1570).

Mémoires de Bailly, ed. Berville and Barrière (3 vols, Paris, 1821–2).

Mémoires de Daniel de Cosnac, ed. Le comte Jules de Cosnac (2 vols, Paris, 1852).

Mémoires de Gourville, ed. Léon Lecestre (2 vols, Paris, 1894–5).

Mémoires de la cour d'Espagne, ed. M. A. Morel-Fatio (Paris, 1893).

Mémoires de Mlle de Montpensier, ed. A. Chéruel (4 vols, Paris, 1858–9).

Mémoires de Mme de Motteville, ed. F. Riaux (4 vols, Paris, 1855).

Mémoires de Saint-Simon, ed. A. de Boislisle et al. (43 vols, Paris, 1879–1930).

Mémoires du duc de Luynes sur la cour de Louis XV, 1735–1758, ed. L. Dussieux and E. Soulié (17 vols, Paris, 1860–5).

Mémoires du maréchal de Villars, ed. le marquis de Vogüé (6 vols, Paris, 1884–1904).

Mémoires du marquis de Sourches sur le règne de Louis XIV, ed. le comte de Cosnac and Édouard Pontal (13 vols, Paris, 1882–93).

Mémoires touchans le mariage de Charles II., Roy d'Espagne, avec la Princesse Marie Louise d'Orléans (Paris, 1681).

Mémoriaux du Conseil de 1661, ed. J. de Boislisle (3 vols, Paris, 1905–7).

Ménestrier, Père, 'Dissertation sur l'usage de se faire porter la queue', *Archives historiques et statistiques du département du Rhone*, x (1829[1704]), 246–65.

Mercier, Louis Sébastien, *Tableau de Paris*, ed. Jean-Claude Bonnet (2 vols, Paris, 1994).

Mercure François; Mercure Galant; Mercure de France.

[Milleran, René], *Le Nouveau Secretaire de la Cour* (Paris, 1723).

La Pompe Fvnebre faite à l'honnevr de tres-havte tres-excellente et tres-puissante princesse Marie Therese d'Avstriche (Montpellier, [1683]).

'Le Président Bouhier', *Le Cabinet historique*, vii (1861), 92–3.

[Puget de la Serre, Jean], *Le Secretaire de la Cour: ou, La Maniere d'ecrire selon le Tems* (Lyon, 1713).

Recueil des actes, titres et memoires concernant les affaires du clergé de France (12 vols, Paris, 1716–50).

Recueil des instructions données aux ambassadeurs et ministres de France (Paris, 1884–).

Saint-Simon, duc de, 'Matériaux pour servir a un mémoire sur l'occurrence présente—aoust 1753', in Jean-Pierre Brancourt, *Le duc de Saint-Simon et la monarchie* (Paris, 1971), pp. 242–56.

Saint-Simon, duc de, *Traités politiques et autres écrits*, ed. Yves Coirault (Paris, 1996).

Saint-Simon, duc de, *Hiérarchie et mutations: écrits sur le kaléidoscope social*, ed. Yves Coirault (Paris, 2002).

Savile Correspondence, ed. William Durrant Cooper ([London], 1858).

Sévigné, Madame de, *Correspondance*, ed. Roger Duchêne (3 vols, Paris, 1972–8).

Spanheim, Ézéchiel, *Relation de la cour de France en 1690*, ed. Émile Bourgeois (Paris-Lyon 1900).

Tillet, *Chronique bordeloise* (Bordeaux, 1703).

'Trois mémoires du duc du Maine', ed. A. de Boislisle, *Annuaire-Bulletin de la Société de l'Histoire de France* (1895), pp. 215–47.

Wicquefort, [Abraham] de, *L'ambassadeur et ses fonctions* (2 vols, The Hague, 1681).

PRINTED SECONDARY WORKS

Adamson, John, ed., *The Princely Courts of Europe: Ritual, Politics and Culture under the Ancien Régime, 1500–1750* (London, 1999).

Althoff, Gerd, and Witthöft, Christiane, 'Les services symboliques entre dignité et contrainte', *Annales HSS*, lviii (2003), 1293–318.

Anselme, et al., *Histoire généalogique et chronologique de la maison royale de France*, 3rd edn (9 vols, Paris, 1726–33).

Aribaud, Christine, and Mouysset, Sylvie, eds, *Vêture et pouvoir: XIIIᵉ–XXᵉ siècle* (Toulouse, 2003).

Arizzoli-Clémentel, Pierre, and Gorguet-Ballesteros, Pascale, eds, *Fastes de cour et cérémonies royales: le costume de cour en Europe* (Paris-Versailles, 2009).

Arriaza, Armand, 'Mousnier and Barber: The Theoretical Underpinning of the "Society of Orders" in Early Modern Europe', *Past & Present*, lxxxix (1980), 39–57.

Asch, Ronald G., 'The Princely Court and Political Space in Early Modern Europe', in Beat Kümin, ed., *Political Space in Pre-industrial Europe* (Farnham, 2009).

Baecque, Antoine de, 'From Royal Dignity to Republican Austerity: The Ritual for the Reception of Louis XVI in the French National Assembly (1789–1792)', *The Journal of Modern History*, lxvi (1994), 671–96.

Balsamo, Jean, ed., *Les funérailles à la Renaissance* (Geneva, 2002).

Bassenne, Marthe, *La vie tragique d'une reine d'Espagne: Marie-Louise de Bourbon-Orléans, nièce de Louis XIV* (Paris, 1939).

Beaulieu, Michèle, and Baylé, Jeanne, *Le costume en Bourgogne de Philippe le Hardi à la mort de Charles le Téméraire (1364–1477)* (Paris, 1956).

Béguin, Katia, *Les princes de Condé: rebelles, courtisans et mécènes dans la France du Grand Siècle* (Seyssel, 1999).

Béguin, Katia, 'De la finance à l'intendance: la reconversion réussie de Jean Hérauld de Gourville (1625–1703)', *Revue d'histoire moderne et contemporaine*, xlvi (1999), 435–56.

Béguin, Katia, 'Louis XIV et l'aristocratie: coup de majesté ou retour à la tradition?', *Histoire Économie et Société*, xix (2000), 497–512.

Beik, William, 'The Absolutism of Louis XIV as Social Collaboration', *Past & Present*, clxxxviii (2005), 195–224.

Beik, William, *A Social and Cultural History of Early Modern France* (Cambridge, 2009).

Bély, Lucien, *La société des princes: XVIᵉ–XVIIIᵉ siècle* (Paris, 1999).

Blanc, Odile, 'Le manteau, vêtement de l'autorité', in Christine Aribaud and Sylvie Mouysset, eds, *Vêture et pouvoir: XIII*^e*–XX*^e *siècle* (Toulouse, 2003), pp. 53–66.

Blanquie, Christophe, 'Entre courtoisie et révolte: la correspondance de Condé (1648–1659)', *Histoire Économie et Société*, xiv (1995), 427–43.

Blanquie, Christophe, 'Saint-Simon épistolier?', *Cahiers Saint-Simon*, xxix (2001), 75–84.

Blet, Pierre, *Richelieu et l'Église* (Versailles, 2007).

Boislisle, A. de, 'La désertion du cardinal de Bouillon en 1710', pts 2–3, *Revue des questions historiques*, 2nd ser., xli (1909), 61–107, 444–91.

Bojani, F. de, *Innocent XI: sa correspondance avec ses nonces* (3 vols, Rome, 1910–13).

Bonvallet, Adrien, 'Le bureau des finances de la généralité de Poitiers', *Mémoires de la société des antiquaires de l'ouest*, 2nd ser., vi (1883), 137–424.

[Boppe, Auguste], *Les introducteurs des ambassadeurs, 1585–1900* (Paris, 1901).

Bossenga, Gail, 'Estates, Orders and Corps', in William Doyle, ed., *The Oxford Handbook of the Ancien Régime* (Oxford, 2011), pp. 141–66.

Bottineau, Yves, 'Aspects de la cour d'Espagne au XVIIe siècle: l'étiquette de la chambre du Roi', *Bulletin Hispanique*, lxxiv (1972), 138–57.

Boucher, Jacqueline, *Société et mentalités autour de Henri III* (Paris, 2007).

Boureau, Alain, *Le simple corps du roi: l'impossible sacralité des souverains français, XVe–XVIIIe siècle* (Paris, 1988).

Boureau, Alain, 'Les cérémonies royales françaises entre performance juridique et compétence liturgique', *Annales ESC*, xlvi (1991), 1253–64.

Braddick, Michael J., ed., *The Politics of Gesture: Historical Perspectives* (*Past & Present* Supplement 4, 2009).

Brancourt, Jean-Pierre, *Le duc de Saint-Simon et la monarchie* (Paris, 1971).

Braun, Friederike, *Terms of Address: Problems of Patterns and Usage in Various Languages and Cultures* (Berlin, 1988).

Bray, Bernard, 'Recherchez la brièveté, évitez l'extrême concision: théorie et pratique du billet à l'époque classique', *Révue de l'AIRE*, xxv–xxvi (2000), 52–64.

Briggs, Robin, 'The Theatre State: Ceremony and Politics 1600–60', *Seventeenth-Century French Studies*, xvi (1994), 15–33.

Brocher, Henri, *À la cour de Louis XIV: le rang et l'étiquette sous l'ancien régime* (Paris, 1934).

Brown, Penelope, and Levinson, Stephen C., *Politeness: Some Universals in Language Usage* (Cambridge, 1987).

Brown, Roger, and Gilman, Albert, 'The Pronouns of Power and Solidarity', in Thomas A. Sebeok, ed., *Style in Language* (Cambridge, Mass., 1960), pp. 253–76.

Brunot, Ferdinand, *Histoire de la langue française des origines à nos jours*, new edn (13 vols, Paris, 1966–79).

Bryson, Anna, *From Courtesy to Civility: Changing Codes of Conduct in Early Modern England* (Oxford, 1998).

Buc, Philippe, *The Dangers of Ritual: Between Early Medieval Texts and Social Scientific Theory* (Princeton, 2001).

Burke, Peter, *The Historical Anthropology of Early Modern Italy: Essays on Perception and Communication* (Cambridge, 1987).

Burke, Peter, *The Fabrication of Louis XIV* (New Haven-London, 1992).

Bush, M.L., ed., *Social Orders and Social Classes in Europe since 1500: Studies in Social Stratification* (London, 1992).

Caiani, Ambrogio A., *Louis XVI and the French Revolution, 1789–1792* (Cambridge, 2012).

Campbell, Peter R., *Power and Politics in Old Regime France, 1720–1745* (London-New York, 1996).

Cañeque, Alejandro, 'On Cushions and Chairs: The Ritual Construction of Authority in New Spain', in Laurie Postlewate and Wim Hüsken, eds, *Acts and Texts: Performance and Ritual in the Middle Ages and the Renaissance* (Amsterdam-New York, 2007), pp. 101–48.

Carroll, Stuart, *Blood and Violence in Early Modern France* (Oxford, 2006).

Chabaud, Gilles, ed., *Classement, DÉclassement, REclassement de l'Antiquité à nos jours* (Limoges, 2011).

Chartier, Roger, *Cultural History: Between Practices and Representations* (Cambridge, 1988).

Chartier, Roger, 'Des "secrétaires" pour le peuple? Les modèles épistolaires de l'Ancien Régime entre littérature de cour et livre de colportage', in Roger Chartier et al., eds, *La Correspondance: les usages de la lettre au XIXᵉ siècle* (Paris, 1991).

Chatenet, Monique, *La cour de France au XVIᵉ siècle: vie sociale et architecture* (Paris, 2002).

Chatenet, Monique, 'Quelques aspects des funérailles nobiliaires au XVIᵉ siècle', in Jean Balsamo, ed., *Les funérailles à la Renaissance* (Geneva, 2002), pp. 37–54.

Chatenet, Monique, 'Habits de cérémonie: les mariages à la cour des Valois', in Isabelle Poutrin and Marie-Karine Schaub, eds, *Femmes & pouvoir politique: les princesses d'Europe XVᵉ–XVIIIᵉ siècle* (Rosny-sous-Bois, 2007), pp. 218–32.

Collins, James B., *The State in Early Modern France*, 2nd edn (Cambridge, 2009).

Coraillon, Cédric, 'Les deux morts de Louis XIII', *Revue d'histoire moderne et contemporaine*, lv, no. 1 (2008), pp. 50–73.

Corp, Edward, *A Court in Exile: The Stuarts in France, 1689–1718* (Cambridge, 2004).

Cosandey, Fanny, *La reine de France: symbole et pouvoir XVᵉ–XVIIIᵉ siècle* (Paris, 2000).

Cosandey, Fanny, ed., *Dire et vivre l'ordre social en France sous l'Ancien Régime* (Paris, 2005).

Cosandey, Fanny, 'L'insoutenable légèreté du rang', in Fanny Cosandey, ed., *Dire et vivre l'ordre social en France sous l'Ancien Régime* (Paris, 2005), pp. 169–89.

Cosandey, Fanny, 'Entrer dans le rang', in Marie-France Wagner, Louise Frappier, and Claire Latraverse, eds, *Les jeux de l'échange: entrées solennelles et divertissements du XVᵉ au XVIIᵉ siècle* (Paris, 2007), pp. 17–46.

Cosandey, Fanny, 'Les préséances à la cour des reines de France', in Isabelle Poutrin and Marie-Karine Schaub, eds, *Femmes & pouvoir politique: les princesses d'Europe XVᵉ–XVIIIᵉ siècle* (Rosny-sous-Bois, 2007), pp. 267–78.

Cosandey, Fanny, 'Classement ou ordonnancement? Les querelles de préséances en France sous l'Ancien Régime', in Gilles Chabaud, ed., *Classement, DÉclassement, REclassement de l'Antiquité à nos jours* (Limoges, 2011), pp. 95–103.

Coutelle, Antoine, 'La robe rouge comme enjeu: l'exemple du présidial de Poitiers au XVIIᵉ siècle', in Christine Aribaud and Sylvie Mouysset, eds, *Vêture et pouvoir: XIIIᵉ–XXᵉ siècle* (Toulouse, 2003), pp. 149–67.

Croq, Laurence, 'Des titulatures à l'évaluation sociale des qualités: hiérarchie et mobilité collective dans la société parisienne du XVIIᵉ siècle', in Fanny Cosandey, ed., *Dire et vivre l'ordre social en France sous l'Ancien Régime* (Paris, 2005), pp. 125–68.

Daloz, Jean-Pascal, *The Sociology of Elite Distinction: From Theoretical to Comparative Perspectives* (Basingstoke, 2010).

Darnton, Robert, 'A Bourgeois Puts His World in Order: The City As a Text', in Robert Darnton, *The Great Cat Massacre and Other Episodes in French Cultural History* (New York, 1984), pp. 107–43.

D'Aumale, le duc, *Histoire des princes de Condé pendant les XVIᵉ et XVIIᵉ siècles* (8 vols, Paris, 1885–96).

Da Vinha, Mathieu, *Les valets de chambre de Louis XIV* (Paris, 2004).

Daybell, James, *Women Letter-Writers in Tudor England* (Oxford, 2006).

Deloye, Yves, Haroche, Claudine, and Ihl, Olivier, eds, *Le protocole ou la mise en forme de l'ordre politique* (Paris, [1997]).

Delpierre, Madeleine, *Se vêtir au XVIIIᵉ siècle* (Paris, 1996).

Descimon, Robert, 'Le corps de ville et le système cérémoniel parisien au début de l'âge moderne', in Marc Boone and Maarten Prak, eds, *Statuts individuels, statuts corporatifs et statuts judiciaires dans les villes européennes* (Leuven, 1996), pp. 73–128.

Descimon, Robert, 'Un langage de la dignité: la qualification des personnes dans la société parisienne à l'époque moderne', in Fanny Cosandey, ed., *Dire et vivre l'ordre social en France sous l'Ancien Régime* (Paris, 2005), pp. 69–123.

Descimon, Robert, and Haddad, Élie, eds, *Épreuves de noblesse: les expériences nobiliaires de la haute robe parisienne (XVIᵉ–XVIIIᵉ siècle)* (Paris, 2010).

Dewald, Jonathan, *Aristocratic Experience and the Origins of Modern Culture: France, 1570–1715* (Berkeley, 1993).

Duindam, Jeroen, *Myths of Power: Norbert Elias and the Early Modern European Court* (Amsterdam, 1995).

Duindam, Jeroen, *Vienna and Versailles: The Courts of Europe's Dynastic Rivals, 1550–1780* (Cambridge, 2003).

Duindam, Jeroen, 'Early Modern Court Studies: An Overview and a Proposal', in Markus Völkel and Arno Strohmeyer, eds, *Historiographie an europäischen Höfen (16.–18. Jahrhundert)* (Berlin, 2009), pp. 37–60.

Duma, Jean, 'Les formes de la civilité au XVIIIᵉ siècle: la correspondance protocolaire du duc de Penthièvre', in Pierre Albert, ed., *Correspondre jadis et naguère* (Paris, 1997), pp. 85–99.

Elias, Norbert, *Gesammelte Schriften* (Frankfurt, 1997–).

Elias, Norbert, *The Collected Works of Norbert Elias* (Dublin, 2006–).

Ellis, Harold A., *Boulainvilliers and the French Monarchy: Aristocratic Politics in Early Eighteenth-Century France* (Ithaca, 1988).

Fantoni, Marcello, Gorse, George, and Smuts, Malcolm, eds, *The Politics of Space: European Courts ca. 1500–1750* (Rome, 2009).

Faudemay, Alain, *La distinction à l'âge classique: émules et enjeux* (Paris, 1992).

Feyel, Gilles, *L'Annonce et la nouvelle: la presse d'information en France sous l'Ancien Régime (1630–1788)* (Oxford, 2000).

Fogel, Michèle, *Les cérémonies de l'information dans la France du XVIᵉ au milieu du XVIIIᵉ siècle* (Paris, 1989).

Ford, Franklin L., *Robe and Sword: The Regrouping of the French Aristocracy after Louis XIV* (Cambridge, Mass., 1953).

Fracard, M.-L., *Philippe de Montaut-Benac, duc de Navailles, maréchal de France (1619–1684)* (Niort, 1970).

Gallo, David M., 'Royal Bodies, Royal Bedrooms: The *Lever du Roy* and Louis XIV's Versailles', *Cahiers du dix-septième*, xii (2008), 99–118.

Gerber, Matthew, *Bastards: Politics, Family, and Law in Early Modern France* (Oxford-New York, 2012).

Gibson, Jonathan, 'Significant Space in Manuscript Letters', *Seventeenth Century*, xii (1997), 1–9.

Giesey, Ralph E., *The Royal Funeral Ceremony in Renaissance France* (Geneva, 1960).

Giesey, Ralph E., 'The King Imagined', in Keith Michael Baker, ed., *The French Revolution and the Creation of Modern Political Culture* (4 vols, Oxford, 1987–94), i, 41–59.

Giesey, Ralph E., *Rulership in France, 15th–17th Centuries* (Aldershot, 2004).

Goffman, Erving, *Interaction Ritual: Essays on Face-to-Face Behavior* (New York, 1967).

Grassi, Marie-Claire, *L'Art de la lettre au temps de La nouvelle Héloïse et du romantisme* (Geneva, 1994).

Grassi, Marie-Claire, 'Lettre', in Alain Montandon, ed., *Dictionnaire raisonné de la politesse et du savoir-vivre: du Moyen Age à nos jours* (Paris, 1995), pp. 543–66.

Greig, Hannah, 'Faction and Fashion: The Politics of Court Dress in Eighteenth-Century England', in Isabelle Paresys and Natacha Coquery, eds, *Se vêtir à la cour en Europe, 1400–1815* (Villeneuve d'Ascq, 2011), pp. 67–89.

Guarino, Gabriel, *Representing the King's Splendour: Communication and Reception of Symbolic Forms of Power in Viceregal Naples* (Manchester, 2010).

Hanley, Sarah, *The Lit de Justice of the Kings of France: Constitutional Ideology in Legend, Ritual, and Discourse* (Princeton, 1983).

Hardman, John, *Overture to Revolution: The 1787 Assembly of Notables and the Crisis of France's Old Regime* (Oxford, 2010).

Haroche-Bouzinac, Geneviève, '"Billets font conversation". De la théorie à la pratique: l'exemple de Voltaire', in Bernard Bray and Christoph Strosetzki, eds, *Art de la lettre, art de la conversation à l'époque classique en France* (Paris, 1995), pp. 341–54.

Havard, Henry, *Dictionnaire de l'ameublement et de la décoration* (4 vols, Paris, 1894).

Hennings, Jan, 'The Semiotics of Diplomatic Dialogue: Pomp and Circumstance in Tsar Peter I's Visit to Vienna in 1698', *International History Review*, xxx (2008), 515–44.

Herzog, Tamar, *Upholding Justice: Society, State, and the Penal System in Quito (1650–1750)* (Ann Arbor, 2004).

Himelfarb, Hélène, *Saint-Simon, Versailles, les arts de cour* (Paris, 2006).

Hodson, Simon, 'The Power of Female Dynastic Networks: A Brief Study of Louise de Coligny, Princess of Orange, and Her Stepdaughters', *Women's History Review*, xvi (2007), 335–51.

Horowski, Leonhard, '"Such a Great Advantage for My Son": Office-Holding and Career Mechanisms at the Court of France, 1661–1789', *The Court Historian*, viii (2003), 125–75.

Hourcade, Philippe, *Bibliographie critique du duc de Saint-Simon* (Paris, 2010).

Hours, Bernard, *Louis XV et sa cour: le roi, l'étiquette et le courtisan* (Paris, 2002).

Jackson, Richard A., 'Peers of France and Princes of the Blood', *French Historical Studies*, vii (1971), 27–46.

Janneau, Guillaume, *Les Sièges* (Paris, 1967).

Jones, Colin, *The Great Nation: France from Louis XV to Napoleon* (London, 2003).

Kaiser, Thomas E., 'Ambiguous Identities: Marie-Antoinette and the House of Lorraine from the Affair of the Minuet to Lambesc's Charge', in Dena Goodman, ed., *Marie-Antoinette: Writings on the Body of a Queen* (New York, 2003).

Kamen, Henry, *Spain in the Later Seventeenth Century, 1665–1700* (London, 1980).

Kane, Brendan, *The Politics and Culture of Honour in Britain and Ireland, 1541–1641* (Cambridge, 2010).

Kerbrat-Orecchioni, Catherine, 'From Good Manners to Facework: Politeness Variations and Constants in France, from the Classic Age to Today', *Journal of Historical Pragmatics*, xii (2011), 133–55.

Kessler, Amalia D., *A Revolution in Commerce: The Parisian Merchant Court and the Rise of Commercial Society in Eighteenth-Century France* (New Haven-London, 2007).

Kettering, Sharon, 'Patronage in Early Modern France', *French Historical Studies*, xvii (1992), 839–62.

Klaits, Joseph, *Printed Propaganda under Louis XIV: Absolute Monarchy and Public Opinion* (Princeton, 1976).

Klingensmith, Samuel John, *The Utility of Splendor: Ceremony, Social Life, and Architecture at the Court of Bavaria, 1600–1800* (Chicago, 1993).

Knecht, R.J., *Renaissance Warrior and Patron: The Reign of Francis I* (Cambridge, 1996).

Kühner, Christian, ' "Quand je retournai, je trouvai toutes les cabales de la cour changées": Friendship under the Conditions of Seventeenth-Century Court Society', in Bernadette Descharmes et al., eds, *Varieties of Friendship: Interdisciplinary Perspectives on Social Relationships* (Göttingen, 2011), pp. 59–75.

La Mure, Jean-Marie de, *Histoire des ducs de Bourbon et des comtes de Forez* (4 vols, Paris, 1860–97).

Labatut, Jean-Pierre, *Les ducs et pairs de France au XVIIᵉ siècle* (Paris, 1972).

Lassaigne, Jean-Dominique, *Les assemblées de la Noblesse de France aux XVIIᵉ et XVIIIᵉ siècles* (Paris, 1965).

Le Mao, Caroline, *Parlement et parlementaires: Bordeaux au Grand Siècle* (Seyssel, 2007).

Le Roux, Nicolas, *La faveur du Roi: mignons et courtisans au temps des derniers Valois* (Seyssel, 2001).

Le Roux, Nicolas, 'La cour dans l'espace du palais: l'exemple de Henri III', in Marie-France Auzépy and Joël Cornette, eds, *Palais et pouvoir: de Constantinople à Versailles* (Saint-Denis, 2003), pp. 229–67.

Le Roy Ladurie, Emmanuel, with Fitou, Jean-François, *Saint-Simon, ou le système de la Cour* (Paris, 1997).

Lecestre, Léon, 'La mission de Gourville en Espagne (1670)', *Revue des questions historiques*, lii (1892), 107–48.

Leferme-Falguières, Frédérique, *Les courtisans: une société de spectacle sous l'Ancien Régime* (Paris, 2007).

Lemay, Edna Hindie, *La vie quotidienne des députés aux États Généraux 1789* ([Paris], 1987).

Levantal, Christophe, *Ducs et pairs et duchés-pairies laïques à l'époque moderne (1519–1790): dictionnaire prosographique, généalogique, chronologique, topographique et heuristique* (Paris, 1996).

Lizerand, Georges, *Le duc de Beauvillier, 1648–1714* (Paris, 1933).

Mansel, Philip, *Dressed to Rule: Royal and Court Dress from Louis XIV to Elizabeth II* (New Haven-London, 2005).

Maquart, Marie-Françoise, *L'Espagne de Charles II et la France, 1665–1700* (Toulouse, 2000).

Maral, Alexandre, *La chapelle royale de Versailles sous Louis XIV: cérémonial, liturgie et musique*, 2nd edn (Wavre, 2010).

Merlin-Kajman, Hélène, ' "Une troisième espèce de simple dignité", ou la civilité entre l'honneur et la familiarité', in Fanny Cosandey, ed., *Dire et vivre l'ordre social en France sous l'Ancien Régime* (Paris, 2005), pp. 231–79.

Mettam, Roger, *Power and Faction in Louis XIV's France* (Oxford, 1988).

Mettam, Roger, 'Power, Status and Precedence: Rivalries among the Provincial Elites of Louis XIV's France', *Transactions of the Royal Historical Society*, 5th ser., xxxviii (1988), 43–62.

Mettam, Roger, 'The French Nobility, 1610–1715', in H. M. Scott, ed., *The European Nobilities in the Seventeenth and Eighteenth Centuries*, 2nd edn (2 vols, Longman, 2007), i, 127–55.

Mouysset, Sylvie, ' "Pensan d'esse creniat, lou capairou sul col…": jeux et enjeux de la robe consulaire dans le Sud-Ouest de la France (XVIᵉ–XVIIIᵉ siècle)', in Christine Aribaud and Sylvie Mouysset, eds, *Vêture et pouvoir: XIIIᵉ–XXᵉ siècle* (Toulouse, 2003), pp. 35–50.

Mouysset, Sylvie, 'Au premier rang, à main dextre, de rouge et noir vêtus: les signes du pouvoir municipal dans le Sud-Ouest de la France à l'époque moderne', *Revue de l'Agenais*, cxxxi (2004), 131–48.

Muir, Edward, *Civic Ritual in Renaissance Venice* (Princeton, 1981).

Neu, Tim, 'The Importance of Being Seated: Ceremonial Conflict in Territorial Diets', in Jason Philip Coy, Benjamin Marschke, and David Warren Sabean, eds, *The Holy Roman Empire, Reconsidered* (New York-Oxford, 2010), pp. 125–42.

Neuschel, Kristen, *Word of Honor: Interpreting Noble Culture in Sixteenth-Century France* (Ithaca, 1989).

Nevala, Minna, *Address in Early English Correspondence: Its Forms and Socio-Pragmatic Functions* (Helsinki, 2004).

Nevalainen, Terttu, and Tanskanen, Sanna-Kaisa, eds, 'Letter Writing', special issue of *Journal of Historical Pragmatics*, v, no. 2 (2004), 181–341.

Newton, William Ritchey, *L'espace du roi: la cour de France au Château de Versailles, 1682–1789* ([Paris], 2000).

Newton, William Ritchey, *La petite cour: services et serviteurs à la Cour de Versailles au XVIIIᵉ siècle* (Paris, 2006).

Nicolich, Robert N., 'Sunset: The Spectacle of the Royal Funeral and Memorial Services at the End of the Reign of Louis XIV', in David Lee Rubin, ed., *Sun King: The Ascendancy of French Culture during the Reign of Louis XIV* (Cranbury, NJ-London-Washington, 1991), pp. 45–72.

Paresys, Isabelle, and Coquery, Natacha, eds, *Se vêtir à la cour en Europe, 1400–1815* (Villeneuve d'Ascq, 2011).

Parrott, David, 'Richelieu, the *Grands*, and the French Army', in Joseph Bergin and Laurence Brockliss, eds, *Richelieu and his Age* (Oxford, 1992), pp. 135–73.

Pitts, Vincent J., *La Grande Mademoiselle at the Court of France: 1627–1693* (Baltimore, 2000).

Potter, David, and Roberts, P. R., 'An Englishman's View of the Court of Henri III, 1584–1585: "Richard Cook's Description of the Court of France"', *French History*, ii (1988), 312–44.

Poutrin, Isabelle, and Schaub, Marie-Karine, eds, *Femmes & pouvoir politique: les princesses d'Europe XVᵉ–XVIIIᵉ siècle* (Rosny-sous-Bois, 2007).

Rabinovitch, Oded, 'Versailles as a Family Enterprise: The Perraults, 1660–1700', *French Historical Studies*, xxxvi (2013), 385–416.

Ranum, Orest, 'Courtesy, Absolutism, and the Rise of the French State, 1630–1660', *The Journal of Modern History*, lii (1980), 426–51.

Reure, Abbé, 'Notes Bourbonnaises: d'après les manuscrits de la Bibliothèque de Lyon', *Bulletin Revue—Société d'Émulation & des Beaux-Arts du Bourbonnais*, ix (1901), 100–6.

Roosen, William, 'Early Modern Diplomatic Ceremonial: A Systems Approach', *The Journal of Modern History*, lii (1980), 452–76.

Rousset, Camille, *Histoire de Louvois et de son administration politique et militaire* (4 vols, Paris, 1862–3).

Rowlands, Guy, *The Dynastic State and the Army under Louis XIV: Royal Service and Private Interest, 1661 to 1701* (Cambridge, 2002).

Rudd, Jon D., 'A Perception of Hierarchy in Eighteenth-Century France: An Epistolary Etiquette Manual for the Controller General of Finances', *French Historical Studies*, xvii (1992), 791–801.

Sabatier, Gérard, *Versailles ou la figure du roi* (Paris, 1999).

Sabatier, Gérard, and Torrione, Margarita, eds, *¿Louis XIV espagnol? Madrid et Versailles, images et modèles* (Versailles, 2009).

Saguez-Lovisi, Claire, *Les lois fondamentales au XVIIIᵉ siècle: recherches sur la loi de dévolution de la couronne* (Paris, 1984).

Sarmant, Thierry, 'Quand le noir est couleur: costume et portrait des ministres en France du XVIIᵉ au XXᵉ siècle', in Bernard Barbiche, Jean-Pierre Poussou and Alain Tallon, eds, *Pouvoirs, contestations et comportements dans l'Europe moderne: mélanges en l'honneur du professeur Yves-Marie Bercé* (Paris, 2005), pp. 513–27.

Sarmant, Thierry, and Stoll, Mathieu, 'Le style de Louvois: formulaire administratif et expression personnelle dans la correspondance du secrétaire d'État de la Guerre de Louis XIV', *Annuaire-Bulletin de la Société de l'Histoire de France* (1997), pp. 57–77.

Schneider, Robert A., *The Ceremonial City: Toulouse Observed 1738–1780* (Princeton, 1995).

Sicard, L'Abbé, *L'Ancien clergé de France*, 5th edn (2 vols, Paris, 1912).

Smith, Jay M., *The Culture of Merit: Nobility, Royal Service and the Making of Absolute Monarchy in France, 1600–1789* (Ann Arbor, 1996).

Solnon, Jean-François, *La Cour de France* (Paris, 1996[1987]).

Spangler, Jonathan, *The Society of Princes: The Lorraine-Guise and the Conservation of Power and Wealth in Seventeenth-Century France* (Aldershot, 2009).

Sternberg, Giora, 'The Race for the Mantle: Dress and Status at the Court of Louis XIV', *Zmanim*, xcv (2006), 70–85.

Sternberg, Giora, 'Are *formules de politesse* Always Polite? The Bauffremont-Villars Incident, Discursive Struggles and Social Tensions under the *Ancien Régime*', *Zeitsprünge*, xiii (2009), 219–34.

Sternberg, Giora, 'Epistolary Ceremonial: Corresponding Status at the Time of Louis XIV', *Past & Present*, cciv (2009), 33–88.

Sternberg, Giora, 'Manipulating Information in the Ancien Régime: Ceremonial Records, Aristocratic Strategies, and the Limits of the State Perspective', *The Journal of Modern History*, lxxxv (2013), 239–79.

Stollberg-Rilinger, Barbara, 'La communication symbolique à l'époque pré-moderne. Concepts, thèses, perspectives de recherche', *Trivium*, ii (2008) (http://trivium.revues.org/1152).

Stollberg-Rilinger, Barbara, 'On the Function of Rituals in the Holy Roman Empire', in R. J. W. Evans, Michael Schaich, and Peter H. Wilson, eds, *The Holy Roman Empire, 1495–1806* (Oxford, 2011), pp. 359–73.

Taavitsainen, Irma, and Jucker, Andreas H., eds, *Diachronic Perspectives on Address Term Systems* (Amsterdam, 2003).

Tessier, Alexandre, 'Des carrosses qui en cachent d'autres: retour sur certains incidents qui marquèrent l'ambassade de Lord Denzil Holles à Paris, de 1663 à 1666', in Lucien Bély and Géraud Poumarède, eds, *L'incident diplomatique (XVIᵉ–XVIIIᵉ siècle)* (Paris, 2010), pp. 197–240.

Tittler, Robert, 'Seats of Honor, Seats of Power: The Symbolism of Public Seating in the English Urban Community, *c*. 1560–1620', *Albion*, xxiv (1992), 205–23.

Trexler, Richard C., *Public Life in Renaissance Florence* (New York, 1980).

Turrel, Denise, 'L'identité par la distinction: les robes syndicales des petites villes de Bresse (XVᵉ–XVIIIᵉ siècle)', *Cahiers d'histoire*, xliii (1998), 475–87.

Valtat, Monique, *Les contrats de mariage dans la famille royale en France au XVIIᵉ siècle* (Paris, 1953).

Van der Cruysse, Dirk, *La mort dans les Mémoires de Saint-Simon: Clio au Jardin de Thanatos* (Paris, 1981).

Van der Cruysse, Dirk, *Madame Palatine, princesse européenne* ([Paris], 1988).

Waddy, Patricia, 'Many Courts, Many Spaces', in Marcello Fantoni, George Gorse, and Malcolm Smuts, eds, *The Politics of Space: European Courts ca. 1500–1750* (Rome, 2009), pp. 209–30.

Walter, John, 'Gesturing at Authority: Deciphering the Gestural Code of Early Modern England', in Michael J. Braddick, ed., *The Politics of Gesture: Historical Perspectives* (*Past & Present* Supplement 4, 2009), pp. 96–127.

Watts, Richard J., *Politeness* (Cambridge, 2003).

Weigert, Roger-Armand, *Jean I Berain, dessinateur de la chambre et du cabinet du roi (1640–1711)* (2 vols, Paris, 1937).

Zanger, Abby E., *Scenes from the Marriage of Louis XIV: Nuptial Fictions and the Making of Absolutist Power* (Stanford, 1997).

Zitzlsperger, Philipp, *Gianlorenzo Bernini Die Papst- und Herrscherporträts: Zum Verhältnis von Bildnis und Macht* (Munich, 2002).

UNPUBLISHED THESES

Leferme-Falguières, Frédérique, 'Le monde des courtisans: la haute noblesse et le cérémonial royal aux XVIIe et XVIIIe siècles' (Univ. of Paris I Ph.D. thesis, 2004).

Nguyen, Marie-Lan, 'Les grands maîtres des cérémonies et le service des Cérémonies à l'époque moderne, 1585–1792' (Univ. of Paris IV *mémoire de maîtrise*, 1999).

Sternberg, Giora, 'Interaction Ritual at the Court of Louis XIV: Codes of Status Rivalry' (Tel Aviv Univ. MA dissertation, 2005).

Sternberg, Giora, 'The Culture of Orders: Status Interactions during the Reign of Louis XIV' (Univ. of Oxford D.Phil. thesis, 2009).

VISUAL SOURCES

Bibliothèque nationale de France, Paris
Estampes et photographie, Réserve ED-8B(1)-FOL; QB-201(47)-FOL; QB-201(54)-FOL; QB-201(58)-FOL; OA-18-FOL

Les Arts Décoratifs, Paris
Inv. 12056; 36422; PE 715

Index